RAF TORNADO
1974 onwards (all marks and models)

COVER CUTAWAY: Panavia Tornado F3.
(Mike Badrocke)

Crown Copyright

In the chapter describing Tornado weaponry, some of the text has been drawn from the RAF official website and from other official publications. This text is Crown Copyright and is reproduced with permission.

Disclaimer

The views and opinions expressed in this book are those of the author alone and should not be taken to represent those of HMG, MOD, the RAF or any government agency.

© Ian Black 2014

All rights reserved. No part of this publication may be reproduced or stored in a retrieval system or transmitted, in any form or by any means, electronic, mechanical, photocopying, recording or otherwise, without prior permission in writing from Haynes Publishing.

First published in July 2014
Reprinted May 2019

A catalogue record for this book is available from the British Library

ISBN 978 0 85733 247 9

Library of Congress control no: 2012955429
Published by Haynes Publishing,

Sparkford, Yeovil,
Somerset, BA22 7JJ, UK.
Tel: 01963 440635
Int. tel: +44 1963 440635
Website: www.haynes.com

Haynes North America Inc.,
859 Lawrence Drive, Newbury Park,
California 91320, USA.

Printed in Malaysia.

RAF TORNADO

1974 onwards (all marks and models)

Owners' Workshop Manual

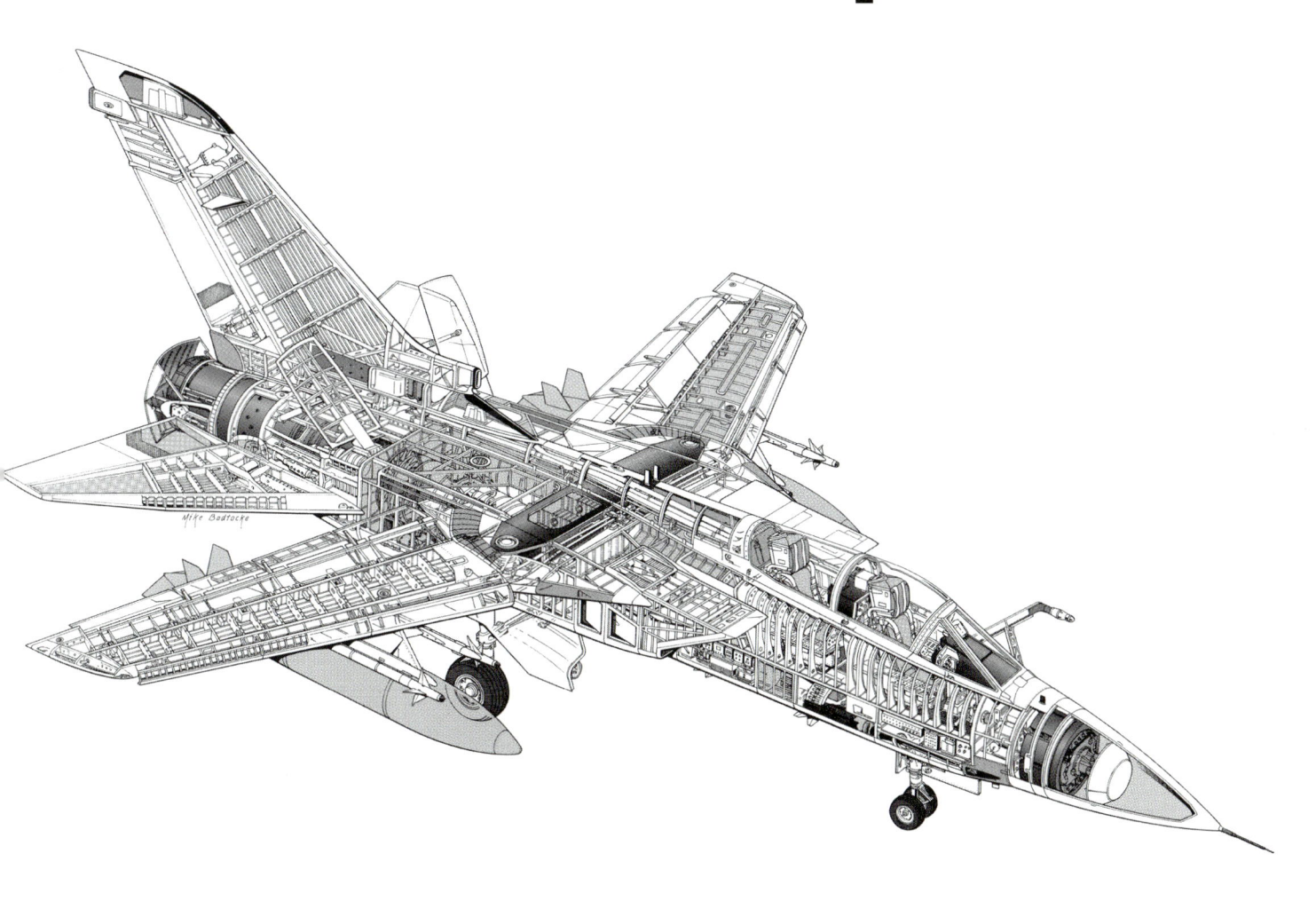

An insight into operating, flying and maintaining the air defence and strike versions of the swing-wing jet

Ian Black

Contents

| 8 | Introduction and acknowledgements |

| 10 | The Tornado story |

Tornado – the birth of a legend — 12

| 28 | Tornado Variants – past and present |

Tornado F3 – the fighter version — 30
Tornado ADV/F2 trials story — 36
Tornado reconnaissance – the GR1A — 48
Tornado anti-shipping – the GR1B — 52
GR1 into the GR4 –
  the Mid-Life Update (MLU) — 54
Tornado current capability –Tornado
  Ground Reconnaissance Force (TGRF) — 57

OPPOSITE Fast and low: A Tornado F3 leads a Dutch F-16 Viper over the Yorkshire countryside. *(All photographs by the author except where credited)*

BELOW Afterburner take-off by Tornado GR4, ZA405.

| 62 | Tornado at War |

| 80 | Anatomy of the Tornado |

Airframe structure — 82
Centre section — 91
Systems — 100

| 110 | The RB199 Engine |

Background to the RB199 — 112
RB199 Mk103 (GR4) amd Mk104 (F3)
  in detail — 115

| 120 | Tornado Weaponry |

Current weapons — 122
The Armourers — 129

| 134 | 'Flying the Fin' |

Tornado from the cockpit — 136
Tornado training 2013 — 144

| 146 | Maintaining the Tornado |

Tornado maintenance — 148
Routine servicing for normal operations — 151

| 154 | Appendix |

| 156 | Index |

Introduction

My association with the mighty Tornado goes back as far as the early 1980s. I visited Warton when my then squadron commander had a back-seat ride in 'A02', one of the prototype ADVs. We arrived in our grubby F-4M with its upturned wings and downturned tailplane and parked next to this sleek swing-wing futuristic jet called the 'Tornado F2'. It would be nearly another 5 years before I strapped myself into the back seat of a shiny new production F2.

BELOW The author post-Combat Air Patrol (CAP) during Gulf War 1.

I had progressed from the back seat of the F-4M Phantom, through pilot training, to end up on an even older air defence fighter – the single-seat Lightning. Thanks to my brother who was then serving on the newly formed Tornado F2 OCU (and who later became boss of the Tornado OEU) I had been given the chance to fly with the then current Tornado aerobatic pilot, on a low-level fighter affiliation sortie. Was I impressed? Well, I was quiet! It was fast but it certainly was not operational. As a former back-seater (there was no radar fitted) I could see it had potential; and from the front seat perspective I could see it was functional but not jaw dropping.

Some months later I left the Lightning and transferred to the Tornado OCU at Coningsby, which had recently equipped with the Tornado F3 version. Had it got any better? Well at least the radar was now fitted and the aircraft had the bigger engines, but there was still a long way to go. With my conversion complete I joined the newly-formed 23 Squadron at RAF Leeming and had the privilege of going to Warton to collect brand new aircraft on two occasions. Later that year I moved across to 25 Squadron who were reforming before deploying to the Gulf in August 1990.

Perhaps this was the pivotal moment in my association with the Tornado. In quick sharp time the aircraft matured into a credible interceptor: rapid improvements under urgent operational requirements had turned it into a capable aircraft. In theatre my respect for the Tornado grew again as I watched and worked with GR1 crews from Bahrain and Tabuk who displayed a level of professionalism I had not encountered. As the shooting war started our squadron had returned to Leeming where I sat glued to CNN watching with admiration as the pilots and ground crews sent wave after wave of Tornados on what proved to be the most dangerous missions of the Gulf War.

In the run-up to war I had been lucky enough to fly against GR1s during fighter affiliation sorties south of Dhahran. My lasting memories are of my late friend Bob Brownlow in his desert painted GR1 trying to evade me as I took a missile shot against him. As he punched out infra-red decoys they simply fell from the pod and flopped onto the ground smouldering. I have no idea how low he was but it cannot have been more than 40ft. My admiration for mud movers remains unwavering.

Post-conflict we developed our tactics and improved the F3 until I left for an exchange posting in 1993 with the French Air Force. Converting to the Mirage 2000C was tremendous fun but I did miss having a back-seater during those dark and dirty nights. I flew the F3 briefly on my return in 1997 and it was clear it had been transformed further still. JTIDS gave the F3 a quantum leap forward in capability as well as ASRAAM and AMRAAM. In the meantime the IDS Tornado was evolving from the GR1 into the GR4. the scale of improvements seemed relentless.

The GR Tornado was constantly in action, with air and ground crews taking part in operations for lengthy periods of time. Since Gulf War 1 the ground attack force Tornadoes have been in the thick of it, like no other RAF aircraft: back to the Gulf again, then Kosovo, the Balkans, Afghanistan and more recently over Libya. Has there ever been a more combat proven aircraft in the RAFs inventory than the Tornado? I doubt it.

When I was asked to write the Haynes Manual on the Tornado it was pretty clear the sub-title of 'owning and operating the RAF's Tornado' was a

BELOW The Leeming Wing puts up a joint nine-ship formation with three aircraft from each of the resident squadrons – 11, 23 and 25.

ABOVE Tornado F3 above the clouds.

RIGHT Author with General Sir Peter de la Billière and Tornado F3.

bit of a tall order. I think the chances of any of us seeing a civilian Tornado operated as a war bird in the future is pretty remote! Then there was the issue of trying to cover everything the Tornado has achieved – again, impossible in a book of this size. This book therefore deals with just the aircraft as operated by the Royal Air Force. Because of its influence on the overall story of Tornado a detailed look at its origins is important to complete the picture. Initially I planned to cover all the weapons used and all the roles the Tornado had undertaken, but again it would need volumes. What I have tried to achieve is a balance between how the Tornado works, how it flies and what the current aircraft are capable of and what they carry. As the aircraft is still actively engaged on operational missions I have deliberately avoided specifics on weapon aiming, accuracy and mission planning and tactics. It is only right these things remain classified for the moment.

Hopefully there is something for everyone. If you worked on the Tornado perhaps it has triggered some happy memories of what the aircraft was like under the skin. If you flew the Tornado I hope it reminds you of what a capable machine both variants were, and still are. If you watch from 'outside the fence' I hope it gives you an insight into just how skilled the people are who keep the Tornado force at the top of its game.

In the preparation of this book I was privileged to be hosted by 41 (F) Squadron, the Tornado test unit, as well as air and ground crews from RAF Marham. Big thanks to you all for answering my questions and for giving me so much access.

My thanks are also due to Air Chief Marshal Sir Simon Bryant; Jim Robinson, CRO RAF Coningsby; OC 41 (F) Squadron and squadron members; Tornado Maintenance School, RAF Marham; Clare Smith, CRO; Staneval, RAF Marham; MBDA; Goodrich; BAE Sytems; Nikon UK; photographers Jamie Hunter and Peter Foster, Geoff Lee, Rick Brewell, Mark Jones, Mark Tyson, Denis Calvert and Neil Bury. Daz Hallworth, long-time Tornado engineer, who looked after me at RTP RAF Leeming. Thanks also to Tornado crews, Stu O, Gaz C, Nige I and Gareth W, as well as all the crews who posed for my air-to-air shots! Of note Archie N, Swanny, K9, Kato, Don M, Doof, Mork, Mick M (Boss!), RPE, Sir John A, Spoons (DH), and all my patient back-seaters.

I hope, too, that this book will inspire young would-be air and ground crews that, while the RAF might be smaller than it ever was, being part of a team that does such a vital job for the freedom we all enjoy is an ambition worth having.

Tornado – Multi-Role Combat Aircraft – second to none.

Ian Black
Surrey, February 2014

Note

All photographs have been taken by the author unless otherwise credited.
The camera bodies and lenses I used to photograph the Tornado were:
Nikon FE, F4, D200, D600, D700, D4;.
lenses 14–12mm, 24–120mm, 80–400mm.
Canon T90, Sony HX300.

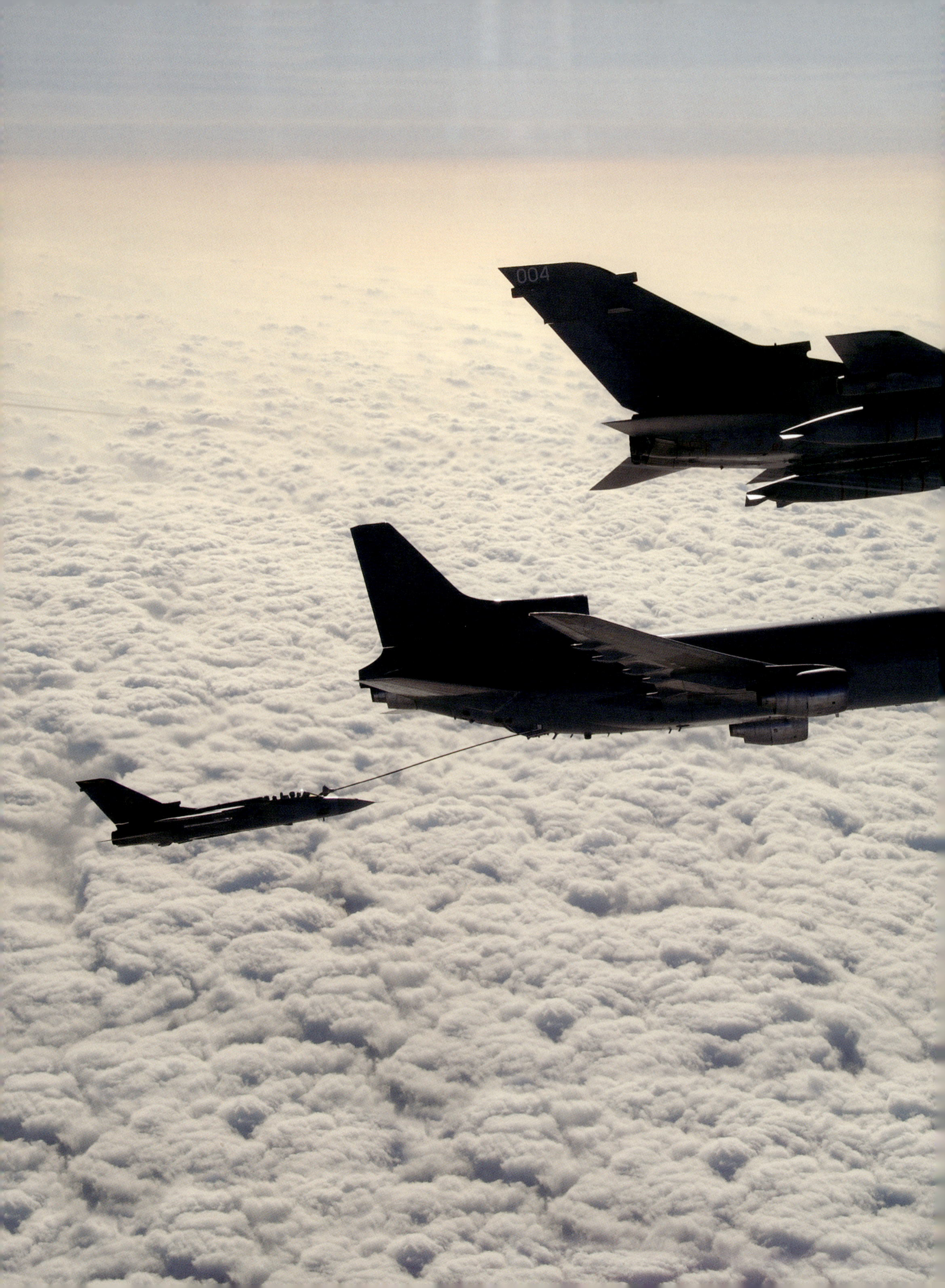
004

Chapter One

The Tornado story

As the Royal Air Force (RAF) approaches its 100th anniversary in 2018, the Tornado stands out for having served with distinction for almost half a century. Now in the twilight of its service life the swing-wing jet will go down in history as one of the greatest aircraft ever operated by the RAF.

OPPOSITE Tornado GR4 and F3 with an RAF TriStar tanker up above the clouds.

ABOVE September 1990 marked the 50th anniversary of the Battle of Britain. As a tribute to 'The Few' a joint 5 and 11 Squadron formation was flown as it returned from an operational CAP over Saudi Arabia. Led by the OC 5 Squadron, the author sits in echelon right in ZE961 'DH'.

Tornado – the birth of a legend

The Tornado is an aircraft that, for once, those who were involved in the project all those years ago can be justifiably proud and say 'we got it right'. Praise must go to the Royal Air Force staff officers who at the time, without the aid of a crystal ball, chose an aircraft that would serve the RAF with distinction for nearly half a century (by its out-of-service date currently 2019), a remarkable feat indeed. Charismatic fighters and bombers have come and gone but none can claim the capability or longevity that one sole type has performed since the early 1980s – the Tornado. Indeed, what other RAF combat aircraft has seen continuous combat operation since 1990 to the present day, nearly 25 years on?

Whilst the purpose of this book is to focus in detail on how the Tornado works, perhaps of equal interest is how the Tornado came in to service. Its birth was arguably the most labour-intensive of any postwar RAF combat aircraft, but as is sometimes the case a difficult birth can produce the best offspring.

RIGHT When the TSR2 first flew in 1964 it represented a radical departure in British aircraft design. XR219 (pictured) was the prototype and the only example of this revolutionary strike/reconnaissance aircraft to fly. *(Author's collection via RPB)*

12

RAF TORNADO MANUAL

Although the very first Tornado flew on 14 August 1974 (in the guise of MRCA – Multi Role Combat Aircraft) its origins can be traced back to an era before swing-wing. In the early 1960s Britain had embarked upon an ambitious military aircraft programme known as TSR2 which, on paper, was set to deliver a world-beating strike aircraft that would become the envy of the Western world. To say the least it was an ambitious project, developing a totally new aircraft with a radical design and crammed full of the very latest weapon aiming devices in an era where valves became transistors. The TSR2 was the aircraft the RAF were pinning their hopes on into the year 2000 and beyond. Yet within a short space of time the TSR2 project had been cancelled – literally axed into oblivion. The programme could never be resurrected and the future of the RAF's bomber fleet then took an Anglo-American turn with the order of fifty General Dynamics F111Ks. The swinging sixties were turning swing-wing.

In the mid-1960s the RAF had a real hotchpotch of assets. What was left of the V Force had been relegated to new roles. The Vickers Valiant had been withdrawn due to wing spar cracks caused by high fatigue in its new low-level role. The Vulcan force had changed from an all-white anti-flash high-level nuclear role to (slightly later) wraparound European grey-green camouflage and a new low-level role. This change in role had come about as it was clear that Soviet air defences would make short work of V-bomber raids at high level. Lastly the futuristic Handley Page Victors had been converted from bombers into strategic reconnaissance aircraft and then ultimately air refueling tankers. The once proud V force of Valiant, Victor and Vulcan was a shadow of its former self. MRCA would be the last chance to get it right.

ABOVE The RAF's trio of V-bombers: Avro Vulcan, Vickers Valiant and Handley Page Victor, pictured in 1957. *(Author's collection)*

BELOW An Avro Vulcan B2 (XM571) of the Scampton Wing is prepared to receive a Blue Steel stand-off nuclear missile. The Scampton Wing consisted of 27, 83 and 617 Squadrons. *(IWM T4855)*

13

THE TORNADO STORY

Problems intensified during 1957 with Conservative Minister of Defence Duncan Sandys' infamous Defence White Paper. Having served in the Army in the Second World War during which time he had been wounded, Sandys became closely involved with the War Cabinet in dealing with the threat from German pilotless V-weapons. Perhaps this is what swayed him some years later to believe that the future of RAF air power lay not in manned fighter aircraft but in unmanned missiles. His White Paper impacted heavily on what was a national treasure – the development of futuristic manned aircraft – an act that contributed to the decline of parts of the British aircraft industry.

The British aviation industry was in difficulty and the premature cancellation of a succession of innovative projects did not help. The consequent 'rationalisation' of British aircraft and aero engine companies led to an amalgamation that became the multi-faceted British Aircraft Corporation (BAC) with main hubs at Warton and Weybridge. BAC were pinning their hopes on Tactical Strike Reconnaissance 2 (TSR2). No other aircraft in the Western hemisphere looked or flew like the TSR2 and it had the makings of being the backbone of the RAF's strike force until well into the 21st Century. We will never know for sure if TSR2 would have been as good as it was said to be, but its potential was certainly plain to see. Axed by the Labour government, it now seems ironic that Britain then embarked on replacing the 'Great White Hope' with a series of acquisitions which came to nothing. Turning to the United States, General Dynamics were given a British order for 50 F-111Ks, two of which were almost complete before that programme, too, was axed.

The British government then joined the French to collaborate on two projects – the Anglo-French Jaguar and the swing-wing AFVG (Anglo-French Variable Geometry Aircraft. Britain). Under the helm of the brilliant engineer and designer Sir Barnes Wallis, Britain had investigated tailless variable geometry aircraft as early as 1949, but despite a manned experimental aircraft being built (the Heston JC-9) it never left the ground. Notwithstanding millions of pounds of funding being poured into the AFVG programme, within two years it ground to a halt when the French pulled out, leaving Britain alone once again . Defence Secretary Denis Healey announced to Parliament amid jeers that Britain would continue with studies into variable geometry aircraft. Nearly a decade had now passed and the RAF had nothing to show for three successive failures – TSR2, F-111K and AFVG. Now the RAF was faced with the quandary of an aging bomber fleet up against a rapidly developing Soviet threat. The Cold War was beginning to turn hot and the RAF needed to regain the edge – and fast.

The RAF was faced with a dilemma: the Air Chiefs wanted a top-performing aircraft; the engineers and designers wanted an aircraft that would be futuristic and capable; while the politicians wanted an aircraft at an economical cost that would protect British jobs. It was clear from early on that the Vulcan concept (long range high level) was totally outdated. Its impressive range of 1,500 miles would not

BELOW What might have been – the RAF cancelled its order for F-111Ks soon after the termination of the TSR2.

have stopped it from being engaged for most of its track by sophisticated Soviet weapons platforms, both air- and ground-based. As already mentioned Britain had abandoned the AFVG project and only really dabbled in what might have been a good aircraft, the Buccaneer 2* (improved). Good as the Buccaneer was, some aerodynamic factors and a lack of reheat always meant it was only ever going to be a capable – but subsonic – bomber.

While most other Western countries were in the same boat and looking for the Holy Grail of modern third generation fighter/bombers, Britain staved off advances from the US to buy off-the-shelf as well as an ambitious offer from the French to re-engine their Mirage IV design with reheated Spey engines. It was clear in the late 1960s that Britain was effectively broke and any attempt to produce an indigenous low-level strike aircraft was going to be too expensive.

Being an island nation the range requirement for the RAF was always going to be greater than that of Britain's European neighbours who shared land borders with the potentially hostile Warsaw Pact countries. Most NATO countries were also users of the F-104

Starfighter and the RAF definitely did not want a Starfighter replacement. Negotiations would be delicate in the extreme if they were to walk away with the correct aircraft that fitted their needs. Trying to pull together a collective of countries to produce an aircraft with common requirements was not going to be easy. In NATO the following F-104 users were all keen to collaborate – Germany, Italy, Canada, Holland and Belgium.

In the late 1960s the RAF was pulling back from the Far East and Middle East leaving Cyprus as its only long distance asset (a small helicopter force was maintained in Hong Kong but combat aircraft had long gone). Ministers wanted a clear appraisal of Britain's future aspirations in terms of global influence and how any new combat aircraft would fit into that. Whilst the other NATO countries persisted with an 'F-104 replacement', with group studies based on a single-engine single-pilot aircraft Britain stood alone with its solution, insisting the way forward was two-man twin-engine with a price tag of around £1.6 million per airframe. On reflection it is perhaps fortuitous that Britain was even asked to attend the F-104 replacement

ABOVE A mixed formation of Tornado F3s and Italian F-104s led by Sqn Ldr Mark Graham. It is ironic that the Italian Air Force, which had originally dismissed the idea of an interceptor Tornado, became users of 'previously enjoyed' ADVs when the RAF found they had a surplus.

group meetings considering it did not actually operate the aircraft!

In terms of historical dates perhaps 17 July 1968 could be described as the 'birth of Tornado' with the signing of a memorandum of understanding (MOU) between, Britain, Germany, Italy and Holland. The Belgians and Canadians had already dropped out. By March 1969 the consortium was down to three nations – Britain, Germany and Italy – now brought together under the umbrella of one company, Panavia Aircraft GmbH. Whilst Panavia was responsible to the governments of all three countries, NAMMO (NATO MRCA Management Organisation) was the link between governments and the companies located in the same building as Panavia in Munich.

Initial requirements were simple: a high-speed low-level aircraft that could operate in all weathers and perform tactical reconnaissance as well as strike missions. Coupled to this Britain and Germany clung on to the idea that a nuclear option must be retained. From the outset the planned production run was in the order of 1,500 aircraft, but eventually there were just shy of 1,000 Tornados built. In 1968 the order book stood at Britain 300, Germany 550, and Italy 200, with the rest simply being allocated to 'others'. Four years later the figures stood at Britain 385, Germany 324 and Italy 100. Total 809. Of course, Britain kept its hands close to its chest by not revealing that out of its planned purchase of 385, 165 would be Air Defence Variants. Similarly, by overstating their initial order book the Germans may have played clever in securing the Headquarters for Tornado at Munich, which probably hampered to some degree Britain's influence on initial design.

When the prospect of a NATO-led design for a new combat aircraft looked certain the British aviation industry, which had been pruned to its bare bones, had little in the way of latitude in its choice of manufacturer. The winner was obvious: BAC – the British Aircraft Corporation.

Fighter design was always undertaken at Warton in Lancashire and much work had already been carried out behind closed doors on variable sweep geometry, despite the setbacks of TSR2. At an early stage the idea of a collaborative aircraft programme between three countries would need careful management. Of great significance is why at this early stage the Tornado (as it became) adopted the swing-wing design. Two main reasons are clear: first, with the swing-wing design then in vogue BAC had based most of its research on projects designed around swing-wing aircraft. From classified projects such as the P45 to AFVG and aircraft simply known as 'Aircraft D' they all had one thing in common – wing design.

Second, the proposed aircraft would need to be capable of flying at high speed and low level as well as carrying heavy loads; at the end of the mission it would need to land on semi-prepared strips that were often much shorter than the 6,000–7,000ft needed by current RAF aircraft types.

At this time the only other company with knowledge of variable geometry wing structures was MBB in Germany, which had worked with the Americans who were pressing ahead with the F-111 and F-14. MBB relied on Grumman for its expertise in wing box structures. Additional studies were carried out into virtually every aspect of swing-wing philosophy. Aircraft weight was estimated to be reduced by 5% to that of a fixed wing. As well as a reduction in fuel burn of 6%, maximum speed, endurance and manoeuvrability would all be increased. On the down side maintenance would increase by 5% while airframe development costs were up to 9% higher than with a conventional wing.

BELOW This F-14 Tomcat was photographed from the back of a French Air Force KC-135 and shows to good effect the Grumman approach to the swing-wing design – a huge centre box section with engines wide apart.

With most parties convinced of the swing-wing concept the next stumbling block was how to agree on where the wing pivot should be and where the tailplane would sit on the rear fuselage. The consortium was fortunate in acquiring substantial work from the Dutch company Fokker, who gave the information on how best to employ the wing flaps and slats as well as the leading edge high-lift devices.

With swing-wing technology in its infancy the details for flying controls needed to be resolved. In the early 1950s, when a rapid surge in futuristic aircraft designs was gripping every British schoolboy, aircraft manufacturers came up with belt-and-braces approaches to new concepts. Standard procedure was to build working, flying prototypes to investigate new wing shapes, tailplane designs or power plants. With MRCA time was critical and no flying test-beds were built to prove the theory of wing position relative to tailplane position.

With initial progress on MRCA being rapid the one major stumbling block lay in the reluctance of the Germans to adopt a two-seat approach, which is strange when one considers the high loss rate of the F-104 that was often due to the high workload involved in single-seat operations. Luckily this was quickly overcome and by 1970 all nations had agreed on the standard, two-man twin-engine airframe with national variations on avionics and weapons.

Initially MRCA was known as MRA75 and Britain's BAC would be working with MBB (Germany) and Fiat (Italy). With BAC then leading the field in wing sweep technology and ideas, they sought solutions to difficult problems such as where to locate the pivot point on the wing sweep, how to overcome the differing loads applied during sweeping the wings and crucially trying to find a solution as to what materials to choose for wing pivots and seals. What the aerodynamicists wanted was a fuselage-mounted pivot, which permitted the provision of a full-span leading edge high-lift device with the wing in the forward sweep position (although this resulted in a considerable shift in the aerodynamic centre of pressure when the wings were swept).

Ingeniously they came up with the idea of a Teflon-coated bearing for the pivot, while the wing sweep seal was initially an inflatable rubber bag. Indeed, looking at final drawings for what AFVG would have looked like one can see the similarity to what became MRCA. By 1969 the collaboration was making progress but needed to start firming up on some of the following design criteria.

- One or two engines – quickly established as two on safety/and battle damage reasons
- Wing and tailplane position on the fuselage
- where the wing pin pivot point would be
- Intake type
- Single or two-seat – this was pretty much decided
- wet or dry wings
- Type of Flight Control Systems
- Wing centre box material
- Hydraulic pressure and pipe material

At the time many combat aircraft employed a slide-out engine system – Hunter, F-104 etc. BAC argued that the drop-out system was better and in the end as BAC were going to be

ABOVE At this stage (1971) the most 'classified' part of the MRCA programme was the intake design. In fact, early display models simply had moulded shapes over the intakes to disguise the design workings. *(Author's collection)*

ABOVE Showing to good effect the extra fuselage plug that gave room for the four Skyflash missiles, with wings swept back at 67 degrees the F3 takes on a delta shape – but without the turn performance!

building the rear of the aircraft it was decided a drop-out system would be best. This was a major plus in the Tornado story. To change an engine does not require you to change the aircraft's 'footprint' – which means aircraft can undergo engine changes inside purpose-built Hardened Aircraft Shelters (HAS) without the need for large hangars. Accessibility was also to be built into the airframe from day one so the number of fuselage panels was more than on any previous aircraft types.

With the airframe being built by three different countries it fell logically into a division of Britain building the front and rear, Germany the centre section and Italy the wings. With BAC designing the rear section they also had the greatest influence in terms of how the new aircraft would be controlled. A close inspection of the rear of TSR2 shows some striking similarities to what became the rear of Tornado. Side-by-side engines, single fin and control using tailerons. An all-moving tailplane, which moved up or down together to provide pitch and differentially to provide roll – or a combination of both to give pitch and roll. Similarly for roll control the Tornado again borrowed TSR2 technology with wing spoilers for increased roll performance. With its state-of-the-art swing-wing concept the consortium needed a state-of-the-art fly-by-wire system and MBB advocated the triplex analogue system of fly-by-wire technology, with a mechanical back-up provided to the tailplane only. The triplex system relies on comparing signals from two of the lanes – should there be a double failure it would freeze the rudder and allow roll and pitch by mechanical means from the tailerons only.

Part of the beauty of Tornado is the simplicity of the airframe, which hides the highly complex and innovative structure underneath. After much debate regarding structure and aerodynamics the wing pin was positioned just outboard of the fuselage. The wing box was placed just above the unbroken centre section, and a way was found to run strong longerons across the longitudinal slits on each side at the rear for the wings in the fully swept position. This allowed the tailplane to be located high enough roughly midway up the fuselage, allowing the lower portions of the strong rear frames to be detachable to allow the engines to be dropped out for maintenance. This concept also allowed the engines to be fed by intakes under the wing box, as well as allowing space inside to fit the main landing gear. Comparisons to the F-111 prove the Panavia concept was right with the entire under-fuselage area being clear for weapons carriage.

With Britain designing and building the rear fuselage it was logical that they were tasked with the power plant choice. In an effort to divide the work share equally the engine was built by Turbo Union, a consortium of Rolls-Royce, Fiat in Italy and MTU. MRCA would be powered by an engine that incorporated the latest technological developments and promised to be considerably smaller and more powerful than existing power plants. The engine chosen was the RB199, which was a huge risk to the entire programme – un-flown, un-tested and existing only on paper it had huge expectations to live up to. Whilst early engines were slightly underpowered, Turbo Union soon ironed out any problems and the RB199 has remained part of the Tornado success story for the entire period of the aircraft's life.

As the basic airframe shape was becoming set in stone efforts were made to keep within the target empty weight of the airframe. In an era before composites the aircraft was made up of light alloy, 71% Titanium 18% Steel 6% and other materials 5%. With design frozen MBB began work on the centre section, Fiat the wings whilst BAC the front and rear fuselage as well as the fin and tailerons. Avionics and radomes were manufactured according to individual country needs.

As this book is focused solely on the RAF version of Tornado it is appropriate to cover in detail the British development of the airframe.

ABOVE The air defence swing-wing MiG-23 was a million miles away from the sophistication of the Tornado, but it was still produced in large numbers. The ground-attack version was designated the MiG-27 (NATO codename 'Flogger'). *(US Dept of Defense)*

With BAC tasked with the front fuselage the designers at least got the cockpit well laid out, as well as creating the roomiest environment for aircrew in a modern fighter. Part of the uniqueness of the project was the task of trying to co-ordinate all the various groups and meetings in three different countries in an age that pre-dated fax machines let alone the internet and e-mail. Nevertheless Britain forged ahead prior the first flight with a variety of airborne test beds fulfilling vital roles of developing Tornado equipment prior to the first flight. A Vulcan carried the RB199, a Buccaneer the avionics and radar and a Lightning carried the new Mauser cannon fitted into a ventral tank.

With three nations all trying to work together a fair amount of give and take had to be assumed while trying to preserve national interests. It is natural then that the first flight of the MRCA should be regarded as a coup for one or another country. With Germany then having the largest order book it was decided that they should have the first prototype fly in Germany, but they agreed to let the first pilot be British. As airframe P01 took shape Paul Millett, who was BAC Chief Test Pilot, moved to Manching to prepare for the first flight.

In a change to traditional testing where engineers performed all the initial ground running Millett and his opposite number, Nils Meister, undertook most of the initial ground runs to gain in-cockpit experience. The start of the programme nearly ended in disaster. Carrying out their final pre-flight engine runs the RB199 was accelerated to full power when it exploded with spectacular results. Fortunately no damage was done to the airframe and in August 1974 on the fourteenth day the airframe was again ready to fly. Using the call sign 'Luna 23' test pilot Paul Millet lifted German prototype P01 (D-9591) aloft at 17.21hrs on 14 August 1974 – now some 40 years ago.

The weather was clear and calm with the temperature a balmy 30 deg C. The purpose of the first flight was simply to accelerate the aircraft to 300kts in the clean configuration and perform basic handling checks in the approach configuration. With just 3,700kg of internal fuel and an aircraft weight of 17,350kg the take-off run was quick and rotation occurred as predicted at 165kts. Climbing to 10,000ft the aircraft was cleaned up and accelerated to 300kts. A short period of engine handling was carried out before the aircraft was slowed down

BELOW MRCA prototype D-9591 made its first flight on 14 August 1974 flown by Paul Millett, British Aircraft Corporation (BAC) Military Aircraft Division's Chief Test Pilot, with MBB's Chief Project Test Pilot, Nils Meister, in the rear cockpit. *(Jonathan Falconer collection)*

and descended to the airfield at Manching. One dummy circuit was flown before a final landing was performed – total flight time just 33mins.

The flight had been accompanied by German Air Force G91 and F-104 chase planes. The maiden flight of any new aircraft is particularly important but none more so than Tornado. Britain desperately needed an aircraft that was fit for purpose after the cancellation of TSR2/F-111. The Germans were keen to show that a postwar Germany was still able to produce home-grown (almost) aircraft of quality, while the Italians were undergoing some major political upheavals. The Italian Communist Party was in power and they were sceptical about the entire Tornado programme. The successful first flight proved that the tripartite approach was the way forward, securing Italian jobs as well as giving Italy a degree of independence from making American equipment purchases.

With the first flight an unmitigated success the road ahead was set to be long and challenging if the MRCA was going to achieve its full potential. What was remarkable for the RAF was that in just six short years from the ashes of failed dreams they had seen the MRCA take to the air. At last the future looked bright for the service as they embarked upon the Tornado programme – a story that was to last for nearly half a century. With flight one complete subsequent flights examined the wing-sweep facility, initially from 45° and then to fully aft at 67°.

While Sir Barnes Wallis might have preferred a wing-sweep schedule that allowed the pilot to either manually or automatically sweep the wings as a function of load and airspeed (to any degree, and not set figures or limits), what the MRCA had initially was adequate for a new generation of variable geometry aircraft. Early test pilots were pleasantly surprised that contrary to the scare mongering among traditional pilots, wing-sweeping was really a non-event.

With confidence now established in the aircraft's wing-sweep mechanism the MRCA was accelerated to speeds of up to Mach 1.5. Indeed, with its good serviceability the MRCA had achieved some significant milestones in its first six flights. The wings and high lift devices had all been tested satisfactorily, basic handling proved positive and engine behaviour was also tested without major incident

By October 1974 the second prototype was ready for flight – a significant occasion as this was the first British aircraft to take to the skies. Described at the time by the Prime Minister Harold Wilson as 'one of the wonder birds of aviation' the maiden flight of P02, XX946, was indeed a significant achievement for BAC, back in the business of building combat aircraft. It was on 30 October 1974 that BAC would begin a love affair with an aircraft that would serve the RAF for over four decades, provide a bulging order book to the Royal Saudi Air Force (RSAF) with orders for IDS and ADV aircraft, as well as lay the foundations of future European collaborations such as Eurofighter Typhoon. Painted in what was the standard red and white colour scheme of the early MRCA prototypes, the aircraft looked anything but war like. P02, assembled in Britain, was aloft with Paul Millet at the controls again with Pietro Trevisan from Italy in the back seat. In recognition of the tri-national programme the aircraft wore a roundel that incorporated the colours of all three nations. With prototype 02 joining the programme development took on a new pace, with Britain employing Victor tankers early on to extend sortie lengths of the trials. Worthy of mention is that Test Pilot Paul Millet undertook the first flight of P02 in what is known as 'Direct Link' – a degraded CSAS mode that requires a fair degree of pilot skill. The aircraft was also not yet fitted with a Head-Up Display (HUD).

From an early stage it was decided the pre-production phase would consist of ten aircraft – numbers 1, 4 and 7 would be with MBB; 2, 3, 6 and 8 at BAC; and numbers 5 and 9 with Aeritalia in Italy. The tenth airframe was a static test airframe. Each aircraft was allocated a specific task in the test schedule, with some individual trials being allocated to the host nation's airframes. The task of clearing the airframe and weapons for entry into service would take a few short years, with responsibility for clearance in the areas of the flight envelope and the dual control version falling to Britain's airframes.

As BAC's main centre in Britain for Tornado testing, Warton also became responsible for trials of the engine that was slung beneath an aging Vulcan flying test-bed. A pair of

Buccaneers was used to test the radar and avionics, while a Lightning was fitted with the Tornado gun. Hindsight has shown that the Vulcan with its under-fuselage RB199 was perhaps more trouble than it was worth. The host airframe was pretty antiquated and unable to properly represent the full flight spectrum of the high speed Tornado. With ten aircraft initially assigned to the test programme it was clear that these numbers were insufficient, so Britain took an extra pair of pre-production airframes as part of an order of six. These were P12 and P15.

One of the Tornado prototypes was lost on 12 June 1979 when P08 crashed into the Irish Sea with the loss of both crew, while the other five aircraft survive to this day in museums. Although Britain lost only one Tornado aircraft in trials, they were fortunate not to lose P02 early in the programme during April 1975.

Soon after take-off with Paul Millett at the controls the Central Warning Panel (CWP) displayed an engine fault with low oil pressure and high temperature. Millett throttled the engine back and aborted the planned test

ABOVE Prototype P03 (XX947) is seen wearing the early 1970s-style camouflage with the light grey undersides, but with toned-down roundels. Many foreign pilots who were watching the display were impressed by the Tornado's agility, but some suggested that the under-fuselage stores might not have been very heavy! This photograph was taken in September 1978 by the author, who was then aged 19 and just starting his navigator training.

LEFT P03, carrying iron bombs, drop tanks and Sky Shadow pods, tucks up its main gear after take-off in 1978. *(Author's collection)*

flight, switching to the secondary plan of some low-level fly-bys of the tower to check altimeter readings. On his first run past with one engine back at idle (luckily not shut down) the aircraft ingested a large bird (a Herring Gull) down the intake of the remaining good engine. With the gear down and the left engine now severely damaged Millet had no choice but to bring up to full re-heat the faulty engine he had only just brought back to idle. Selecting gear and flap up the aircraft continued its downward trajectory.

Unfortunately the only good engine decided not to light its reheat. Instead the nozzle opened fully, further decreasing the available thrust. Now in an unenviable position of one engine failed and one engine producing limited power, Millet prepared to eject. Luckily the engine surged just when it looked like P02 was doomed, which had the effect of closing the nozzle and the aircraft climbed away from its dangerously low altitude. P02 led a fairly charmed life as a test airframe, surviving a landing with wings stuck at 41° and a double-engine flame-out. Other noteworthy feats were speeds of 809kts and Mach 2 twice, as well as part of the fin snapping off during high AOA spin trials. The aircraft survives today at the RAF Museum, Cosford.

Readers should not underestimate just how much work was required of the tri-national development team if Tornado was to go from first flight in 1974 to introduction to service in 1980. The aircraft would need to be cleared throughout the flight envelope as well as being flown with the vast array of weapons it was due to carry. Coupled to this BAC had to develop the ADV version, which had different release to service limitations to that of its IDS cousin. Despite the fact that the acronym 'MRCA' sounded quite sexy and seventies, all three nations wanted a name for their new aircraft and settled on one that would mean something in all their languages. 'Tornado' was christened in September 1974 having pipped Panavia Panther as an alternative – perhaps wisely, as Panther was the name of an older US Navy fighter aircraft that was fairly vapid and also the name of a leading toilet detergent of the period!

With P02 airborne and then in quick succession the rest of the trials fleet, Panavia faced a hard task in silencing the Tornado bashers. Like every aircraft built since the Second World War, other aircraft manufacturers and indeed countries have taken great delight in highlighting the failings of other nations' new aircraft programmes. Tornado was no different and despite some formidable achievements there were people who were quick to knock it at every opportunity.

P02 was soon flying at speeds in excess of 800kts at low level and nudging Mach 2.0 at altitude – speeds that TSR2 aspired to and figures the aircraft it was to replace could only dream of. The British Tornado trials aircraft were soon repainted in the standard RAF grey and green camouflage and in the process adopting a more serious look for the work of testing weapon release. Soon the aircraft began flying with external wing tanks and a wide variety of under-wing and under-fuselage stores. While the first ten aircraft could be considered true prototypes, the first real Tornado for the RAF flew in March 1977 (XZ630) and it was quickly assigned to the A&AEE at RAF Boscombe Down in Wiltshire.

June 1979 should have been a time to celebrate at BAC's Warton factory but it was marred with the tragic loss of P08, XX950, the dual-control prototype, which was lost in circumstances that might never have been established had the aircraft not been fitted with instrumentation. Sadly it seemed the aircraft flew into the Irish Sea in between simulated loft manoeuvres, the sea conditions at the time being

BELOW Paul Millett and Ray Woollet aloft in Prototype P08 (XX950) on its first flight on 15 July 1976. P08 was the first Tornado to be lost in a flying accident when it crashed into the Irish Sea on 12 June 1979, claiming the lives of BAE's Russ Pengelly and Sqn Ldr John Gray of the A&AEE Boscombe Down.

described as treacherous. Tragic, as only days before Warton had rolled out Tornado BT001, ZA319 (the 'B' standing for British, the 'T' for Trainer, and the airframe '001' of the production run). BT001 was the first true RAF Tornado.

With the first flight of the RAF's new strike/attack aircraft taking place on 10 July 1979, work began on training the first generation of Tornado pilots at an RAF base in England called Cottesmore, under the title of the Tri-National Tornado Training Establishment (TTTE) – popularly known as Triple T-E. The TTTE was to be based in England, but it was run by all three nations with aircraft from all three nations operating as one single unit to teach pilots and navigators the basics of how to fly the Tornado. With the ground engineering side set up as early as October 1979, the Tornado maintenance school eagerly awaited its first airframes.

While I don't undervalue the part played by TTTE in the Tornado story, I feel that the most relevant first unit to be formed by the RAF on the IDS version was the Tornado Weapons Conversion Unit (TWCU). It may have been that the consortium's original intention was for the Tornado programme to remain as a cohesive whole single unit, both in training crews at the initial stage and latterly on the weapons phase, with Britain used for initial training then a move to Sardinia where weapons training would be undertaken on the ranges. However, whilst the aircraft were all similar the weapons carried by host nations – and indeed the tactics they adopted – differed significantly and hence the reason why the RAF decided (wisely) to keep the weapons and tactics training 'in-house'.

Students who passed through the TTTE are pretty unanimous in their verdict that the course was probably the most gentlemanly

ABOVE Talking up the Tornado – 'now in production for three NATO air forces and one navy', in 1979.

LEFT Tri-National Tornado Training Establishment (TTTE): in the foreground is GR1, ZA322, the second production Tornado for the RAF. The fin flash 'B-50' indicates this is a British aircraft. G-39 and I-43 are German and Italian respectively.
(Author's collection)

in the RAF – but they had a rude awakening when they arrived on the TWCU formed at RAF Honington. The TTTE aircraft were always flown in a 'clean' configuration and lacked the under-chin Laser Ranger and Marked Target Seeker (LRMTS), whereas the TWCU aircraft (that came from Batch 2 off the production line) were more combat capable. TTTE eventually closed its doors in March 1999 having trained a staggering 4,500 pilots and navigators and its aircraft having flown some 162,000hrs. Today all the RAF's Tornado training is undertaken by 15 (R) Squadron at RAF Lossiemouth. With around 25 aircraft on strength the TWCU soon adopted the shadow squadron number plate of 45 Squadron, and then 15 Squadron, giving them a reserve war role.

Having been taught to fly the IDS by the tri-national unit at Cottesmore the serious matter of operating the GR1 was left to the experienced instructors at RAF Honington. With TWCU in full swing the RAF geared up for what was to become a historic moment when 9 Squadron accepted its first aircraft in January 1982. Finally, after nearly two decades of waiting, the RAF could replace the aging Vulcan with an aircraft that was all-weather day/night capable and able to hit targets with extreme accuracy in high ECM environments.

The first Tornado aircraft (ZA586) was delivered to the RAF in January whilst the squadron officially stood up in June 1982 with crews taken from the TWCU. Initially the RAF would retire the long-serving Vulcan squadrons on a one-for-one basis, with 617 'Dambusters' forming next in January 1983 at RAF Marham (which would become one of two Tornado main bases). Next to receive the Tornado was 27 Squadron, again a former Vulcan unit, and also based at RAF Marham.

These early days of Tornado operations were a time of great change in the RAF. Simply introducing a new aircraft type into service is not just about building aircraft, and training pilots and navigators. From an engineering perspective the logistics of entering into service a brand new type are huge. The pressure on engineering support is immense – trying to train new engineers on a brand new type and ensure they can fix the aircraft as quickly as possible is never easy. Being a brand new aircraft it was hard to predict which parts would need replacing and then set up sufficient stocks of spare parts to allow the fleet to remain serviceable. Equal praise must go to the engineers and logistics people for the smooth introduction to service, as to the aircrew and manufacturers.

With the British Tornado re-equipment up and running the next forces within the RAF to re-equip were the Buccaneer squadrons at RAF Laarbruch, followed by the Jaguars at RAF Bruggen. Despite the Buccaneer serving with distinction in its role it was nevertheless an aircraft the RAF had inherited from the Royal Navy. With

BELOW GR1, construction number CN278, with 'BS095' painted on its side (later ZA465), pictured ground-running at BAe Warton prior to its maiden flight in 1983. It went on to serve with 16 Squadron and was much photographed in Gulf War 1 as *Foxy Killer*.

Tornado replacing the Buccaneer it could now be reassigned to the more suitable role of anti-shipping. Likewise, the Jaguar had proved its worth as a low-level strike/attack aircraft, but was simply not in the same league as the Tornado GR1. From November 1983 to late 1984, RAF Laarbruch re-equipped with the Tornado GR1 in the guise of 15, 16 and 20 Squadrons. Just down the road at RAF Bruggen four more squadron were set to get the new Tornado in the shape of 14, 17, 31 and eventually 9 Squadrons, which were transferred from Britain to Bruggen and re-equipped with new-build aircraft. By the end of 1986 the RAF was up to full strength of seven RAF Germany (RAFG) squadrons and two in Britain. All that was needed now was the replacement of the two dedicated recce squadrons with the Tornado.

From an early stage it was clear the Tornado was a leap forward in capability compared to some of the 'steam driven' aircraft it replaced. The RAF had successfully introduced the aircraft into service, ably helped by BAe Warton and the A&AEE, but what it needed now in order to maximise the effectiveness of its new weapons platform was a unit that was dedicated to developing the aircraft operationally, ironing out any problems as quickly as possible. Under the guise of the RAF's Strike Command Central Trials and Tactics Organisation (CTTO) there was a push for a specialist unit to be known as the Tornado Operational Evaluation Unit (TOEU). Based at RAF Boscombe Down it undertook urgent trials on how best to employ JP233, LGB delivery, and how to employ the WE177 strike weapon. Initially the unit was formed on a temporary basis, but due to the success of the trials they undertook – such as the work to clear the aircraft for NVG use – the unit's life was extended, and indeed under the guise of 41 (F) Squadron it still exists today.

By 1986 the RAF had pretty much re-equipped with the Tornado GR1 and the only remaining task was to introduce the Tornado GR1A with 2 Squadron at Laarbruch, and latterly with 13 Squadron at Marham in the specialist recce role. Now, as the aircraft began to settle into an era dominated by Cold War fever, the RAF rapidly found itself in new territory.

ABOVE ZA328, the BAe Trials Fleet's Tornado GR1, was intercepted and photographed by a French Air Force Mirage 2000 on its return from weapon trials in Sardinia.

ABOVE The RAF's combat force gathered together in one unique formation post-Gulf War 1. Flying the ADV is RAF Leeming's Station Commander, Grp Capt Rick Peacock Edwards.

The Cold War ended virtually overnight, and the RAF suddenly found itself engaged in a conflict far removed from what it had previously trained for. The end of the Cold War led to a pull back from RAF Germany and a reduction in the numbers of combat aircraft in the RAF's inventory. Under a policy known as 'Options for Change' the RAF was going to be shrunk in size to a peacetime force that bore little resemblance to the era when Tornado was conceived. Despite the Iraqi invasion of Kuwait in August 1990, political forces did not appear to appreciate the fact that despite the Cold War ending, new threats would still emerge that required the RAF to force-project. Now more than ever it needed aircraft that were able to adapt to rapidly changing threats in a variety of scenarios. In August 1990 both types of Tornado began to deploy to the Middle East in what came to be called Gulf War 1. (See Chapter 3 'Tornado at War'.)

With the conclusion of Gulf War 1 it should have been a time for reflection among both the ADV Tornado force and the GR1/1A force. Future conflicts would probably run along similar lines – out of area, rapid deployment against a threat that was probably less capable but still able to fight back.

'Options for Change', however, had been set in motion and no sooner had the Tornado squadrons begun returning home from the Gulf and their aircraft stripped of their desert paint schemes than they were faced with the prospect of disbandment. With the decision to pull the Tornado force back from RAF Germany a rationalisation of British assets meant there would be just two main British Tornado bases – RAF Lossiemouth in Scotland and RAF Marham in Norfolk.

With Gulf War 1 not even a distant memory the Tornado force was soon heading back to the Middle East. Whereas the RAF's Jaguar and Harrier forces mainly operated out of NATO bases in Turkey the Tornado aircraft were soon back in action at bases in Saudi Arabia and Kuwait under the guise of operations to police 'no-fly zones'. Indeed, Tornado aircraft even deployed to bases in the Middle East they had previously bombed. In addition to the Gulf,

Tornados served with distinction in the Balkans, Afghanistan and more recently over Libya.

On reflection no-one could have predicted all those years ago in 1968 what the Tornado would ultimately have been asked to perform. History has shown that by choice or by chance the RAF bought an aircraft that was able to grow into a platform that now delivers smart weapons with pinpoint accuracy and at far less cost than ever before. With its design philosophy of keeping munitions and stores either podded or under-slung, the Tornado airframe has avoided the expensive and time consuming task of major airframe reworking. It has enjoyed only one major mid-life upgrade in its service history, which has proved a great success. Above all the Tornado has formed the backbone of the RAF's ability to deploy to any part of the world and undertake a variety of missions, both air-to-air and air-to-ground, for nearly thirty years. What other aircraft has achieved such success?

ABOVE *Foxy Killer* (ZA465 'FK') was one of the best-known RAF Tornado GR1s of Gulf War 1 (see also page 24).

RIGHT See here at Dhahran Air Base during the run-up to hostilities in Gulf 2, the F3 force tried many new configurations without the need to go through the usual testing regimes of different weapon fits. *(RAF)*

27

THE TORNADO STORY

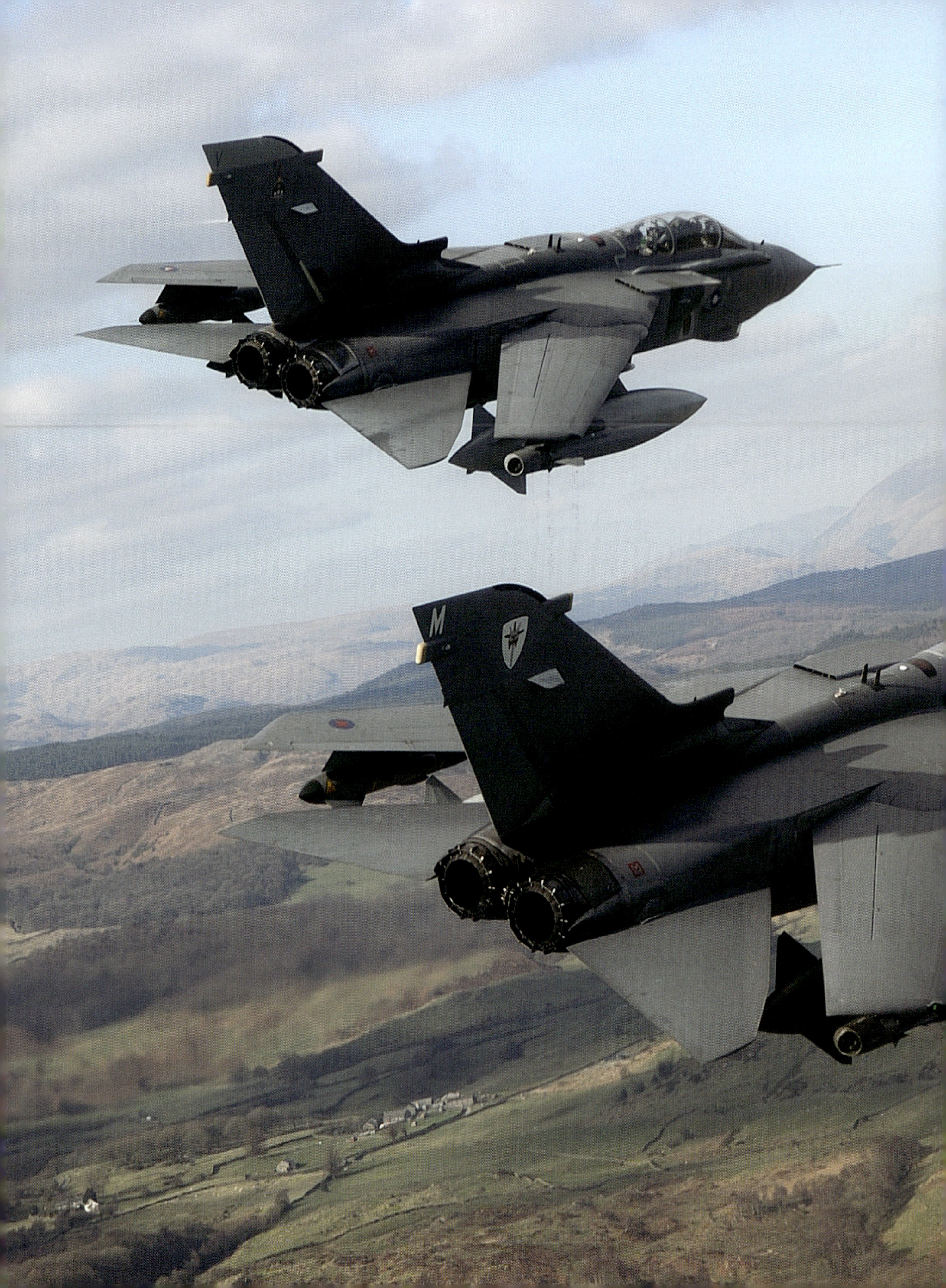

Chapter Two

Tornado variants – past and present

Since 1997 the RAF has employed the Tornado GR4 as a front line combat aircraft. This chapter looks in detail at the versions no longer in service – the GR1A, GR1B and the F3/ADV. The Mid-Life Update, which morphed the GR1 into the GR4, turned a capable airframe into a superb weapons platform, giving the RAF's Tornadoes a new lease of life.

OPPOSITE A pair of Tornado GR4s of 13 Squadron based at RAF Marham pictured over Western Scotland. *(RAF)*

Tornado F3 – the fighter version

With headline-grabbing words like 'fighter', perhaps the correct title should be 'interceptor' because from the outset that is what the ADV (Air Defence Version) was – and was designed to be. From a difficult conception and tricky birth the Tornado became one of the great unsung success stories of the modern fighter era in the postwar Royal Air Force. My association with the Tornado ADV/F3 started in 1984 and ended in 1997. Even though I flew 1500-plus hours on the aircraft I am fully aware that I missed the best years of its life.

I was privileged to visit 111 (F) Squadron just days before they disbanded in March 2011, and the aircraft and crews I saw were so much more capable than the force I had left in 1997. It was indeed ironic that just as the aircraft was reaching the height of its powers in terms of capability the RAF decided to retire it. The Typhoon is a worthy successor, but the ADV in its role of bomber interceptor was unequalled. As an airframe designed to sit on Northern QRA and intercept Russian bombers day or night, 365 days a year, and in all weathers, there was no match. It was simply the best at its job.

ABOVE Tornado ADV – this is F3, ZE835 'EE'.

BELOW On 10 March 2010, two Tornado F3s of 111(F) Squadron were scrambled from RAF Leuchars in the early hours of the morning to intercept two Russian Tu-160 'Blackjack' aircraft, which were approx 100nm to the west of Stornoway on the North-West coast of Scotland. The Tornadoes shadowed the Russian aircraft as they progressed south before the 'Blackjacks' turned north, short of the Northern Irish coast, exiting UK airspace. *(RAF)*

Once an aircraft is withdrawn from service there is usually a wave of sentiment about how good it was and people tend to forget its shortcomings. This can be true of the ADV; initially it was lack-lustre, but the last few years of its life proved its critics wrong. It was never meant to be an F-15 or F-16: it was designed for a specific task and that was defending British airspace. Armchair critics pontificate on how it was no match for the Soviet Su-27 or MiG-29. I would counter that with 'if we had been fighting MiG-29s over the coast of Norfolk, then chances are it was all over anyway'.

I've flown the MiG-29 and the F3 and I know where I'd rather be. Performing at an air show or close-in combat on base defence – give me a MiG-29. Going to war on Offensive Counter Air (OCA) or Defensive Counter Air missions (DCA) with forces of 60 plus aircraft – give me the F3. No contest.

The Tornado was a remarkably easy aircraft to fly, though some might say difficult to operate, and the F3 never once put me in a situation where I felt uncomfortable – few pilots can say that after 1,500hrs on any fighter.

Making a fighter out of a bomber

The Tornado can be described as multi-role so it is perhaps a touch ironic that the type it was due to replace was in fact one of the first true multi-role combat aircraft in its class. Whilst the Americans take the theory that if you start with an excellent fighter it is easy to turn it into a bomber, the British (naturally) decided to do it the other way round. The British Phantom FGR2 had been introduced in the air-to-ground strike role, but publicity pictures from the 1970s show 41 (F) Squadron Phantoms flying with almost every known weapon in service slung underneath in a role that encompassed just about every current task.

So, how would the British be able to persuade their partner nations to produce a fighter version of the Tornado? In truth the tactic they employed was fairly astute. By sticking to their beliefs in the two-man, two-engine bomber version it was in theory a relatively easy job to convert the GR1 into a fighter. The basic airframe would remain the same while an elongated nose would house a powerful radar and the rear fuselage stretched to accommodate the bigger RB199 Mk 104 engines needed for fighter performance

Coupled to this was a forward fuselage plug (just behind the navigator) housing an 'O' tank, which gave the interceptor an increased range equivalent to about 10–15mins extra flying. Although all the British versions have a 'wet' fin, like the GR1/4 the F3s were capable of filling the fin with around 600/440kgs of additional fuel. Not gauged when you refuelled from a tanker, the only clue you had was a light in the cockpit to tell you 'Fin F' (full) – or your wingman telling you your fin fuel was pouring from the dump mast! Other Tornado operators, German and Italy, decided against having a wet fin.

The Cold War threat

At the design phase Germany and Italy aided the RAF's approach to a fighter variant by insisting the bomber had a Mach 2.0 performance – a capability only Britain had on its 'wish list'. This was pivotal in airframe design, especially in the area of intakes, where variable ramps were incorporated to allow for supersonic performance, as well as the large fin that was big enough to give controllability at high Mach numbers.

The Lightning is certainly regarded as one of the all-time great interceptors, but Air Staff members were well aware of its shortcomings – lack of range, poor radar, under-armed, single-seat and with little or no self-defence capability. Even its startling performance could not mask these deficiencies in a wartime scenario. Equally

ABOVE The Phantom, which the Tornado replaced, was another true multi-role combat aircraft.

ABOVE A Tornado F3 (ZE808 'FA') of 25 (F) Squadron shadows a Russian 'Bear-F' over the North Sea. The Bear's massive turboprop engines were surprisingly noisy.

BELOW The Tornado's onboard Foxhunter AI radar represented a vast leap forward in capability over earlier British interceptors like the Lightning.

it was known the Lightning was an engineer's nightmare, and its accident record in the late sixties and early seventies was giving serious concern to senior planners. With a loss rate of nearly one airframe a month it was doubtful the RAF would even have enough airframes to maintain a viable Lightning force.

As early as 1967 high-ranking British officers were aware that the RAF needed a fighter that was fit for purpose. The military might of the Soviet Union was growing at an alarming rate and interceptions of 'Bear' bombers were an almost daily occurrence off the coast of Scotland. Initially the RAF was content to introduce the Tornado ADV (Air Defence Variant) in the mid-1980s once the GR force was up and running. With delays this is pretty much what happened in any case.

The RAF defined the (then) Cold War threat as Tu-22M 'Backfire' bombers, and Su-24 'Fencer' low-level strike aircraft as well as the odd high-level high-speed MiG-25 'Foxbat' recce aircraft. With hindsight the Su-24 'Fencer' would have been a long way from home to penetrate British airspace; and the 'Foxbat', too, was a long way even from its forward operating bases. If the Cold War turned hot these attacks on British airspace would probably occur at night in all weathers under heavy ECM (electronic countermeasures) coverage. These threats added to the already existing long-range probing flights of British airspace by Soviet 'Bear' and 'Bison' bombers. It was indeed a tall order to expect 150 or so ADVs to protect the whole of British airspace 24 hours a day, 365 days a year.

Replacing the Lightning and the Phantom

When whispers of a replacement for the Lightning and Phantom reached the front line, many thought that we would leave the Tornado IDS version as it was and turn westwards to buy off-the-shelf US fighters. At that time the shopping list included the F-16, deemed too small and single-seat for British ops. The F-15 would have been ideal, but was not the capable machine then that it is today. The F-14 Tomcat was another obvious contender, but early engine problems and huge costs made it a non-starter. (Recently de-classified government documents reveal that the RAF wanted the F-15 twin-seat fighter as its first choice, but aircraft procurement is a matter of balance.) In the end the ADV won the day and although Britain was the sole operator and bore all the development costs, it was really only the radar and internal cockpit changes that Britain was developing, piggybacking on the already budgeted-for airframe development costs. With the Royal Saudi Air Force the only other operator (Oman pulled out of a small order) the unit cost of the ADV was much higher than the GR version. Specific figures are hard to find but between £20–23 million per airframe would seem reasonable – probably double that of the GR.

Perhaps worthy of mention was why the other two nations shied away from an interceptor version. The Italian Air force did not need a long-range interceptor and early on bought the upgraded F-104S as they already operated the F-104. It is ironic that later on the Italian Air Force would operate Tornado ADVs borrowed from the RAF. Despite the RAF lending the ADV to Italy it was never a real success for them. It was also agreed that Britain would lend them Skyflash missiles, but the Italian F3s were seldom seen in a full UK-style war fit, except during Operation Allied Force in 1999. The West German Air Force (WGAF) also had no need for a long range interceptor; Germany's coastline is tiny. They opted early on for the F-4 Phantom, initially wanting a unique single-seat version, but then chose the F-4F (due to retire in June 2013). The German F-4F was eventually upgraded with APG-65 Radar and AMRAAM missiles as the Eurofighter Typhoon programme slipped behind schedule.

Once again the emphasis was placed on building the Tornado ADV 'in-house', so all subcontractors were from Britain. The radar was to be built by GEC/Marconi with help from Ferranti. The RAF were painting a picture of what they wanted from the ADV – an aircraft that could loiter on its own with or without tanker support some 400 to 500 miles from base. In the big plan the RAF would operate modern AWACS to fully integrate with the ADV force. At this time the AEW support was in the form of the venerable Shackleton, which was also well past its sell-by date. In an ambitious programme the RAF was trying to modernise the entire Air Defence System in one go, whilst introducing the GR version in large numbers.

ABOVE The RAF looked at buying the F-14 but deemed it too costly.

BELOW Part of the Tornado story should have seen the AEW Nimrod replace the venerable AEW Shackleton (pictured) and integrated within the RAF's air defence network. But this never happened because the Nimrod was scrapped.

33
TORNADO VARIANTS – PAST AND PRESENT

ABOVE Pictured at the SBAC Farnborough Air Show the ADV prototype is seen here with a fin-mounted camera and 1,500-litre fuel tanks.

BELOW Tornado ADV showing Mauser cannon and Skyflash AAM. *(Jonathan Falconer collection)*

Guns and missiles

Armament from the outset was to be four radar-guided missiles (AIM-7 Sparrow) but eventually home-produced TEMP (Tornado Embodiment Modification Programme) Skyflash, with four short-range AIM-9L Sidewinder missiles. From day one the ADV would be equipped with a single gun, after painful lessons deleting the gun on early Lightnings as well as the gun being an afterthought on the F-4. Under Air Staff Target 395 the RAF formally ordered 165 ADVs on 5 March 1976. This would include a pair of the prototype ADVs (this later became three) known as F2s. The plan was that the ADV should be 80% common to the GR1. Having won over the other nations for an airframe that needed Mach 2.0 performance, turning the GR1 into a fighter was still an ambitious programme.

Now being toted amongst the RAF as a 'bomber destroyer' the Service chiefs and crews of 11 Group (formally RAF Fighter command) had high hopes for the new fighter. The task of replacing two iconic fighters like the Lightning and the Phantom with a single type was never going to be easy. One journalist cruelly noted that the new fighter weighed as much as a wartime Sunderland flying boat – a strange analogy. With a production run of just 165 airframes the RAF would, in hindsight, probably have been better off buying the US off-the-shelf American F-14 or F-15, but as ever British industry was hoping for export sales despite its approach to a UK-bespoke fighter.

BAe had enjoyed huge success as a defence exporter to the Royal Kingdom of Saudi Arabia with a massive arms deal that included Strikemasters and Lightnings, and the Lightning force operated by the RSAF was due for replacement. Equally, Oman looked traditionally to Britain for its defence needs and could have bought British. In the end only the RSAF bought the ADV – in fact discounting the loan to Italy, it became the only other user of this specialised variant. Had the US bought the Tornado (it was, supposedly, interested in buying the GR version), history may have been written differently. As it is, hindsight shows that there was much posturing between nations and the prospect of the US buying a European combat aircraft was never on the cards. The idea of the US buying foreign-built aircraft for the defence of the homeland was always unlikely.

During the development phase it was really only the Germans who offered some hope of a purchase to replace the F-4 had the ADV lived up to expectations. With the framework of what would become the ADV set in stone, some advantages fell naturally into place. The carriage of four Skyflash missiles was a non-negotiable option and initial thoughts were that they would be wing-mounted. Fortunately, a better solution was to increase the fuselage length with a plug behind the rear cockpit and fit them semi-recessed beneath the fuselage. (An additional benefit from the fuselage plug was the increased internal fuel capacity it conferred.)

Mounting the radar-guided Skyflash on the wings would have been interesting. The F-4 Phantom did on occasion mount the Sparrow on the wing pylons, but the Tornado would have needed to overcome the problem of launching with wings sweeping. The Skyflash would often take some pretty savage initial geometry turns post-launch, which could have proved interesting to say the least to crews in combat. Part of the initial launch sequence post-trigger-press for Skyflash is to push the missile down and away from the fuselage. Placing the missile under the wings would have meant an additional clearance requirement as the wings are shoulder-mounted, not to mention the risk of scorching the tailerons as the rocket motor fired.

Britain's view at the time was correct in the fact the Tornado ADV would be unlikely ever to encounter agile Soviet fighters close to home. The MiG-29 has pretty short legs and the prospect of a MiG-29 versus Tornado ADV over British airspace would mean things had gone badly wrong in the NATO Central Region. What Britain was building was a comprehensive plan covering the whole UK ADR (United Kingdom Air Defence Region) – an amalgamation of Ground Control Stations (GCS), Ground Controlled Interception (GCI), AWACS and the fighter force backed up with tanker support. It was colloquially known as ADGE – or UK Air Defence Ground Environment.

While the RAF had never planned the ADV to be intercepting Russian MiGs in British airspace it is perhaps ironic that one of the first public viewings of the new Tornado F3 was when

5 Squadron aircraft escorted Russian MiG-29 fighters into the Farnborough Air Show in September 1988.

ABOVE The F3 was in a different league to the Su27 'Flanker'.

Foxhunter radar

Perhaps the biggest thorn in the side of the ADV programme from the outset was the Foxhunter radar. Called the AI24 by Ferranti/GEC Marconi, one must first put this version into context with the previous radar which was the AI23 used in the Lightning. First used in the late 1950s, by the 1980s the Ferranti AI23 was positively prehistoric compared to the AI24. Ferranti were trying to go from a post-Second World War pulse-only radar, whose display was not much bigger than a cigarette packet, to a

BELOW Foxhunter AI radar inside the nose cone of the Tornado F3.

radar that would track while scan target shoot missiles BVR (beyond visual range) and allow the navigator a God's-eye view of the battlefield on his plan display TV tab. The task was huge ... and it was. The world had gone from pulse-only, Pulse Doppler to FMICW (Frequency Modulated Interrupted Continuous Wave). With a pulse radar, targets over land would be hard to see; with Pulse Doppler, targets with a forward velocity even at low level could be detected. Now with FMICW, targets could hopefully be tracked and crews shown vital information such as altitude, speed and aspect angle in the read-out line. The new radar was developed in about 1976 but strangely there seemed to be no urgency in achieving operational status; most fighter development leads to multiple test-bed flying to try and iron out any problems that may occur prior to service release.

With the ADV a reliable working radar only really appeared just prior to Gulf War One. This radar consisted of eight liquid-cooled LRUs clustered around a central transmitter. The traditional twist-Cassegrain antenna system was light and simple and boasted a target detection range of over 100 miles, in theory. The radar also incorporated a J-band transmitter used to guide the Skyflash missile to impact. Other functions allowed the radar to work in low PRF (Pulse Repetition Frequency) enabling the ADV to track slow-speed targets.

For any air defence fighter the range of targets its radar needs to deal with is formidable. It might be tracking a Mach 2.5 MiG-25 'Foxbat' at 60,000ft plus, or the fighter might need to shadow a slow-speed civilian target lost over the sea at 150kts. Encompassing the latest technology the aircraft was fitted with a Cossor IFF-3500 interrogator to detect both friendly and enemy targets.

Tornado ADV/F2 trials story

The first ADV, ZA254, flew on 27 October 1979 and quickly began making development sorties. Initially the aircraft showed promise. There were three ADV prototypes, known as A01, A02 and A03. The IDS version was now well developed so many of the early

BELOW The first ADV (ZA254) Tornado F2 is rolled out on 9 August 1979. *(Denis Calvert)*

teething problems had been ironed out. Indeed, on its first flight the prototype ADV was aloft for 1hr 32min flown by Dave Eagles with Roy Kenward in the back seat. Within weeks the aircraft had achieved speeds of Mach 1.6 as well as making night landings. Having a fully retractable forward refueling probe incorporated from day one (unlike the IDS version) it made use of airborne tankers to speed up the development process. Initially flown clean, the aircraft soon adopted a more representative war fit with additional wing tanks and was seen demonstrating its ability to loiter 375 miles from base for over 2hrs early in the development phase.

RAT and SPILS

Work also continued apace on spinning trials and operation of the newly fitted RAT (Ram Air Turbine). It was deemed that because the ADV would be operating a long way from base (unlike the GR1 which had only an emergency power supply) the ADV needed a RAT to generate electrical and hydraulic power in the event of a double flame-out or total electrics failure at night over the sea. With the RAT operating sufficient control would be maintained to allow the crew time to try and relight the engines. The other major trial work involved numerous sorties to expand and evaluate the SPILS system, which gave the aircraft its carefree handling.

Frazer-Nash launchers

Other trials work involved live Skyflash firings, although these were actually unguided rockets as the aircraft carried no radar (the Skyflash needs a working radar to guide the missile to the target). Because the missiles were located underneath the fuselage a system was developed that on launch the Skyflash would be physically pushed down and away from the fuselage. These units, known as Frazer-Nash launchers, were specifically designed for the ADV. They consist of two cartridge-powered two-stage rams that impart sufficient velocity on the missile to clear it from the launch aircraft whilst not exceeding its airframe limits. The aim was to control the missile in pitch during launch. A yoke on each launcher also controlled the missile in roll during launch. All of this occurring milliseconds after trigger-press and rocket motor ignition. However, initial trials showed that the launchers were too powerful and were actually bending the missile body as it launched.

27mm Mauser cannon

On the starboard side of the forward fuselage was the 27mm Mauser cannon, an essential must-have accessory for the ADV. Unfortunately, on the ADV the cannon was located that bit further away from the intake than it was

ABOVE Fitted with four Skyflash AAMs ZA254 tucks up her gear. *(Jonathan Falconer collection)*

LEFT Skyflash missile firing trials by the second ADV prototype (ZA267) on 19 November 1981. *(Jonathan Falconer collection)*

LEFT The Tornado ADV was fitted with one Mauser 27mm cannon (the IDS version has two).

37

TORNADO VARIANTS – PAST AND PRESENT

ABOVE The Nimrod was a fantastic maritime patrol aircraft but attempts to turn it into an AEW platform were unsuccessful.

BELOW The short career of the F2 came to an end after the F3 entered service.

on the IDS, and initial firings proved almost catastrophic. As the gun was fired, exhaust gases from the spent cartridges (the cases are kept inside) was fed straight into the right-hand engine intake – into the optical devices used to determine turbine blade temperature. This caused the engine to surge (at best) and it was many months before the ADV could fire its guns without the worry of a flame-out or surge.

Trials and tribulations

Other trials looked at the high altitude capability of the ADV, which was never going to be in the same league as the Lightning, especially with the early Mk 103 engines. The initial radar sets began arriving in 1981 and such was the extent of the problems that trials to cure a host of problems were still ongoing at Warton as late as 1990.

Troubles with the Foxhunter continued and it was nearly two years before an ADV flew with a working radar, at which stage the programme was nearly four years behind schedule and 50% over budget. Indeed, things became so serious with the ADV programme that ministers decided that either the ADV or the Nimrod AEW would have to be scrapped. In the end the Nimrod fell on its sword allowing the ADV to continue by the skin of its teeth.

Enter the F2

Some five years after the ADV's first flight the RAF began to accept what was known as the Tornado F2 at RAF Coningsby. Prior to introduction a handful of crews had undergone training at BAe Warton on the new fighter and initial reports were not rosy. Most of the crews had flown the Lightning, the F-4 Phantom or some of the US fighters on exchange programmes. The ADV initially fell way short of expectations. The radar was still pretty non-existent and most of the time the aircraft flew 'lead-nosed' (that is, with ballast in the front). This was particularly frustrating for back-seaters who were left with a nice plan display in front of them, but generally their only contribution to a mission was as an extra pair of eye balls.

Initially the RAF received 18 of the interim F2 versions. Although it is only 30 years ago it is hard to see why the RAF persisted with an aircraft that was way below the standard of what was to become the F3. Rumour has it that that the intention was to rework the F2 into F3 standard but it was never really looked on as a serious option. The F2 had the same Mk 103 engines as the GR version but just one Inertial Navigation System (two was a prerequisite for AD ops) and it was only able to carry two AIM-9L missiles on wing-mounted pylons. It was indeed far inferior to the Phantom FGR2 it was supposed to replace.

No 229 OCU was formed and despite the lack of credible radars it was declared to NATO as an emergency air defence unit in 1985. This was unusual as the OCU had declared itself to NATO even before the arrival of the first F3s to 29 (F) Squadron, an operational unit. Of the F2s delivered to the RAF eight were twin-stick/dual-control aircraft, although like the F3 it was impossible to tell from the outside if they had a dual role. In total the RAF operated 18 F2s. Despite a huge amount of work the OCU served little purpose other than bringing the AD version of the Tornado into the RAF's peripheral vision – and highlight its deficiencies.

The F2's turn in the public spotlight was short-lived and in January 1988 it was effectively withdrawn from service. Most of the airframes had less than 250 hours on the clock and had never flown with under-wing tanks. For the most part they had been used as day fighters in the air combat role. On a positive note the F2 had been displayed at air shows and performed a stunning mixed routine with an RAF Battle of Britain Memorial Flight Spitfire. If nothing else it had shown the ADV did have some agility.

While the F2 may have had a fairly inglorious service life it is perhaps sadder to report that while they were in storage most of the aircraft were reduced to spares to provide replacement parts for F3s damaged during a re-work programme. With the Cold War thawing rapidly the idea of forming an aggressor squadron with F2s also melted away before it had set. Although the F2 vanished from RAF service almost as quickly as it had entered, a handful soldiered on with BAe Warton and A&AEE Boscombe down as trials aircraft.

With the F2 consigned to the role of spare parts the F3 was certainly a major improvement. The radar, however, still remained substandard but the airframe was enhanced dramatically by fitting the Mk 104 RB199 engine. At this point it is probably worth reflecting on where we

BELOW Tornadoes and Lightnings fly together in formation in March 1988.

39

TORNADO VARIANTS – PAST AND PRESENT

were in the world of the late 1980s. The digital camera was in its infancy, the mobile phone was the size of a block of flats and the internet a glint in the eye of Tim Berners-Lee. At its launch in 1985 the Enterprise home computer with 64KB RAM may have seemed the stuff of science future, but no-one could have dreamed that by 2010 almost every person would be walking around with a 64GB mobile phone. The Tornado ADV was being introduced into service with the RAF at a time of unprecedented technological development. With no disrespect to the plane builders the world was moving forward more quickly than defence companies were able to keep pace with. While mobile phone manufacturers might be able to develop and produce to market a new mobile phone in a matter of months, trying to introduce upgrades to a new fighter aircraft took years after it had gone through designers, flight-testers, and then service release. It is no wonder, then, that the ADV was probably a victim of this era, an era that was racing ahead of itself.

F3 into service

With the first F3 (ZE159) delivered to the RAF in July 1986 it was decided to form an Operational Evaluation Unit (OEU) co-located at RAF Coningsby. Similar to the introduction of the Lightning in the 1960s, it was clear that ADV development was going to be a long process requiring constant upgrading. Initially work had taken place at Warton, but the RAF was keen to keep development in-house avoiding any delays incurred by manufacturers or indeed Boscombe Down. With around four aircraft on strength the OEU would be crucial to the success of the F3 in service.

The F3 looked similar to the F2 but was stretched at the back to accommodate the pair of RB199 Mk 104 engines – to be accurate, this is a 14in (36cm) extension to the afterburner section. At the back of the fin a small fillet was extended, giving an easy recognition of the two types. From a pilot and engineer's perspective the instillation of the Lucas Aerospace Digital Engine Control Unit (DECU) was a big step forward. From an operator's perspective it was the world's first full authority digital engine control unit and gave the magic carefree handling, improved combat power and better fuel consumption. Small problems remained that needed fixing: the de-selection of re-heat always purged the fuel lines and gave a distinctive puff of fuel vapour – a give-away in combat as to your throttle setting. From the ground engineer's perspective the DECU 500 allowed improved post-flight fault diagnosis as well as engine health monitoring. At the front the ADV had the single 27mm Mauser cannon on the right side. On the left side the cannon was replaced by a retractable refuelling probe that extended forward and upward just ahead of the pilot's left quarter light. If nothing else the gun was a huge step forward from the Aden cannon in the Lightning or the SU-23 Gatling gun on the Phantom FGR2. Accuracy with radar-ranging leapt from around 15% to an easily achievable 50% hit rate, in fact one or two pilots achieved the unthinkable 100% hit rates when firing in the air-to-air mode. The back-seater had a cockpit environment that was finally tailor-made to his needs: a roomy cockpit that was quiet and superbly air conditioned with no bulkhead between him and the front-seater.

Unlike the early GR1s the F3 had a 64KB computer as opposed to 32KB. The comms suite was extensive and the radar could be filmed with an over-technical Epsylon CVR/Video system. Initially the aircraft lacked the American Have-quick secure comms essential for combat operations. The back-seater now also had dual INS – the FIN 1010 three-axis digital INS – with the two INS's

BELOW Pilot's view.

RIGHT Wings swept, but not fully, give some idea of just how large the rear tailerons are.

monitoring each other giving indications in the pilot's HUD if an error was developing. (Of course, history has shown that to work properly you need three not two INS to detect if one is failing.)

A lot of mistruths have been written about the F3 and Auto Wing Sweep and Manoeuvre flaps. It was installed in RAF aircraft at manufacture but never used. I had the pleasure of collecting ZE964 from Warton for delivery to RAF Leuchars as one of 43 Squadron's first aircraft and it worked perfectly. Basically, as the aircraft accelerated and decelerated the wings moved forward and aft on schedule with no need to move the wing sweep lever. Likewise as you pulled 'G' the manoeuvre flaps came up and down automatically to improve your turn performance. Quite why the RAF never adopted it in service was always a matter for conjecture. The RSAF certainly used it with no problems. (One theory was that should two aircraft be in formation, with each aircraft having slightly different tolerances on the auto wing sweep, there was a possibility that one of the aircraft could be in a different wing sweep to the other, although this would really not be a flight safety issue.) If nothing else, by not having auto wing sweep it gave the back-seater great delight in shouting at the pilot 'Wings!' when he had forgotten to sweep them forward and was trying to turn with a target in swept wing mode! Other theories are that test pilots felt pilots could better control the wing sweeping themselves. Sad, then, that the RAF's first F3 loss was due largely to not having auto wing-sweep fitted. (The pilot was accelerating away from a known threat and in an effort to increase his acceleration he swept the wings back too early and the aircraft mushed into the sea.)

With a main computer now up to 128KBs the F3 also had the weapon carriage upgraded to four AIM-9Ls. This was a simple fix of adding extra stubs on the inner wing pylons to carry four not two Sidewinders. Initially the ADVs were delivered with just the inner pylons operational

41
TORNADO VARIANTS – PAST AND PRESENT

ABOVE Illustrating 20 (or even 30) years of advancements in aerospace technology – swing-wings and engines mounted in parallel (Tornado) compared to fixed 60-plus degree swept wings with twin vertically-mounted engines (Lightning).

but fortuitously, perhaps, the manufacture had built the F3 with virtually identical wings to the GR version – a feature that would prove vital later in life as the F3 developed. Initially aircraft were delivered with AI24 – 'W' list standard radars or indeed 'N' standard, 'N' standing for None!

With RAF Coningsby re-equipping, first the OCU swapped its F2s for F3s then 29 (F) Squadron traded its Phantom FGR2s for new-build F3s. Next to form was 5 Squadron, a former Lightning operator, which moved from RAF Binbrook 20 miles down the road to Coningsby. With only one former Lightning unit left ,11 (F) Squadron they were next to receive the ADV. Extended in service partially due to a need to provide targets for Foxhunter trials, 11 Squadron was the first to move to a newly upgraded Tornado base at Leeming. While this should have seen the end of the Lightning in service, BAe had to buy back four of the lowest-houred airframes to support the ongoing development of Foxhunter radar. With 11 Squadron installed at RAF Leeming next to re-equip was 23 Squadron, which had previously operated the FGR2 in the Falkland Islands. No 23 Squadron was the first to move into a newly

built Hardened Aircraft Shelter (HAS) site at Leeming. The transformation of Leeming was massive. Two fully operational HAS sites totally integrated for two squadrons of Tornado as well as a new QRA site dedicated to two aircraft. With RAF Binbrook now closed Leeming took on the role of Southern QRA. Last to form was 25 (F) Squadron. With Leeming complete it only remained for RAF Leuchars operating the tired FG1 Phantoms to transform. Initially 43 Squadron converted to the F3 then 111 (F) Squadron, which became the final operators of the ADV.

With the introduction of the F3 into RAF service complete it was now mid-1990. The radar was already up to 'Z' list standard and improvements to the radar and Marconi Hermes (RHWR) were coming into service, albeit at a very slow place. Navigators faced an increased workload. To actually fire a FOX1 (radar-guided missile) was a complex and difficult task. In the old F-4 it was simply a case of finding the target, locking it up, waiting for the lock to settle and then firing the missile. Now everything was done in the twin-TV tabs using the lower read-out lines. Back-seaters were frequently performing up to 16 separate tasks just to launch a missile and complete an attack. The OEU were gravely concerned about the deficiencies of the aircraft as a weapons platform and in particular the shortcomings of the radar. This led to trial 'Bunbury', which formally identified all of the radar's problems and tried to fix them. The cost was huge and quoted figures at the time were in the region of £395 milllion – in 1990 that was a huge expense on 150 airframes. (at this point each radar cost a staggering £3m)

Gulf War 1

With the start of the Gulf War in August 1990 the RAF Lightning had gone. The FGR2 was in the twilight of its years and the F3 was still a long way off being fully combat capable. It lacked so many vital things that the shopping list was long, very long. Added to this was the integration of fifteen ex-US Navy F-4J Phantoms into the UK air defence system at an awkward time. The first problem for the ADV was a lack of self-defence capability. Unlike the FGR2, which had ALE-40 scabbed to the back of the inner wing pylons, the F3 had no such luxury – in any case the fitment of flares onto the wing pylons would not work due to the close proximity of the tailerons. Luckily the fix was quick and the aircraft was fitted with twin ALE-40(V) under the rear engine doors. Due to its angular shape (especially with the carriage of four Skyflash missiles under the fuselage and the triangular fins sticking down) the RAF tried to make the airframe more stealthy. Under a veil of secrecy aircraft began emerging from 11 Squadron's old Second World War hangar at RAF Leeming with dark grey paint on the leading edges of the fin and wings. Known as Radar Absorbing Material (RAM) it also masked a further improvement – material known as RAM tiles were glued to the inside of the engine intakes. The theory was that the fast moving compressor blades gave off turbine modulations that fighter radars could detect. The RAM tiles were not a great success as the glue required several days to cure and when it failed the tiles would come off and enter the engines.

With the RAF receiving a budget for the F3 they made sure it was well spent. In the front cockpit the original stick-top was replaced with an F-18 stick-top giving much better Hands on Throttle and Stick (HOTAS) ability. Now the front-seater could cycle between Skyflash, Sidewinder and guns just with his thumb. Similarly the pilot could put the radar into an

BELOW No 11 Squadron's F3, ZE206 'DC', photographed over the desert. Note the dark grey fin and wing leading edges covered in RAM (Radar Absorbent Material) – otherwise known as paint!

LEFT F3, ZE968 'DJ', sporting the combined RAF Leeming 'Desert Eagle' badge on the fin.

ABOVE Combat fit with Phimatt chaff dispenser under the right wing pylon.

LEFT F3 with 2,250-litre tanks and full weapons fit.

air-to-air override mode, locking on to the target visible in the HUD and relieving the pressure on the back-seater.

In terms of capability the F3 now received the latest radar known as the Stage 1 or Stage 1+. Finally the aircraft had a radar that was performing well, with improved cooling and ECCM resistance; the back-seater now had a reliable piece of kit that worked, although it was still in need of minor improvements. One of the advantages of the RHWR was the fact it was fully programmable so re-programming to perceived Gulf threats was relatively simple. Have-quick radios were added allowing the F3s to work with the USAF, but sadly it was decided not to use the F3 forward of the Saudi border during Gulf War 1. To overcome the lack of CHAFF the F3s deployed to the Gulf were fitted with the Phimat chaff dispenser normally seen on the Harrier or Jaguar. Initially the Phimat pod was fitted under the inner wing pylon where the 1,500 or 2,250-litre fuel tanks would be – obviously not a great war-fit as the F3 relied on carrying external fuel tanks. It was later remounted to a Sidewinder pylon.

Other internal modifications were trialled including the use of Night Vision Goggles (NVG), which involved painting the cockpit black and trying to cover up stray light that degraded the goggles' performance, as well as full integration of the AR5 into the F3. The AR5 was a particularly unpleasant piece of aircrew clothing/equipment that allowed crews to operate in a full nuclear/biological threat environment. Whilst the ground crew would be expected to wear full NBC (Nuclear, Biological, Chemical) suits and S6 respirators, the pilots and navigators needed protection from the point when they were walking out to the aircraft and strapping in, to returning again, without removing the standard S6/S10 gas mask. Whilst the ground crew would have the unenviable job of servicing in such conditions, re-loading and re-arming the Tornado in full NBC kit, the aircrew was also not well placed. The AR5 was a full rubber hood worn under the helmet along with the carriage of a portable ventilator. As you climbed into the cockpit you switched from portable ventilator to main 100% oxygen supply. Quite how this would have felt in the 45° heat of a desert I never tried.

With no aspect of the F3 safe from 'enhancement' the RAF turned to the US Navy to obtain improved AIM-9Ls for the start of the conflict. These arrived in the shape of the AIM-9M fitted with the WGU-4A/B seeker head that gives better target discrimination as well as a flare rejection capability. In simple terms the seeker can detect an aircraft's jet plume, say, at 600° Centigrade, which it locks on to, guiding the missile to the jet pipe area. In older missiles should the target drop a decoy flare the seeker head will see this brighter, hotter source and transfer its lock on to the flare and track the new heat source, diverting away from the jet pipe. This was the shortcoming of the AIM-9L. In the AIM-9M the missile is clever enough to lock to the target jet pipe (or hot spot) and, seeing the flare launch, the seeker initially tracks the new hotter source but as it burns so hot and so bright it is able to shift back to the original heat source and not be fooled by the decoy. The AIM-9M also has an improved rocket motor.

Engine-wise there was a small improvement in top line temperature, which gave a small increase in thrust, though this meant a big decrease in engine life so its use was not encouraged. In truth, the F3s deployed to the Gulf were only really in need of extra power under certain flight regimes, for example remaining above the upper level of various surface-to air-missile threats.

Apart from flying QRA missions over Britain most pilots had never really flown the F3 at its all-up maximum weight, which proved challenging. On day to day operations in Britain the F3 flew in 'K' fit, which equates to clean wings, with perhaps a Sidewinder training round and little else. Now the crews were flying in 'L+' fit – that is, everything: 4 x Skyflash, 4 x AIM-9Ms and 2 x full 2,250-litre tanks. The maximum take-off weight now meant the aircraft would need specially modified high-speed tyres – the temperatures in the Gulf were 40 degrees plus, giving rotation speeds near 200kts with maximum weight. Actually, take-off weights were in the region of 25 tons with 9 tons of this being fuel, both internal and external.

At maximum all-up aircraft weight (25-plus tons) thrust now became an issue, despite the fact the F3 was never comfortable above 35,000ft. During the Gulf War the F3 was limited in height during air-to-air refueling in 'L' fit, which forced tankers down to the area of 20,000ft. One fairly revolutionary modification was the fitting to both ADV and GR1s of single-crystal turbine blades as used on German Air Force ECR Tornadoes. This gave a nominal increase in ceiling of 1–2,000ft in dry power, which might seem insignificant but may have given crews the edge on overflying short-range SAMs. Whilst the RAF F3s did not actually engage any Iraqi forces during Gulf War 1, they performed adequately and many of the deficiencies were rectified in a few short months to make the aircraft much more capable for the future.

After Gulf War 1 the Tornado F3 force was in a state of disarray. Even though the aircraft that had deployed to the Gulf were now at a greatly improved standard the Tornado fleet that remained were all at various modification states, so there was a huge amount of shuffling around trying to get commonality between bases rather than units. From an engineer's point of view this was a huge headache as aircraft had normally spent most of their lives allocated to a single squadron. To move aircraft from, say, Coningsby to Leuchars, was a huge amount of work for the engineers let alone the painters and finishers.

The Airwork upgrade

No sooner had the conflict in the Gulf finished than the F3 was suffering fatigue problems. Not designed for hard combat (in truth it was never envisaged the aircraft would deploy and take part in an overseas out-of-area conflict) the airframes were using up fatigue at a much higher rate than had been envisaged. Initially BAe was contracted to upgrade a batch of 15 airframes, but the next batch was put out to tender in a contract won by Airwork Services.

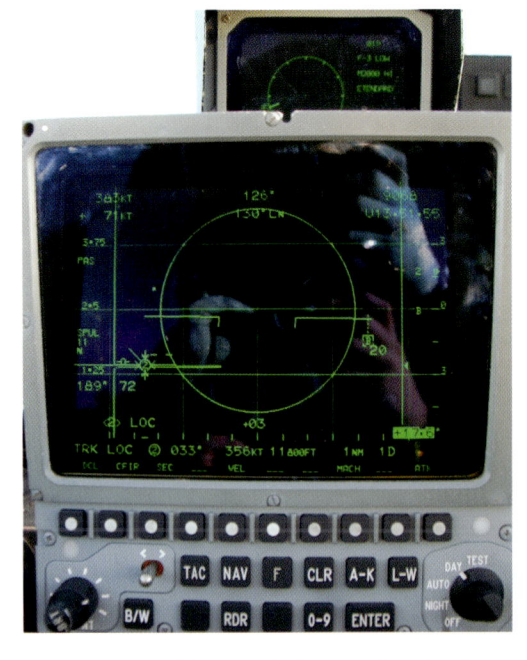

RIGHT Back-seat TV tab showing display of a target locked up by the AI 24.

BELOW Back-seat radar display showing the radar in search mode with horizon bars to give the rear seater an idea of attitude whilst heads-in. The target is the tadpole shape in the top right-hand corner.

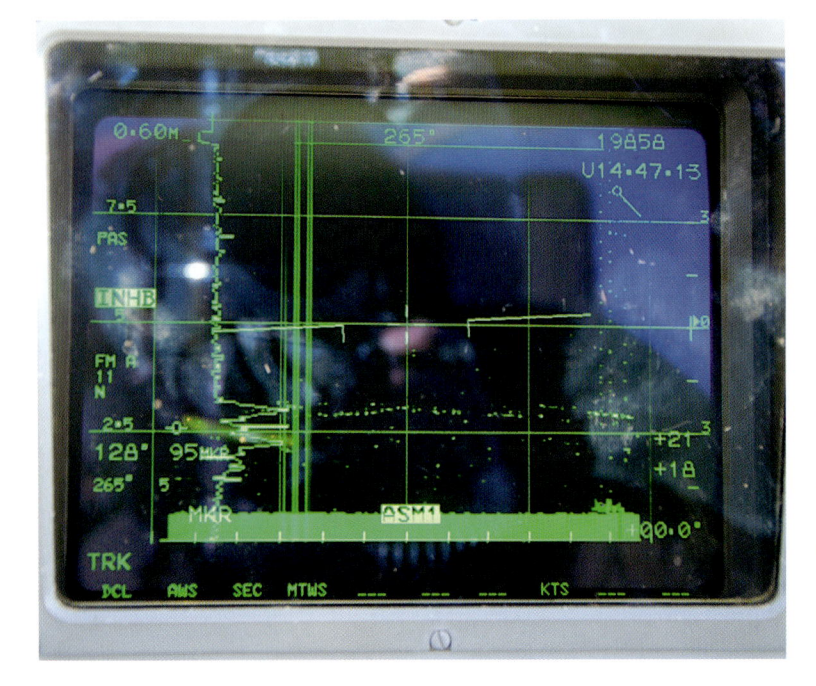

Airwork would upgrade the next batch of Tornadoes at St Athan and re-deliver them to the RAF. The first four aircraft returned to service (ZE292, 295, 343 and 728) soon began developing problems; the pilots who flew them stated they behaved differently. The RAF subsequently discovered that there had been structural damage to the airframes. On inspection a further 12 airframes were found to be badly damaged. The damage was so serious that initial diagnosis was to scrap the aircraft (a plan to return them to have new centre sections manufactured by Panavia was too costly).

In true British fashion an engineer calculated the airframes could be saved by rebuilding them with the centre sections of the original F2s then in storage at St Athan. By incorporating these centre sections a solution had been found to save the damaged F3s. In a twist of fate the contract was given back to BAe and a trial modification was undertaken using ZE154 to be morphed with F2 ZD901, an experiment that was deemed a success and the rest of the damaged fleet was converted back to service. A historic day in Tornado production was 24 March 1993 when the RAF accepted ZH559, the last and final Tornado built for the RAF. It was collected from the BAe factory by AVM Sir John Allison; the aircraft was withdrawn from service in 2008 and scrapped.

Improved missile fits

Whilst Joint Tactical Information Distribution System (JTIDS) deserves a chapter to itself, the next major upgrade to the F3 force came with the welcome addition of the AMRAAM and ASRAAM to enhance its capability and allow it inter-operability with US fighters. The introduction of the Tornado F3 into the RAF's air defence inventory was only a small part of the jigsaw in combining all Britain's air defence assets under one umbrella.

The Big Stick AIM 120 – AMRAAM was a missile F3 crews had wanted since the missile began to be seen on the F-15, while the ASRAAM would overcome the shortcomings of the F3's turning ability and give it the edge of the F-16 class of agile fighters. An advantage to both missile types was the ability to fit them to the F3 airframe without major modifications. In 1997 BAe was awarded a contract worth £125M to fit both missiles to the F3 under a programme, known as Capability Sustainment Programme (CSP). Modifications involved the upgrading of the missile management system as well as the main computer. The carriage of AMRAAM and its fire-and-forget capability was once again another essential upgrade to the F3 in order to overcome some of its shortcomings. When the aircraft was finally retired from RAF Service (not including the trials aircraft that carried METEOR) the F3 AMRAAM/ASRAAM force was on a par with its contemporaries. Other vital upgrades saw the F3s carry towed radar decoys in converted BOZ pods as well as a chance to turn the F3 into a super Tornado (EF3) with the incorporation of ALARM missiles onto some 11 Squadron aircraft, a trial that showed great promise.

JTIDS

As described earlier the introduction of the Tornado F3 into the RAF's air defence inventory was only a small part of the jigsaw of combining all of the UK's air defence assets under one umbrella. Pivotal to this was the introduction of Link 16 JTIDS, arguably the most important advance in capability to air defence aircraft since the invention of radar. JTIDS is a high capacity communications system that provides secure jam-resistant transfer of digital data information to participating aircraft or ground stations, giving an unparalleled level of situational awareness to friendly forces. Suffice it to say that Tornado F3s working with AWACS had some of the best air pictures available – indeed, the amount of information available to the aircraft could saturate the crews, giving credence to the original two-crew concept to reduce individual workload.

ADV retirement

The RAF Tornado ADV era was drawn to a close in 2011, but the legacy of the F3 will live on in the Service. Perhaps not the most charismatic of fighters, it certainly earned the respect of those who flew and serviced it. Whilst its critics were generally lacking in knowledge of what the aircraft could do, it had served the RAF with distinction in the Gulf,

ABOVE The RAFs last three F3s are seen here in the markings of 43, 25 and 111 Squadrons. Having spent some time performing trials work for the Meteor missile these aircraft were finally retired in July 2012.

ABOVE A 2 Squadron GR4 blasts through the Lake District in typical British winter weather.

the Balkans, back again to the Gulf and for many years protecting Britain and the Falkland Islands. Perhaps its greatest achievement was during Operation 'Telic'. Now fully capable it was often tasked flying deep into Iraq escorting Tornado GR4s and allied aircraft sanitising hostile airspace. Nearly twenty years after its entry to RAF service the F3s operating during 'Telic' were universally respected. The fact that no GR4 was lost to enemy aircraft, nor was any F3 ever lost to enemy fire, is proof of the pudding and that the aircraft and crews were up to the task.

Tornado reconnaissance – the GR1A

Perhaps the most commonly know reconnaissance aircraft of the postwar period is the Lockheed U-2 and before that the Canberra, but since the late 1980s the Tornado has been a world leader in the field of aerial recce. Although not able to fly as far and as high as its predecessors, the Tornado cut its teeth and set the bench mark during Gulf War 1 as a 'scud Hunter' *par excellence*. When it entered service in 1989 just prior to hostilities, it was the world's first film-less recce aircraft, thanks to its (then) revolutionary Infra-Red (IR) video system. As the RAF had been late in specifying what they wanted in the production aircraft, initial airframes were converted from Batch 4 GR1s. In total the RAF ordered 30 GR1A aircraft – 14 from the original GR1's, while the last 16 were new-build GR1A from Batches 5 and 14.

The work entailed removing the two forward cannons and replacing them with sensors and recording equipment. In the cockpit additional controls were added allowing the recce system to be integrated with the standard nav/attack system. Although the airframe was now 'gun-less' the aircraft still retained a strike role in addition to the primary role of reconnaissance. Externally the aircraft had small brown di-electric panels under the engine intakes forward of the back-seater, while the area behind the radome was blanked over to keep the redundant gun ports smooth.

Under the fuselage there was a bulge for the Infra Red Line Scan (IRLS) sensor (normally this is covered, but when required for use the window slides open). The package was known as Tornado Infra Red Reconnaissance System (TIRRS). Recording was accomplished by six tape machines easily accessible through drop-down doors. The RAF opted for an Infra Red (IR) system because it allows much greater flexibility than standard 'light' images, as well as giving additional information not readily discernible to the naked eye. Less affected by weather conditions, IR images can be taken day or night with little difference.

At this time a new skill of IR imagery exploitation was growing among RAF analysts. The advantages of IR could be seen with images of parked aircraft – engines that recently had been run showed 'hot' for hours after shutdown; similarly, aircraft fuel tanks could be seen as full or empty due to temperature differences. Recently departed aircraft leave a heat trace, even with no sign of the airframe. Now, with IR it became increasingly difficult for ground troops to camouflage weapons.

As described the Tornado GR1A had three sensors: the Vinten Type 4000 IRLS mounted in the under fuselage blister; Sideways Looking Infra Red (SLIR) sensors; and the Vicon GP1 pod.

The reconnaissance Tornado had three regular missions:

- **Point of interest (POI).** Here a mission is planned with specify targets or a target in mind with the aim of gaining as much intelligence as possible.
- **Traditional line search.** For example on a rail, road link or for capturing specific troop convoys.
- **Strip search.** The aircraft covers large areas of interest to allow Intelligence officers to scour miles of film post-flight looking for activity or items of special interest.

Often the recce Tornado flies alone with no gun or even Sidewinder for self-defence, relying on a low altitude map of the earth or TFR flying or under cover of darkness with the aid of NVGs. As the crew progress to the target the pilot or the navigator can 'tag' events for looking at in detail later on. The pilot uses a switch on his control column whilst the back-seater uses the rear joystick. One of the big advantages of the TIRRS was it allowed navigators to review imagery in the air as they returned to base- This was vital as it gave them a chance to re-attack a positive target for better images - or in extreme cases allow them to transmit back via HF radio - observations that were of extreme urgency. Whilst the Tornado GR1A was cutting-edge technology the advent of the RAPTOR pod has given the GR force a fleet-wide capability that few air forces possess.

BELOW No 13 Squadron GR4A, ZG707 'B'.

ABOVE Loaded with the immensely capable Goodrich RAPTOR Pod, 13 Squadron's GR4A (ZG707 'B') is seen over the Scottish mountains in typical 'Tornado' weather. *(Peter R. Foster)*

GOODRICH RAPTOR POD

'Making a dark world bright'

Without question the current Royal Air Force retains the edge in terms of ISTAR (Intelligence Surveillance Targeting Acquisition and Reconnaissance), thanks in no small way to the Reconnaissance Airborne Pod for Tornado (RAPTOR).

RAPTOR is built by the Goodrich Corporation and is a new stand-off electro-optical and infrared (IR), long-range oblique-photography pod fitted to the Tornado GR4. The images received by the pod can be transmitted via a real-time data-link system to image analysts at a ground station, or can be displayed in the cockpit during flight. The imagery can also be recorded for post-flight analysis. The RAPTOR system can create images of hundreds of separate targets in one sortie; it is capable of autonomous operation against preplanned targets, or it can be re-tasked manually for targets of opportunity or to select a different route to the target. The stand-off range of the sensors allows the aircraft to remain outside heavily-defended areas in order to minimise the aircraft's exposure to enemy air-defence systems.

The RAPTOR pod contains a dual-band (visible and IR) sensor, which is capable of detecting and identifying small targets from either short range or long range and from medium or high altitudes, by day or by night.

The optical sensors gather high-resolution, motion-free images of extraordinary detail. The optical images are supported by IR imagery that can reveal differences in the shape, composition or content of objects from their thermal signatures. Daytime IR also offers superior haze-penetration in poor weather conditions, while the night time imagery can reveal details such as the fuel levels in storage tanks. The aircraft weapon systems officer controls the RAPTOR system using a real-time cockpit video display, enabling verification of target acquisition, and the conduct of tasks such as battle-damage assessment, or recording the images on digital tape for further in-depth, post-operation analysis.

TIW are able to extract minute detail from images gathered by Tornado aircraft flying at medium or high altitudes out of harm of small arms fire and able to view areas ground troops would find difficult. The level of detail is stunning with TIW personnel able to detect and prevent acts of terrorism like no other sensor can. As an illustration of the value Coalition forces place on the RAF RAPTOR equipped aircraft GR4 crews can be tasked with capturing on image hundreds of points of interest on a single sortie – a task it achieves with ease. Such is the capability of the pod that it can actually show at night with thermal imagery the level of fluids kept inside storage tanks not visible to the naked eye. Some of the capabilities of RAPTOR are eye watering, quotes that Tornado crews can read the time on the face of Big Ben whilst sitting over the Isle of Wight – some 60-plus miles away are hard to comprehend. Now the limitation is not on the equipment but on the human interface in terms of analyzing the vast quantities of data received in such a short period.

The capability of the pod should not be underestimated. Recent operations over Afghanistan have seen Tornado GR4 aircraft, equipped with the RAPTOR pod on reconnaissance missions, re-tasked in the air to provide a show of force. Further, when armed only with the 27mm gun the aircraft is still able to perform air-to-ground suppressing fire against insurgents. Despite its size the RAPTOR pod mounted on the right under fuselage shoulder pylon still allows room for the Paveway IV guided munitions on the right pylon, thereby increasing the punch. This is particularly useful when GR4 crews are called on to support TIC (Troops in Combat) scenarios. Coupled with ROVER (Remote Optical Video Enhanced Receiver), RAPTOR allows true real time inter-operability between ground and air forces.

With no other aircraft cleared to carry RAPTOR in the current RAF inventory a new solution will need to be found after Tornado using either a new pod or unmanned airborne vehicles. Modern warfare relies more than ever on real time imagery delivered by airborne assets such as Tornado and it seems inconceivable that any future conflicts won't involve the use of RAPTOR pods from the beginning. The Goodrich RAPTOR pod is perhaps the jewel in the crown in terms of capability to current RAF TGRF operations, indeed as the title says Tornado GR4 equipped with RAPTOR makes 'a dull world bright'.

BELOW A 617 Squadron armourer carefully removes a RAPTOR reconnaissance pod from a Tornado GR4 at Kandahar Air Base in Afghanistan following a mission. *(RAF)*

Tornado anti-shipping – the GR1B

With the withdrawal from operational service of the Blackburn Buccaneer the RAF faced a capability gap in anti-shipping strike. Carrying the BAe Sea Eagle missile the Buccaneer was well suited for the role of maritime strike and had developed tactics that despite the aircraft's age put it way ahead of its contemporaries. Nevertheless the airframes were due for retirement and no type-specific aircraft had yet been built to fulfill the over-sea role.

After Gulf War 1 the RAF effectively withdrew from forward bases in Germany (Bruggen and Laarbruch were the Tornado bases) and returned to Britain, with the Tornado force now located at only two British bases (Lossiemouth and Marham; the TWCU at Honington was also due to close). With 15, 16 and 20 Squadrons giving up their GR1s it left a surplus of aircraft suitable for a new role – that of maritime strike/attack.

At the time of the Buccaneer's withdrawal there was a shuffling around of squadrons – the two Buccaneer units (12 and 208) became a Tornado GR1 squadron and a reserve Hawk unit respectively. The TWCU at Honington (which was 45 Squadron) became 15 Squadron, while 16 Squadron became the Jaguar OCU, and finally 20 Squadron took up the mantle of the Harrier OCU.

Early in the development phase of the ADV it became clear that the airframe was every bit as good as the GR1, if not better. Bigger engines, more fuel and improved SPILS meant that it would be an easy conversion to turn the F3 into a 'Super Tornado' adapted for a variety of tasks. BAe had ideas of a 'Super Tornado' carrying ALARM, Sea Eagle or indeed as a dedicated ECR/Wild Weasel aircraft. Of course history has shown that none of this came to fruition (although a few F3s did get ALARM capability). With a surplus of GR1s it was an easy choice to convert them from overland bombers to overwater bombers.

Designated the GR1B the Tornado was able to carry 4 Sea Eagle missiles – 2 under the fuselage and 2 under the wings. With the RAF's need to replace two squadrons of Buccaneers it was decided to convert 26 former GR airframes to GR1B status. Externally it was impossible to tell from the GR1, the 1B hosted an improved software modification as well as taking the Buccaneer's control panel from the rear cockpit and using it to control the launch of the Sea Eagle missiles. The two squadrons chosen to be Sea Eagle operators were 12 and 617, both appropriately co-located at RAF Lossiemouth. With no major airframe changes the only internal modifications involved the main

BELOW The short-lived GR1B is seen here heading to the tanker armed with a pair of dummy Sea Eagle missiles on the fuselage pylons.
(Author's collection)

computer software – allowing the missiles to be detected by the aircraft and the modification of the under-wing inner and under-fuselage shoulder pylons. For reasons unknown the airframes were modified in-house at RAF St Athan rather than at BAe Warton, and as early as 19 September 1993 the first GR1B (ZA407) had flown. (The aircraft converted to GR1B were all in the range of ZA374-ZA492 but were not sequential.) While undergoing conversion to GR1B standard the aircraft began to appear in a new all-over dark sea grey paint scheme replacing the traditional grey and green low-level European camouflage of the Cold War era.

Initially the aircraft were modified to either Batch 1 or Batch 2 standard. The Batch 1 aircraft were capable of merely employing Sea Eagle in a point-and-shoot mode, whilst the Batch 2 aircraft were able to use the missile's own radar and fire at targets up to 110km away. As mentioned the first Buccaneer unit to transfer to GR1B was 12 Squadron, which formerly had been 27 Squadron, and which then became a helicopter unit. When 617 Squadron moved north to take up 208 Squadron's role the former Honington recce units of II (AC) Squadron and 13 Squadron moved in to Marham to form the nucleus of the RAF's reconnaissance wing.

Now fully established at RAF Lossiemouth the GR1Bs also had an overland role and were not dedicated solely to Sea Eagle missions. As good as the Buccaneer was at employing the Sea Eagle it lacked the sophistication of the Tornado's avionics suite and the ability of the GR1B to fly at night in all weathers with the aid of its TFR, still retained on the GR1B. Attack profiles relied on the use of AWACS or Nimrod MPA aircraft, or the Tornado could prosecute attacks autonomously. Specific attack profiles remain classified, but normally the force would launch with six aircraft all spaced apart to allow the maximum force of attack on designated targets. The attack runs would be as low as 100ft in peacetime, with the GR1B making use of its extra speed over the older and slower Buccaneer. Using either the GR1B's onboard mapping radar or AWACS and MPA information the formation would be given updated co-ordinates of the surface vessels, which the back-seater could then programme into the Sea Eagle's own computer. With Tornado the RAF had an improved capability with Sea Eagle despite the Buccaneers excellent reputation as a low-level strike aircraft.

With the introduction of GR4 and the withdrawal of the Nimrod aircraft the Sea Eagle role has now been dropped. Similarly GR1Bs have been withdrawn and several have ended up in museums, including the USAF Museum and the RAF Museum at Hendon, London.

BELOW No 2 Squadron's GR4, ZD890, at low level around Dunmail Raise in the Lake District. *(Mark Tyson)*

GR1 into the GR4 – the Mid-Life Update (MLU)

When I asked a former Tornado pilot what the Tornado Mid-Life Update (MLU) involved he jokingly referred to it as the 'Tornado Mid-Life Re-paint'. That, however, is far from the truth for what the RAF has now in the GR4 is a million miles away from what was the GR1 or even the original GR4.

From its inception the MRCA/Tornado was designed and built with longevity in mind. Although the concept of swing-wing proved to be a fashion no more lasting than flared trousers, the basic airframe concept has withstood the test of time. Perhaps initially not future-proofed or designed with planned growth in mind, the aircraft has benefitted from the advancements in technology allowing for more to be packed in to a smaller space. From a manufacturer's point of view BAe was quick to realise that the Tornado airframe had growth potential and the prospect of one nation ordering a completely new bomber within a matter of years from introduction were over. The Tornado would need to be upgraded, incorporating new technologies and benefiting from its combat experience.

With the end of the Cold War, aircraft attrition and changing perceptions on Britain's future air power strategy deemed that a re-work of 142 airframes would see the Tornado force through to its planned retirement of 2025 – nearly half a century of service. This was after a planned follow-on order of 26 new-build Tornados was cancelled in 1990. Whilst lucrative to BAe, it also proved to be cost effective to the RAF to retain an existing airframe and thus avoid all the high baseline costs of introducing a new type.

Lessons learned from Gulf War 1 and subsequent conflicts proved that no longer would the Tornado be able to continue in its role of low-level strike and attack relying largely on dumb weapons. The future lay in precision 'smart weapons' with the emphasis on a day or night capability, and most importantly the delivery of these weapons with unparalleled accuracy avoiding collateral damage and civilian casualties. The new improved Tornado would need improved FLIR, the integration of a full Night Vision Goggles (NVG) capability as well as improving the defence aids suite. Importantly the aircraft would be capable of carrying existing and future smart weapons. Planned conversion would take around 18 months per airframe. Having been delivered to the RAF in 1981 the airframes were already nearly 20 years old and due for upgrading. The very last Tornado had been built in 1998 (an aircraft for the RSAF) and BAe was hungry for work now production had ceased.

Air Staff Requirement 417 was geared to enhancing an aircraft that was now combat proven and technologically mature. With the advent of Gulf War 1 the RAF rose to the challenge and aircraft had begun to get out of phase due to urgent operational requirements being fitted. The Tornado force (IDS) was becoming an eclectic mix of airframes, trainers, recce aircraft, pure strike aircraft, airframes that were ALARM capable as well as those that carried TIALD, and the new GR1B Sea Eagle airframes. What the RAF wanted was one common standard airframe that could be switched from unit to unit without any difference.

From its combat experiences the RAF now had a fairly long shopping list for its GR fleet. At the front end FLIR was deemed essential. While the TFR is combat-proven it does require the TFR radar to be in transmit mode, which is susceptible to jamming. New avionics architecture would require the 1553 data bus fitting. In the front cockpit the pilot would have a new wide field of view HUD as well as the pilot's multi-function digital map, enhanced digital video recording system and improved computer loading system – essentially a fully night vision-capable cockpit.

When wearing NVGs stray light from dials or instruments in the cockpits need to be dimmed. Initially aircraft were simply painted black inside and copious amounts of 'bodge tape' were used to cover up stray light, so clearly a more robust system was needed. Additionally, the update would have a new armament control system consisting of a stores management system linked to the 1553 databus with a 1760 interface. A covert rad alt (essential for night operations) is a radar altimeter that does not emit radio frequencies and give away your position.

Other important changes were an improved Environmental Control System (ECS). As an aircraft gets older (they term it 'growth' or 'creep') and more new systems are incorporated all this new equipment needs to be cooled, which puts an increased demand on the existing systems. GPS was also added, in addition to the BAe Terprom digital terrain mapping system and a Honeywell H-764G Laser INS. (One of the guns was removed because it was deemed superfluous.) If the RAF had its 'dream list' then it would have added the fuselage plug seen on the ADV to give the aircraft improved internal range. Another nicety (shelved due to budget constraints) was the upgrading of the TFR to be truly covert.

The RAF were hard at work determining the baseline standard for its future fleet when world events began to unfold that would throw the entire programme into jeopardy. After Gulf War 1 the end of the Cold War presented new challenges. Britain had to quickly reassess what it now deemed the 'threat' to be and how it was going to counter it. What no-one could predict was how the GR Tornado would be employed over the next 20 years. Certainly, the RAF was adamant that the primary task of the GR force was to continue in its low-level role, but what no-one knew was that it would be thrust into conflicts far from Britain in Kosovo, Libya, back again to Iraq, and finally in the hostile environment of Afghanistan.

The RAF was faced with additional problems: having had Tornado airframes modified to GR1B standard and now deciding they no longer needed a Sea Eagle capability, industry (BAe) insisted that all aircraft delivered back to them should be to the same modification standard – a tall order in a fleet of 200 plus aircraft that were engaged in conflicts almost continuously for over a decade. As illustrated earlier, while the Tornado GR1 airframe differs little externally from what the RAF accepted back in 1981, it's the internals that have undergone huge changes – namely software. Indeed, the pace of change of software development coupled with the relatively long introduction of changes it meant that on occasion what the RAF may have wanted at the start of the year had now become outdated, and they wanted state-of-the art and then changed their minds. Unfortunately industry is not quite that reactive!

These obstacles were largely overcome into what became known as rolling development. With over 30 miles of electrical wiring inside the Tornado (20% of which would need replacing) this was certainly not going to be what one Tornado pilot mentioned earlier (with tongue in cheek) as a mid-life repaint. With just two years having elapsed from the start of the MLU programme, the final standard was set and work would be done at the Tornado's birthplace at BAe's Warton plant in Lancashire.

The Tornado MLU programme was huge. Each aircraft would have 500 items removed, which were stored, scrapped or refitted. What BAe wanted was a production line where

ABOVE Tornado GR4, ZA400, '*Scud Hunter*', is one of the RAF's most well-known Tornadoes, having distinguished itself during Gulf War 1 hunting mobile Scuds – surely an airframe worthy of preservation one day. This wonderful image shows the leading edge slats fully deployed, Kruger flaps inboard locked up, the intake doors are open (denoting the aircraft is at low speed). Clearly visible beneath the fuselage is the nose-mounted LRMTS (right chin), FLIR (left chin) just aft the rotating camera doors, and on the centre line a CBLS (practice bomb store, right side) and TIALD pod (left side). The aircraft is fitted with 1,500-litre (small) fuel tanks and a Sidewinder training round. *(RAF)*

TORNADO VARIANTS – PAST AND PRESENT

RIGHT The FLIR is mounted on the right chin. To prevent damage to the sensitive glass the optical window is closed until required.

BELOW Tornado GR4, '004', was formerly a GR1A but since its Mid-Life Upgrade it has adopted the tail code of '004' – being the fourth oldest GR4 in service. The centre line has a TIALD pod fitted, which is slimmer and longer than the Litening pod.

aircraft would enter the factory and basically not move for 18 months until the work was complete and flight-testing could take place. It was essential that individual aircraft should be modified on a bespoke basis – the temptation to 'rob' parts from different airframes would only complicate the process. Having opted not to have airframes moving down a traditional production line, BAe had small teams of engineers working on up to three airframes at a time. The RAF MLU was crucial to BAe as its success would offer a potential work stream for the Warton plant if the RSAF undertook the same MLU on its GR1s.

Working from the forward fuselage the front left gun was removed, the area around it strengthened and the chin-mounted FLIR fitted. On the base of the fin the heat exchanger was replaced by the more powerful one used on the ADV. As already mentioned BAe wanted the aircraft to arrive at Warton to a common baseline standard. To achieve this aircraft were flown first to RAF St Athan for major work, allowing them to depart north at the baseline standard required by the manufacturer. Once at Warton the aircraft were prepared for upgrading. The first GR1 arrived in April 1996 and was ready some 12 months later, ahead of the original planned 18 month-schedule. By the seventeenth aircraft turnaround time had been reduced to just eight months, with the entire 142 aircraft completed by 2003.

Re-coding

One by-product of the GR4 upgrade was the re-coding of the RAF fleet. With several aircraft lost in accidents, or scrapped, it was decided to code the remaining GR4 fleet in numbers 001–140 – 001 being ZA365, the oldest in the fleet, with ZG794 the youngest. Of the upgraded aircraft some became GR4As from original GR1As (25 in total), although these are now simply GR4s because the internal cameras have been replaced by the RAPTOR pod. With the programme in full swing BAe was returning an upgraded aircraft to the RAF every eight days. Initially the aircraft were flown back to RAF St Athan, re-accepted into RAF service, then issued to front line units. Although the upgraded aircraft suffered from initial teething troubles these were soon ironed out. With a total cost of around £943million the MLU worked out at around £6.6 million per aircraft – perhaps the RAF's most cost-effective expenditure for a long time. BAe can be justifiably proud of upgrading the Tornado GR1 to GR4.

Tornado current capability – Tornado Ground Reconnaissance Force (TGRF)

Now that the Tornado is approaching the twilight of its autumn years its worth highlighting how the GR4 aircraft of today are configured and what the weapons fit will be for the foreseeable future. While the basic airframe may be almost identical to the GR1 first delivered to the RAF in 1980 (TTTE), the GR4 has slowly evolved into one of the most potent attack aircraft still in service with any air arm in the world today.

Today the airframe is pretty much subsonic due to the intake ramps no longer being moveable at high speed, but the power plant remains the same – the twin RB199 MK103 turbofans. Nevertheless, the aircraft is still capable of low-level all-weather operations day or night using its TFR (Terrain Following Radar) and GMR (Ground Mapping Radar).

The front left blister located beneath the forward fuselage houses the FLIR (Forward Looking Infra Red), an early upgrade of the GR4 Mid-Life Upgrade programme (a lesson learned from the Harrier GR7/9 also fitted with FLIR which demonstrated how capable this piece of kit was). Each cockpit is now fully NVG (Night Vision Goggle) capable. When NVG ops were first considered the cockpit was given a very quick upgrade (normally a splash of black paint), but now the front and back seat are optimised for night operations. This allows crews to operate the aircraft at night, lights out, 'passively'. Crews wearing helmet mounted NVG and using FLIR avoids the need for them to transmit radar and alert enemy forces.

On the forward right-hand side of the chin is the LRMTS (Laser Range and Marked Target Seeker) used to give accurate range to ground targets (not to be confused with the capability of the Litening III targeting pod). Allegedly the LRMTS housing is exactly the same profile as that used on the SEPECAT Jaguar.

Internally the aircraft is fitted with GPINS (Global Positioning Internal Navigation Systems) as well as modern secure radios. A recent

ABOVE The Tornado's LRMTS is the same as that fitted to the SEPECAT Jaguar.

BELOW No 9 Squadron GR4 training for deployment to Afghanistan. *(RAF)*

ABOVE *A GR4 Tornado fitted with Brimstone and Paveway weapons awaits permission to take off from Kandahar Airfield during Operation Moshtarak in Afghanistan. (RAF)*

addition is the T-shaped large aerial located under the rear left door of the right engine. All remaining GR4s will undergo this modification. In terms of smart weapons the Tornado GR4 force has all but abandoned the Alarm missile and other previous legacy munitions to focus on the following newer 'smart' weapons.

Depending on the mission tasking and/or the theatre of operations, the following equipment fits can now be seen on the Tornado GR4. Under-fuselage two Storm Shadow cruise missiles can be mounted side-by-side on the shoulder pylons. Other weapon fits can include up to five Paveway IV smart weapons or DMS (Dual Mode Seeker) Brimstone missiles. These are the small (comparatively) missiles that hang at a downward angle and are normally mounted near the rear hard points (especially if a targeting pod is on the forward mount). To complement these weapons the aircraft carries the TIALD or Litening III self-contained designating pod, again under the fuselage. Litening III is the most modern pod.

Perhaps the largest store to be seen under-mounted is the highly capable RAPTOR pod used for reconnaissance missions. ALARM has been effectively mothballed but future conflicts may see its return, although some consider this to be unlikely.

The under-wing standard training fit is two

RIGHT *No 617 Squadron GR4 with Storm Shadow. (RAF)*

58
RAF TORNADO MANUAL

1500-litre fuel tanks with the option of the bigger 2,250-litre tanks for long range war missions. With four under-wing stores pylons the inner two are normally reserved for fuel tanks while the outer two carry the BOZ-EC countermeasures pod (often on the right wing), and on the port wing the Sky Shadow 2 ECM pod. For self defence the GR4 carried the Sidewinder AIM-9L IR missile but this has now been replaced by the much-improved ASRAAM missile. Sadly, it is unlikely the Tornado will see the implementation of the HMS (Helmet Mounted Sight) to complement the missile's outstanding off-bore sight capabilities, despite the fact that helmet-mounted sights are in use in Afghanistan (under Operation Herrick they are theatre-specific equipment for tasks not associated with missile cueing).

Developed by BAE Systems the HMCS (Helmet Mounted Cueing System) is described by them as greatly enhancing the situational awareness of crews and resource management, enabling the rapid identification of points of interest in the hostile Afghan environment.

The Storm Shadow cruise missile is probably the smartest weapon of all carried by the Tornado. Deadly accurate, it allows the GR4 to launch cruise missiles at high value targets with pinpoint accuracy from a relatively safe distance.

The Tornado GR4 has moved away from the high risk JP233/1000lb iron bomb attacks of the late 1980s with the development and employment of smart weapons. Likewise the WE177 nuclear weapon is now a distant memory because the GR4 is now fully conventional.

With the demise of the GR1, the GR1A and the GR1B the RAF Tornado force is now fully GR4. Erroneous reporting stated the old recce Tornadoes were GR4A but this is not the case. The only difference is the training aircraft, which could be classed GR4T, but in truth when seen from the outside all the RAF Tornadoes are GR4s.

With the fitting of GPS the GR4 can now navigate covertly without the need to transmit radar emissions. Added to this is the full laser Inertial Navigation System and GPWS (Ground Proximity Warning System). In essence what the Tornado Mid-Life Update did was to prepare the airframe for growth and development in future weapons, which has now been combat proven in a multitude of conflicts. By using FLIR and NVG the aircraft is fully capable of passive night low-level operations.

All GR4s still retain a single 27mm cannon (1700 rounds per minute), which can be used either in the ground strafing mode or as a show of force against ground forces.

Both front and rear cockpits have benefited from major re-works. In the front the new HUD (Head-Up Display) and the digital map generator are big improvements over the old system, as well as the F3-style HOTAS stick top. In the rear 'office' the layout has been cleaned up and modified with the TARDIS (Tornado Advanced Radar Display) located between the two active-matrix liquid-crystal displays (AMLCD). Linked to this BAE was awarded a contract to install a new main display processor/computer symbol generator, enhancing the data-link capability when installed.

ABOVE From many angles the GR4 can appear stubby, but this superb wide-angle shot by Jamie Hunter captures the purposeful lines of this 31 Squadron 'Goldstars' jet to perfection. ZA395 is armed with two MBDA Storm Shadow weapons. *(Jamie Hunter)*

ABOVE No 41 Squadron's 95th Anniversary aircraft, Tornado GR4, 'EB-G' – 'EB' was the squadron's Second World War identification letters.

For self-defence the GR4 currently carries a Sky Shadow 2 ECM pod on the left wing outer station and a BOZ countermeasures pod on the right outer station.

At the time of writing (September 2013) the RAF Tornado force comprised three squadrons at Marham (2, 9 and 31), with two more combat squadrons further north (12 and 617 Dambusters), as well as the OCU, 15 (Reserve) Squadron. In August 2013 it was announced that 617 Squadron would disband to become the first unit to equip in 2016 with the F35 Joint Strike Fighter (JSF), while 12 Squadron would also disband in 2014. In charge of all current and future Tornado development is 41 (F) Squadron, which usually has four aircraft on strength and is based alongside the Typhoon OEU 17 (R) Squadron at RAF Coningsby. As the aircraft nears its out of service date of 2018–19 (though this is subject to change), 41 (F) Squadron is tasked with maintaining and enhancing the Tornado's future capabilities.

The SCoT (Secure Coms on Tornado) modification designed by the British company Ultra Electronics allows GR4 crews the ability to have a fully integrated radio system, V/UHF and havequick radios. Ultra's SCoT system provides the critical secure voice and data communications capabilities that are needed to support operations in today's increasingly complex battle space. The SCoT system incorporates software definable radios and cryptographic devices along with secure voice and data distribution systems. It allows secure communications with both air and ground forces vital when working with the new Litening III targeting pod, instant data transfer being the keystone in modern Tornado operations.

All Tornado GR4s will also be fitted Link 16/JTIDS, which is a further boost for its inter-operability with modern platforms. Fitting TIEC (Tactical Information Exchange Capability) allows data to be passed between AWACS and ground stations to Tornado crews. Tactical data link to the GR4 is pretty much a prerequisite to integrating into future conflicts. Most of these upgrades were the indirect result of the early withdrawal of the RAF's Harrier force. With only two combat types in the RAF's current inventory the focus was placed on the TGRF upgrading under a programme known as CUS (P) (Capability Upgrade Strategy (Pilot)) awarded to BAE Systems in 2007. This encompassed the two-stage upgrade of the Tornado GR4 fleet Capability A (CAP A) including the secure communications upgrade already mentioned as well as integration of the Paveway IV. Capability B (CAP B) is the TIEC – the project name for the embodiment of Link 16. Whilst similar to Link 16, TIEC utilises slightly enhanced devices offering increased bandwidth. It is hoped after trials at BAE's Warton plant these modifications can be embodied by the CMU (Combined Maintenance and Upgrade) facility at RAF Marham. Indeed Marham will probably become the Tornado's last lair with a pair of squadrons and a small training unit. This will be sufficient to maintain an offensive capability until the F35 is introduced.

Additional upgrades to the TGRF focus on developing methods to both improve the Raytheon Paveway IV, allowing it greater accuracy and longer release from target, while further upgrades will allow it to attack and destroy moving targets. These improvements to the TGRF will prove beneficial with a seamless transition of the weapon to Typhoon and JSF.

Few aircraft have perhaps matured so gracefully as the Tornado GR4. From the outside it might look the same but under the skin it has evolved into perhaps the RAF's most capable strike aircraft in over a century. As the TGRF force has reduced in size due to the disbanding of squadrons the RAF has retained the most modified and capable airframes and those with the most fatigue/hours left on them. Under a UOR (Urgent Operational Requirement) some of the GR4 aircraft have been fitted with CAGNET (a multi-band transceiver based on a Rohde and Schwarz MR6000L software radio), which embodies the Have Quick II waveform

ABOVE Tornado GR4 crews may yet be called upon to back up Typhoons in combat.

used for air-to-ground communications with JTACs. CAGNET is an interim fit prior to the fleet being fitted with Scott radios.

Sadly, plans to fit a new upgraded radar to the GR4 will no longer happen due to the out of service date of GR4 continually being brought forward – currently, in 2013, its projected out of service date is 2019. At the time of writing the GR4 is the only aircraft capable of carrying DMB, RAPTOR and Storm Shadow.

Typhoon crews gained valuable experience in Libya from the seasoned GR4 crews, but there is still a huge amount of work to be done before the Typhoon can take on all of the GR4's roles. The Tornado might be the senior type in the RAF's fast jet inventory, but it is still the most capable in the air-to-ground role by a considerable margin.

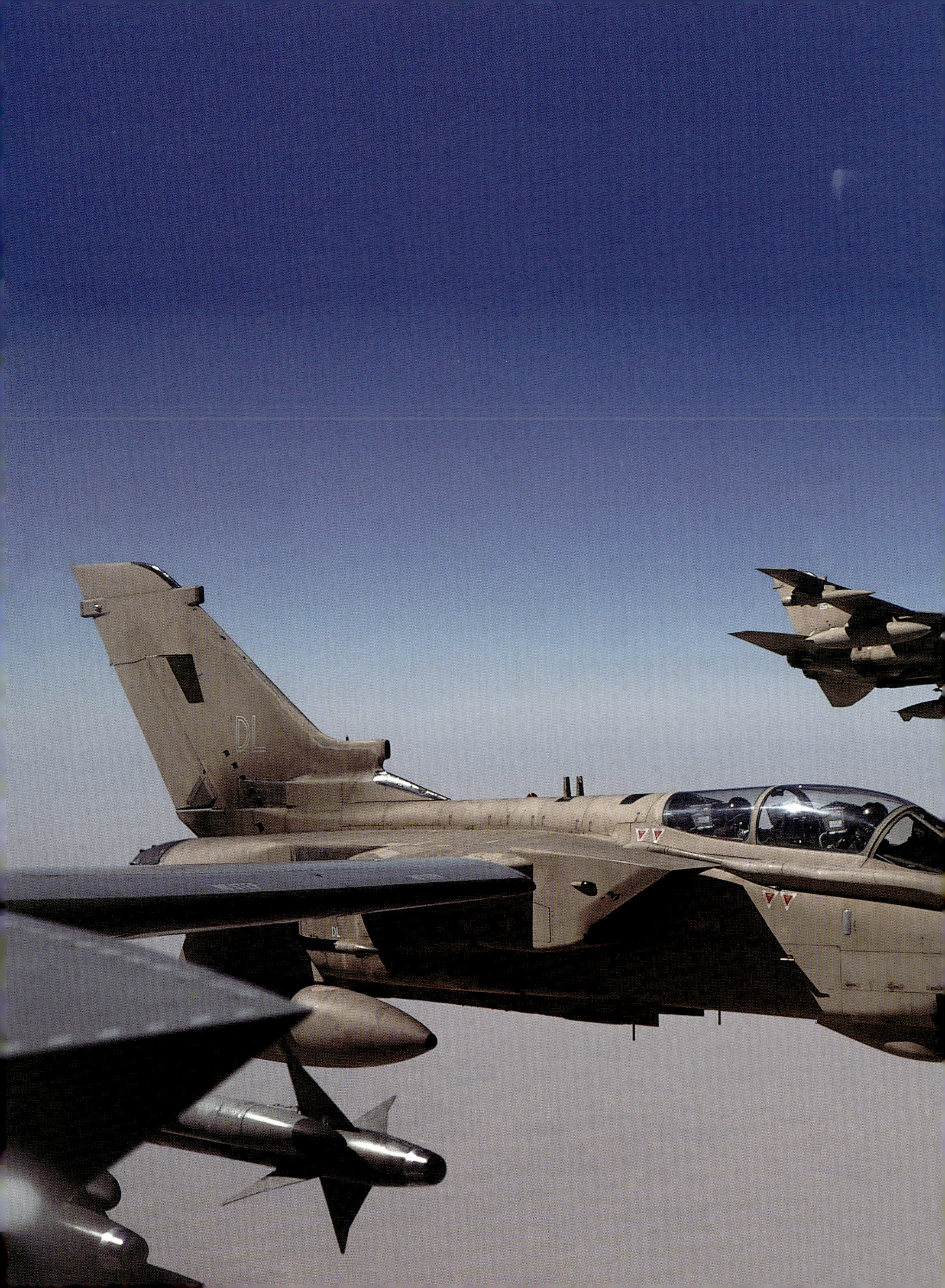
DL

Chapter Three

Tornado at war

When the designers built the MRCA they had a clear vision for its intended use. Three European nations wanted a single type of aircraft that could perform broadly similar roles – low-level day/night all-weather interdiction, capable of both conventional and nuclear weapons delivery. The Tornado has seen more combat than any other RAF type since the Second World War and without question this has been the aircraft's finest hour.

OPPOSITE Rehearsing low-level strike missions over the deserts of southern Saudi Arabia. Tornado GR1s of 31 Squadron with an F3 of 11 (Composite) Squadron banking away from the camera.

Had I been sitting writing this chapter thirty years after the RAF introduced the Tornado into service there is the very real prospect it would be a chapter that either said: 'The Cold War has continued well into the 21st Century and the RAF Tornado has defended us from the awesome might of the Warsaw Pact Forces,' or I wouldn't be writing this at all had the Tornado been employed in its primary role of nuclear strike attack. As it is the Tornado has been engaged on continuous operations since 1990, in areas far removed from its intended role.

First operational call of duty for the Tornado actually fell to the F3 version, with aircraft from 5 Squadron deploying to Saudi Arabia on 7 August 1990. Despite the RAF no longer having a presence much further east than RAF Germany, it still retained a sovereign base on the island of Cyprus. Each year air defence crews deployed for up to six weeks at a time to take advantage of the good weather and undertake air-to-air gunnery. When unannounced the Iraqi Army invaded Kuwait on 2 August 1990 the British Government was quick to respond to the needs of both Kuwait and Saudi Arabia. A decision was taken almost immediately to deploy aircraft into the area in an attempt to prevent the likely invasion of Saudi Arabia. The twelve aircraft deployed were led by Wg Cdr Euan Black, OC 5 Squadron, using a mix of both 5 and 29 Squadron aircraft. Quickly following the aircrew was Gp Capt Rick Peacock Edwards, a well-known and respected RAF fighter pilot who had seen the introduction into service of the early Tornado F2. Dhahran airbase is vast and at the time housed squadrons of both RSAF ADV and IDS Tornadoes, so it was a logical choice to co-locate the RAF's assets here.

Within hours of arriving RAF crews were flying Combat Air Patrols (CAP) along the Iraqi/Saudi border. For now the advancing Iraqi army had been halted. Under the codename Operation Granby the RAF soon established a presence on the base with around 20 aircrew and 200 ground crew. Although the RAF had its own name for the operation the Coalition Forces worked under the unified title of 'Desert Shield'. Immediately, however, it became clear that the F3 was not capable of going to war without some pretty rapid modifications and additions to its weapons systems.

As the Tornado F3s bedded in the RAF took the step of sending a squadron of Jaguars to Oman as a sign to Iraq that they would not be able to simply occupy Kuwait and remain unchallenged. Not since the Second World War had the RAF been involved with a conflict of such magnitude, events were changing by the hour and it was clear this was to be a long term operation. Although the F3 was not in an ideal position to remain in theatre it was still capable of engaging a less capable Iraqi Air Force, and more importantly it bought the RAF time in allowing urgent modifications to take place.

The Tornado GR1s were much better placed operationally, having been in squadron service for nearly a decade. With no sign of the Iraqi government backing down by 23 August 1990, the RAF had announced it would be sending a squadron of Tornado GR1s to be based at the old RAF airfield of Muharraq in Bahrain, a stone's throw from Kuwait. With nearly 50,000 Iraqi troops on the border of Saudi Arabia it was clear their intentions would not stop at re-taking just Kuwait.

With Jaguars from Coltishall turning pink overnight in an effort to blend in with their new surroundings it followed suit that the GR1 force would also adopt a desert camouflage. All GR1 aircraft deployed to theatre received the new paint scheme known as ARTF (Alkali Removable Temporary Finish). Initially choosing aircraft from the Bruggen Wing (with crews from Marham as

BELOW Cruising along at 500kts barely 250ft above the Saudi desert, F3 ZE941 is armed with AIM-9Ms and Sky Flash.

well) that had improved RHWRs and up-rated engines, the first detachment was in position by 26 August. Aircraft came from RAF Bruggen, with a mix of Bruggen and Marham crews.

During the first week of August 1990 I had just flown my 500th hour on the F3 and found myself flying to RAF Alconbury to provide a static display aircraft for the annual air show. Over the weekend the word soon got out that 5 Squadron had deployed to Dhahran and we (the Leeming Wing) were due to replace them. Our flight home was pretty short as we began our work up to deploy as soon as we landed. The next three weeks were pretty much a blur. RAF Leeming had been selected as the next base to deploy the F3 into theatre and the aircraft, crews and ground crews all had three weeks to get ready. It was a tall order.

Within two days our aircraft began to receive the new improved Stage 1 radars and we tried to work out a plan to be as capable as possible as soon as we arrived. Soon we were flying Air Combat down to a base height of 2,000ft above ground level as opposed to our normal limit of 10,000ft. Now 'burying' the nose took on a whole new meaning as the summer fields over the Yorkshire Wolds seemed to get bigger by the day.

Whilst we were aware of the ground attack Tornados working up to deploy, there was no time to swap ideas as we had so much to do ourselves. As Air Defenders air-to-air refuelling was our bread and butter, however the GR1 force (especially RAFG) was very inexperienced in AAR so we let them have priority over tanker assets.

Soon our aircraft were stripped of their unit markings, although luckily we did not turn pink! We began receiving airframes that engineers had identified as suitable for deployment (ie, those that did not require major servicing in the near future). With all three Leeming squadrons amalgamated into one unit the aircraft wore codes in the 11 Squadron range of DA to DZ. As mentioned the GR1 Tornado required only a few modifications to enable it to go to war, while the F3 had its biggest and most numerous upgrades since its introduction to service.

ABOVE ZA492 is another celebrity Tornado with its shark mouth, mission markings and Iraqi 'Cub' transport kill markings. It later became one of two special 617-marked aircraft in 2013. It is seen here over the UK on its way to drop live 1,000lb bombs just after the first Gulf War had ended.

ABOVE Armed and ready to go, a GR1 in Desert Storm camouflage.

Under an initial retrofit of 26 aircraft the F3 finally got a radar that worked; it was known as Stage1+. Other improvements included the fitting of the F-18-style stick top; radar-absorbent paint was applied to the wing leading edges and fin as well; the avionics benefited from improved cooling and the RHWR was re-programmed; and engine thrust was increased slightly. Perhaps the most visible change to the F3 was the addition of the two Tracor AN/ALE-40(V) flare dispensers under the rear engine doors. To complement the self-defence capability the aircraft also carried the Phimat chaff pod. Also added (thanks to the US Navy) were improved AIM-9M Sidewinder missiles. Initially the force comprised 18 aircraft, 27 crews and 350 ground crew.

The GR1s also had radar-absorbent paint applied under the ARTF (Alkali Removable Temporary Finish) as well as various communications upgrades. Like the F3 the GR1 had to be fitted with HaveQuick radios and the MKX11 Mode 4 IFF sets if they were going to operate with other Coalition Forces. With likely targets located deep inside Iraqi airspace the GR1 force swapped the smaller 1,500-litre under-wing fuel tanks and began flying with the larger 2,250-litre tanks associated with the ADV. In order to carry them the GR1s had a small metal stop fitted to the wing sweep lever, restricting them to a maximum sweep of 63.5 degrees (the F3 is 67 degrees). This was due to the GR's shorter rear fuselage and prevented the tanks touching the tailerons.

With the Tornado F3 established at Dhahran under the name of 'Desert Eagles', all three Leeming units (11, 23, and 25 Squadrons) had either an eagle or a falcon incorporated in its badge. Life soon became pretty routine. Initially Combat Air Patrols (CAP) were undertaken 24 hours a day, 7 days a week, alternating between USAF F-15s, RSAF F-15s or RAF and RSAF Tornado ADVs. As the conflict dragged on it was clear that merely flying CAP was denying crews vital training and a method needed to be found to start a training programme.

The Air Defence Force was firmly set up at Dhahran, but as aircraft numbers grew the location of the GR1 force required some shuffling around. At first the Bruggen-based aircraft were located at Muharraq in Bahrain, a civilian airfield that was home to the airline Gulf Air. With the deployment of additional GR1s from Laarbruch in late September, as well as VC10 tankers occupying the pan, space was at a premium. Although not popular at the time (the Bahrain crews were located in comfortable hotels) a decision was made to move half the GR1 force well north to the Saudi base at Tabuk. With time running out and UN Resolution deadlines drawing closer, further GR1s arrived in theatre and as late as the first week in January aircraft from Bruggen were deploying to Dhahran. By far the closest call, though, was the GR1A recce force, which only arrived in theatre between 14 and 16 January, again at Dhahran.

Throughout the period from August 1990 to January 1991 Tornado crews had been training hard developing tactics and getting to grips with working in large packages (parlance for multi-national formations of up to sixty aircraft). Back home the pace of change was no less frantic as urgent trials were undertaken to allow new equipment to be rushed into use. Crucial to the Allies' success was getting the new GR1A reconnaissance aircraft into service. Similarly the RAF had also identified the need to give the Tornado a self-designating pod to allow it to drop precision weapons. This would lead to the rapid introduction of the Ferranti TIALD pod. In terms of breakthrough weapons ALARM was also a brand new and untried munition, but its role as an Air Launched Anti Radiation Missile was going to be crucial in neutralising the Iraqi air defences, which were vast.

Prior to the outbreak of hostilities the crews had a hard time trying to assess the capabilities of their potential adversaries. Equipped with a mixture of French and Soviet weaponry they were definitely not to be underestimated. The RAF had trained pilots for the Iraqi Air Force until at least 1985 so they were assumed to be competent and aware of the RAF's strengths and weaknesses. Tornado crews were familiar with working alongside NATO allies, but apart from Red Flag exercises they were not trained with working alongside the might of US air power. Each day an ATO (Air Tasking Order) would be sent to each squadron by a secure means, and known colloquially as the FRAG (Fragmented Operation Order). This was all pretty new stuff to RAF crews, but basically it was a daily war plan detailing every mission that would be flown in a 24-hour period. The level of detail was incredible: each unit checked the FRAG to see what mission they would be on, what weapon fit was required, and what other assets would be airborne at the time in their 'slot'. It did, however, give crews a pretty good air picture and situational awareness before they launched – a very impressive planning tool.

For Air Defence crews it is pretty straightforward with just an order to put, say, four F3s in combat fit on CAP 'M' between 1400–1700. Added to this would be air-to-air refueling (AAR) 'brackets'. For the IDS Tornado force the detail would be far more specific, with target details including weapons fit, AAR and where they fitted into the overall package, which sometimes could be upwards of 80 aircraft. The learning curve was steep.

The cat and mouse game played by the Iraqi forces typically ran the UN Resolutions right up to the wire, but on the plus side it allowed vital training to continue. By 13 January 1991 the UN Resolution and the Coalition's patience finally ran out. The world waited with baited breath to see how events would unfold. UN Resolution 678 authorised the use of force against Iraq and the scene was set. (Tragically, the RAF also lost a Tornado GR1 on the same day when an aircraft flew into the ground at low level during a training mission just to the east of Bahrain.)

On 16 January Tornado GR1 crews prepared to take their aircraft to war for the first time on missions that were far removed from its original theatre of operations. The first task of any conflict is to neutralise the enemy's air defences and gain air supremacy. The task allocated to the GR1 force was daunting and perhaps the most dangerous given to any of the Coalition aircraft: the shutting down of some of the most heavily defended targets in Iraq – their airfields.

Now based at three different locations the GR1 force included crews from pretty much the entire Tornado force. On the night of 16–17 January 1991 (confusion often occurs with the date because the Gulf is 2–3 hours ahead of GMT) the Tornado was blooded as aircraft set off armed with JP233 and 1,000lb bombs to attack Iraqi airfields. The heavily defended airfields of Al Jarrah and Shaibah were the first targets for the night. Unlike the air bases found in NATO countries the airfields in Iraq are in a different league altogether – they are huge and the task of shutting them down was not to be underestimated. As an indication of their size imagine a major International airport – and then add some. Added to this, many of the airfields in Iraq were purpose-built new structures with a huge selection of runways and taxiways to allow continued ops during time of war. Originally built by British companies they were completed by Yugoslavs. The HAS shelters were almost indestructible and a network of underground tunnels connected various facilities.

The RAF's weapon of choice at the time was the Hunting JP233 airfield denial weapon. Carried in pairs on the under-fuselage hardpoints the weapon resembles a giant canister nearly half the length of the GR1. Inside the canisters are sixty SG357 runway-cratering munitions as well as 430 HB876 area denial mines designed to hamper any airfield repair work. In theory the weapon dispenses its munitions in 6 seconds and then drops the empty canisters.

Just how the weapon was delivered highlights the bravery of the Tornado crews. Typically the mission would be more than four hours long with numerous visits to the tanker. Always undertaken at night, with all lights out, the delivery height was at low level utilising the Tornado's TFR and high speed.

As part of the package the RAF Tornados would not be alone. Supporting them would

ABOVE GR1, ZD747, *Anna Louise.*

BELOW Aircrew of 27 Squadron with their CO, Wg Cdr Nigel Elsdon (extreme left). Elsdon and Flt Lt Max Collier were killed in action when their Tornado aircraft was shot down by anti-aircraft fire during a raid on an Iraqi airfield on 17 January 1991. *(IWM GLF746)*

ABOVE John Peters and John Nichol shortly before 'Desert Storm' in 1991. *(Copyright unknown)*

be the tanker force, F-15C fighter cover, other bombers, with F-4G Wild Weasels and EF-111 Ravens (jammers) in the anti-radiation missile roles. Few crews had ever flown with the JP233 for real and were afforded just one training sortie prior to the live mission to get a feel of just how heavy the aircraft would be. Add to this a perceived threat of MiG-29 fighters, radar-laid anti-aircraft guns and surface-to-air missiles; it was not a mission for the faint hearted.

Led by Wg Cdrs Jerry Witts and John Broadbent (31 and 15 Squadron) 12 aircraft got airborne from Dhahran (4 from Dhahran and 8 from Muharraq) at around 0100hrs, their target Tallil Air Base. The aircraft were in the two JP233 fit as well as carrying 2,250-litre tanks and associated ECM pods. All-up weight was somewhere near 31 tons and the rotation speeds were close to 200kts. In the words of one GR1 pilot they were operating beyond the release to service, but the cool temperatures of the Saudi winter and 12,000ft runways were in their favour.

The first evening saw Tornados operating from Tabuk also in action, with aircraft launching on missions to attack airfields as well as the first combat sorties of ALARM missiles engaged in SEAD (Suppression of Enemy Air Defences). Further waves departed Dhahran and Muharraq on that historic night. As the initial waves returned, elated to have returned safely, the mood soon changed when news broke that an aircraft had been brought down over Ar Rumaylah Southwest Airfield. ZD791 (Flt Lts J.G. Peters and A.G. Nichol) became the first combat casualty with the crew taken prisoners of war. If the horrors of war had not been fully appreciated the Iraqi news agency soon reinforced how dangerous the game was by parading both the pilot and navigator on television.

Having survived their high-speed ejections it was clear their injuries were not entirely caused by leaving their Tornado in a hurry. Worse news was to come when it transpired the Tornado force had suffered a second loss with both its crew presumed killed. ZA392 (27 Squadron, Wg Cdr Nigel Elsdon and Flt Lt Max Collier) crashed near its target. The first night's ops had proved the success of the JP233 but had cost the RAF an aircraft . As the aircraft were parked and ground crew began the task of re-arming, refuelling and repairing the aircraft it soon became apparent how another loss early in the conflict had been narrowly avoided. Flown by (then) Flg Off Nigel Ingle and Flt Lt Paul McKernan, ZD744 had been on one of the first JP233 missions. A conversation with the pilot proved a humbling experience as to how dangerous the missions were.

'As junior pilot, Nigel Ingle found himself as No 4 of a second wave of 4 aircraft. Having lost the toss with the lead four-ship his formation had been allocated the more heavily-defended airfield of Al Jarrah, the lead four-ship taking a closer target that required no air-to-air refuelling and a route initially thought to be less well-defended. The second mission with its target further away would require at least two trips to the tanker.

'The attack plan had four aircraft running in first over the airfield tossing eight 1,000lb bombs, "air bursting" them into the heavily defended airfield defences (the theory being this would keep the Iraqi soldiers' heads down before the JP233 attack arrived and soften them up, but in practice it probably stirred up a hornet's nest). As the lone 617 Squadron crew in formation, Ingle found himself at the back of the 27 Squadron package, which was then further complicated by the No 3 aircraft aborting the mission.

'Approaching the target Ingle was locked up by a SAM-8 and took evasive action. Acutely aware that there were an awful lot of other aircraft in the dark at low level in close proximity around him, he soon returned to track. Having studied the target in detail, crews opted for attacks that either flew down the runway or cut runways and taxiways at an angle, scattering munitions over a wide area.

'With some miles to run and now down to low level, Ingle engaged combat power trying to eke a few more knots out of his over-laden bomber. He described the drag of the massive JP233 fit as "similar to leaving the airbrakes out on the top of the fuselage and on the bottom". With burners blazing they must have made a terrifying sight streaking low over the target. Having felt a thump on the run-in to the target his back-seater responded to his pilot's call that they'd been hit to "carry on". Describing the JP233 release as an "almighty clattering noise like machine gun fire" they pulled off target, the auto pilot tripped out and Ingle climbed his damaged Tornado away whilst trying to assess the situation. Quickly back down to low level they made a dash for the border. Crews chose to either fly the aircraft manually or engage the autopilot, or a mixture of both, using the TFR 'E Scope'. Whatever method was adopted it must still have been attention-getting for the crews involved.

'Close to the Saudi border they climbed up to medium altitude and regained contact with their formation, discussing their predicament. Using a torch they could soon see the leading edge of the wing (where the slats are) was peeled back. At this stage unaware what had hit them they assumed it was an anti-aircraft shell. With the aircraft just controllable in 45° wing sweep they had no option but to refuel in this untried and dangerous configuration.

'Having taken on fuel the crew were now faced with the unenviable task of trying to land their crippled aircraft. Arriving back at Bahrain (the island was bristling with its own defence weapons) they asked for a long straight-in approach, expecting the wings to be stuck back. Gingerly they moved the wings forward until they could reach a final landing configuration of wings forward with flaps down but no leading edge slats. Now minus the heavy JP233s they managed to land the damaged Tornado and turn off the runway. Met by the ground crew and the world's press the gravity of the situation soon sunk in as the saw the damaged wing (actually a high-speed bird strike over the target area). Despite the sceptics the Tornado had survived the bird strike, completed its mission and returned to base, all in a short few hours, testimony to the survivability of the airframe in a wartime scenario. In that first night RAF Tornado detachments carried out 60 missions – by 18 January 1991 they had lost two aircraft and sadly a crew killed.'

While the focus was on JP233, other formations continued to airburst 1,000lb-bombs as well as Tornados firing ALARM for the first time. Having been rushed into service, ALARM

ABOVE Sqn Ldr Gordon Buckley (right) senior flight commander and pilot on 15 Squadron, led the second four-Tornado formation of the first wave at night on 17 January 1991 at low level against Iraqi main operating bases. Flt Lt Paddy Teakle (left) was his navigator in Tornado GR1, ZD790 (nicknamed *Snoopy Airways – Debbie*). Here the pair are interviewed by the international press delegation at Muharraq, Bahrain, after returning from a mission. *(IWM GLF460)*

proved its worth against the vast network of Iraqi air defence radars. This was an incredible achievement when one considers the Tornado only fired its first trial ALARM at the US Naval Air Weapons Station China Lake, California, in October 1990.

At this stage of the Tornado story the RAF tended to allocate specific roles on an individual squadron basis and 20 Squadron was given the ALARM role. The squadron was based at RAF Laarbruch in Germany and was given just one week to get to grips with its new role before deploying to Tabuk. Initially ALARM could only be carried under the wings on pylons, meaning the fuel tanks were moved to the under-fuselage position, resulting in the strange configuration of ALARMs under the wing and fuel tanks under the fuselage. This was soon rectified and ALARM began to be fitted under the fuselage and the aircraft adopted its more normal guise of Sky Shadow, 2,250-litre tanks, ALARM 2,250-litre tanks and BOZ pod. For self defence the GR Tornadoes carried AIM-9L Sidewinders. Eventually the RAF managed to convert nine aircraft to ALARM capability by introducing the MIL STD 1553B data bus. As it was a specialist role, only eight crews were trained to fire ALARM, the tactics and procedures being new to the force. ALARM was still used from day one of the Gulf War. Generally throughout the conflict while operating as part of the Coalition Forces, the RAF tended to only fly 'in-house' missions, (ie, missions that only involve the host nation) although ALARM Tornadoes did work with USAF F-15Es.

BELOW Photographed a couple of months after the end of the first Gulf War, GR1, ZD714 'BE', wears the 'desert pink' paint scheme for service in the Middle East.

Back in Britain the gravity of the unfolding situation in the Gulf was clear with a further four aircraft and crews held on high readiness standby, ready to deploy to replace combat losses. While the F3 force manned CAPs behind the border, the GR1 force was being thrust into the limelight. Operation 'Desert Shield' (as Gulf War 1 was known) was the first major conflict where satellite television brought us the conflict live on television on a minute-by-minute basis. No sooner had a crew shut down their Tornado's RB199s than camera crews were debriefing them on what they had seen. For those of us watching in Britain it was a sobering and humbling experience.

The following night, 18–19 January, the Tornado force was back in the thick of it. Still using JP233 and 1,000lb bombs, the force suffered another loss when ZA396 was shot down by a surface-to-air missile, its crew miraculously surviving the episode. Pilot Dave Waddington, who was injured in the explosion, survived when his back-seater saved them both by using the Tornado's Command Eject system. By 19 January the RAF had already sent three replacement aircraft to cover combat losses.

By 21 January the Tornado force changed tactics and moved away from the dangerous low level night JP233 missions. Contrary to media reports this was not due to the risks involved but more a lack of credible threat put up by the now neutralised Iraqi Air Force. Despite a change of tactics, further losses were incurred on 22 January when ZA467 was lost to undetermined causes (Sqn Ldrs G.K.S. Lennox and K.P. Weekes were killed) and on 24 January when ZA403 was brought down by the premature detonation of one or more bombs, both crewmembers ejected and were taken prisoner. A further combat loss occurred on 14 February when a Tornado was brought down by surface-to-air missiles. The pilot initiated command ejection and survived but the navigator, Flt Lt S.M. Hicks, was found to have been killed.

As the war got under way clearly there would be an urgent need for reconnaissance assets to be in theatre. With Tornado ADV and GR1 aircraft in theatre it was a logical choice to deploy the RAF's GR1As, which filled a gap in the Coalition's ability to gather real-time intelligence. At the time Tornado GR1As equipped two frontline squadrons, 2 and 13, both long-time recce squadrons. Both were relatively new to the Tornado – 2 Squadron had re-equipped from the Jaguar in 1989 while 13 Squadron had operated the GR1A for under a year.

Regardless of all the other urgent trials that were going inside the RAF in the run-up to war, preparation of the GR1A was probably the most pressing. The coalition forces needed real-time imagery of the biggest threat posed to the land forces – 'Scud' missile attacks. Like the V2 rockets of the Second World War, it may have been the fear of the unknown that caused senior commanders so much concern over the launching of 'Scuds'. Coupled to this was always the worry that Saddam Hussein might decide to launch missiles armed with chemical weapons, a threat that was taken very seriously by RAF personnel in theatre. You were never far from your S6/S10 respirator (gas mask) and tin hat. No one actually knew how big an explosion a 'Scud' would make, although I did ask one RAF Regiment instructor who jokingly said that the only risk it posed to me personally was if one landed on my head!

Using its Vinten 4000 infra-red horizon-to-horizon line-scanner, the GR1A was the only aircraft that could achieve the task of searching for mobile 'Scuds' at night deep into Iraq. Without the luxury of any in-theatre work-up, six Tornado GR1As arrived covertly at Dhahran as late as 14–16 January. As described earlier most crews received their mission tasking via the ATO some 24 hours ahead of the planned mission. Because the GR1As were looking for mobile 'Scuds' they often only had a couple of hour's notice of where there mission would head. This also meant that tanker assets could not be allocated and they would need to fly alone and unarmed – and in the words of the squadron motto – unafraid!

It was soon deemed pointless to even carry the AIM-9L, so with no 27mm gun fitted the GR1A was totally 'unarmed'. Led by Wg Cdr Glen Torpy, 13 Squadron's Commanding Officer, the distinction of finding the first 'Scud' fell to Sqn Ldr Dick Garwood and back-seater John Hill flying ZA400. They had found the proverbial needle in a haystack and captured an image of a 'Scud' in its launch position on the first night. This publically displayed just how capable the Tornado was – no other aircraft could have achieved these images. Nevertheless, with real-time reconnaissance being in its infancy, finding the missile was one thing but coordinating other strike aircraft to remove it proved more difficult. Just like the GR1s the 1As were optimising the aircraft's systems by flying at low-level at night using the TFR as well as NVGs – again, another new technology device that had barely been bedded in.

As the conflict moved into February the RAF deployed the venerable Buccaneer equipped with AN/AVQ Pavespike 23E for laser guidance pod to act as targeting aircraft for laser-guided weapons. The GRs were once more in uncharted waters, dropping from altitude onto targets using either internal kit or having the target designated by 'spike' aircraft. Despite losses, General Norman Schwarzkopf, the Coalition commander, stated 'the RAF contribution has been superb and we are damn glad they were with us'.

With the Buccaneers acting as designators to the Dhahran and Muharraq Tornado detachments, the Tabuk aircraft were given the two development TIALD self-designating pods (once more rushed into service with great speed). By 27 February the war was over and the Tornados could return home, albeit a few days later as things were still unclear as to what the future held. Overall the campaign was a great success for the Tornado. It had shown up its weaknesses, certainly, but it had also highlighted that in future conflicts it could be adapted to changing scenarios quickly and effectively. Post-conflict it was calculated that the RAF Tornado

ABOVE Pink GR1 and Buccaneer S2B in a special formation shot to mark the RAF's four fast jet types used in Gulf 1.

ABOVE **GR1, ZA492 FE, flew from Dhahran and Tabuk with 16 Squadron and was heavily involved in anti-airfield sorties with JP233, conventional iron bombs and LGBs. The squadron was disbanded in September 1991.**

with TIALD was the second most successful attack system during Operation Desert Storm, only being beaten by the F-117A Nighthawk.

What should have been an upbeat time for the RAF Tornado force returning from its first conflict was also tinged with sadness: five aircrew had been lost (as well as a further five in the run-up to war including one Jaguar pilot killed in theatre during a training mission) the future of the GR1 force was undergoing rapid change. Aircraft were pulled back from RAF Germany and squadrons that had only recently served with such distinction in the Gulf were being disbanded. Furthermore Air Force chiefs needed to urgently look at how the Tornado could be modified for future conflicts based on lessons learned from the first Gulf War.

While it had been assumed that the end of Gulf War 1 would herald a new era for the people of Iraq, the optimism was short lived. No sooner had aircraft been cleaned of their temporary sand colours than the painters and finishers were again reapplying it for another deployment. Under codename Operation 'Jural' the Tornado was back in action once again. Having withdrawn from Saudi Arabia within weeks and finally left Bahrain by May 1991, the RAF was then forced to re-deployed Tornado aircraft as part of the UN Resolution declaring a 'no-fly zone' north of the 36th parallel and south of the 32nd parallel. Once again the RAF found itself part of a Coalition Force operating missions in both the recce role and attack role, working initially from its previous base of RSAF Dhahran.

The GR1s were not as active as they had been in Gulf War 1, but the mere presence of the aircraft was enough to deter Iraq's further ambitions. The Coalition Force came under the guise of Operation 'Southern Watch'. Eventually the GR force moved north to replace the Jaguars and Harriers in Turkey. The Northern deployment was called Operation 'Warden' while Operation 'Jural' was located at Dhahran. Now fully fitted with TIALD pods the Tornado could use this versatile tool for both designating targets and post-strike recce.

Despite the effects of Gulf War 1 and the increasing presence of Allied aircraft in theatre, Iraq continued to be provocative which culminated in more GR1 strikes on 13 January 1993. Within a week Iraq had declared a ceasefire. With tensions against Allied forces and security issues around Dhahran increasing, it was decided to move the Tornado detachment south to Al Kharj, which was not a popular choice. Dhahran is close to Bahrain and offered crews some of the Western comforts, but Al Kharj is firmly in the desert 80 miles south of capital Riyadh, nicknamed 'Al's Garage'.

The aircraft participating in Operation 'Jural' were primarily tasked with recce missions using either the Vinten GP1 pod (carried by regular GRs and not just GR1As) or the much improved TIALD. With the GR1s busy in the

Gulf the F3 force enjoyed a period of relative tranquilly before they themselves were deployed to the Italian Air Force base at Gioia del Colle as part of the 'no-fly zone' imposed by the UN over Bosnia-Herzegovina. Under the RAF title Operation 'Deny Flight' F3s were based in Italy for nearly three years (they finally left in September 1996). Most of the sorties were long and arduous CAP missions, but the F3s did come under fire from surface-to-air missiles, which prompted an urgent modification to carry towed radar decoys in modified BOZ pods.

Iraq continued to be a thorn in the side of the United Nations and a failure to allow weapons inspectors into the country forced the RAF to deploy more GR1s into theatre under the codename Operation 'Bolton' (1998). Now based at Ali Al Salem Air Base in Kuwait the aircraft could be seen parked outside the still bombed-out HASs that the Tornado force had helped destroy some years previously. As a result of lessons learned from Gulf War 1 aircraft were now flying with Paveway III laser-guided bombs. Operation Bolton aircraft carried a white fin flash and remained in the grey/green scheme.

At this stage the RAF had twenty-four Tornado GR1s deployed in support of operations in the Middle East. Six aircraft were based in Turkey under Operation 'Warden', 6 at Al Kharj and 12 at Ali Al Salem in Kuwait under what became known as Operation 'Bolton'. With the Tornado GR force about to undergo the Mid-Life Update this level of commitment was unsustainable and eventually the GR Tornados were replaced by F3s at Al Kharj, which were deployed to provide offensive counter air support. Once again it seemed the RAF would be using the Tornado to attack Iraq.

This action against Iraq was codenamed Operation 'Desert Fox'. From 16–19 December 1998 the RAF and USAF attacked 1,993 targets in Iraq, mainly around Baghdad, Tikrit in the north and Basra in the south. Of a total of 250 bombing missions 12 Squadron's Tornado GR1s flew 32 medium level sorties and dropped a combination of 61 UK Paveway 2 and Paveway 3 LGBs. One of their targets was a hangar at Tallil containing the so-called 'drones of death', remotely piloted vehicle (RPV) aircraft capable of carrying chemical and biological weapons.

While the eyes of the world were focused firmly on Saddam Hussein the conflict in Bosnia was also gathering pace, but it drew less attention from the world's press. For reasons that are less than clear the GR1 also attracted less attention from its involvement in attacks in the former Yugoslavia than any other conflict. Perhaps the Kosovo campaign can be classed as the Harrier's war. The terrain in Eastern Europe is extremely hilly and the weather often poor, which posed problems for targeting as well as the need to avoid collateral damage at all costs. The rules of engagement had never been tighter. With RAF Harrier and Jaguar aircraft in action over Kosovo, RAF Bruggen put 9, 14 and 31 Squadrons on standby.

With the arrival of better weather in April, operations intensified. On the 5 April 1999, six Tornado GR1s from Bruggen flew their first sorties against bridges and tunnels on the main supply route between Serbia and Kosovo. Leaving their home base in central Germany the GR1s refuelled from RAF VC10s over France and returned to base after some 7 hours airborne. It was the first time the RAF had mounted airstrikes that departed and returned to their home base since the Second World War.

With a planned surge in air strikes as the weather improved twelve Tornadoes deployed to the French Air Force Base at Solenzara on Corsica's west coast to be nearer the action. By June 1999 the Kosovo war was over.

Despite repeated attempts to neutralise the Iraqi war machine matters came to a head after Operation 'Bolton' in 2003. On 6 February the

BELOW Night launch from Kuwait. As most of the Hardened Aircraft Shelters (HAS) in Kuwait had been destroyed or damaged the RAF was forced to construct temporary 'Sun Shelters'. The aircraft is painted in the temporary light grey finish. *(RAF)*

OP TELIC – UK military operations in Iraq

ABOVE **Pre-start – note the covers are kept on till the last minute to prevent sand ingress.** *(RAF)*

ABOVE **Post-mission – as the RAF began to be engaged on permanent overseas combat operations aircrew flying clothing was adapted to the needs of surviving and ejection over hostile territory.** *(RAF)*

BELOW **If the aircraft has been air-to-air refueling the pilot leaves the probe out to allow the groundcrew to check for any damage.** *(RAF)*

British Secretary of Defence announced that a force of 100 plus aircraft would deploy to the Gulf under the codename of Operation 'Telic'. This was against a growing concern that Iraq still possessed weapons of mass destruction and the Iraqi government should abide by UN Resolution 1441. Often referred to as Gulf War 2, Operation 'Telic' was instrumental in finally dismantling the Iraqi war machine and restoring stability to the region.

Although still in its infancy, this was a time for the newly modified Tornado GR4 to be put into action. Still using TIALD the aircraft was now using Paveway II, III and Enhanced Paveway as well as ALARM missiles. Emphasis was now on using these smart weapons in an effective way to topple the Iraqi dictator. Although the GR4 was an improvement, with rear seat grab handles fitted to dispense chaff and flares and the fitting of Celcius Tech BOL chaff launchers, the aircraft was still some way off the capability it has now.

The Tornado force had come a long way in the 12 years since Gulf War 1. Rumours that the RAF would employ Storm Shadow and possibly Brimstone on their operational debut were confirmed when 617 Squadron became the first to launch live Storm Shadow missiles in support of the coalition during the night of 21 March 2003. People might have been fooled into thinking that Iraq was a spent force after ten or more years of bombardment, but little could have been further from the truth as the first pair of aircraft discovered.

Led by the OC 617 Squadron, Wg Cdr Dave Robertson, and his back-seater Sqn Ldr Andy Myers, they had Sqn Ldr David 'Noddy' Knowles and Flt Lt Andy Turk as wingmen when they left Kuwait and headed for their target near Baghdad. Locked up by SA-2 missiles one aircraft jettisoned its tanks in an effort to evade the inevitable. Having defeated the missile, both aircraft prosecuted their attacks and delivered their weapons. Post-flight Battle Damage Assessment (BDA) showed the weapons had scored direct hits with pinpoint accuracy. The RAF had now truly entered the era of smart weapons – poignant, too, because it was also the 60th

RIGHT A sand-painted Tornado GR1 sits in front of the Gulf Air hangar in Bahrain just prior to the start of Gulf War 1. *(RAF)*

anniversary of the famous 'dam buster' raid by 617 Squadron on 16–17 May 1943.

Operation 'Telic' was not without its tragedy when one GR4 was accidentally shot down by a US Patriot missile returning to base. Sadly, both crew were killed. With the Tornado GR4 in action the F3 version was also seeing combat sorties escorting a wide variety of Coalition packages. Early on it had been thought the F3 would be used in a Suppression of Enemy Air Defences (SEAD) role as trials had been undertaken to fit and fire ALARM missiles. Deemed to be superior at the role due to the F3s more sensitive and accurate RHWR the plan never materialised and the 'EF3' remained in Britain. Other improvements to the F3's capability was the carriage of ASRAAM and the towed radar decoy, with all modifications implemented for lessons learnt in other conflicts.

Other notable firsts for the GR4 force during 'Telic' was the integration of the RAPTOR pod

RIGHT A Tornado GR4 takes off from RAF Marham fitted with a RAPTOR pod. The aircraft is also armed with a Paveway weapon should the need arise. *(RAF)*

BELOW Behind the aircraft is a bombed out HAS. In the foreground can be seen a 2,250-litre fuel tank and the rear section of a Storm Shadow stand-off weapon. *(RAF)*

BELOW Staging back via RAF Akrotiri in Cyprus after Gulf War 2. Akrotiri is perhaps the RAF's most strategically vital air base as a gateway to the Middle East.

75

TORNADO AT WAR

LEFT A Tornado GR4 from 617 Squadron takes off from Kandahar air base in Afghanistan on a mission in support of ground troops. The squadron was part of 904 Expeditionary Air Wing based at Kandahar. *(RAF)*

RIGHT A 12 Squadron Tornado GR4 takes off from Kandahar. No 12 Squadron's Tornadoes took over the close air support role in the summer of 2009 from 1(F) Squadron Joint Force Harriers. *(RAF)*

RIGHT A Tornado GR4 flying over Afghanistan. *(RAF)*

BELOW A Tornado GR4 from 617 Squadron pictured at night under a Rapid Erection Shelter (RES) at Kandahar Air Base. *(RAF)*

as well as the RAF adopting the US method of 'hot' turnarounds, where aircraft were refuelled and re-armed while the crews remained in the cockpits before being re-tasked. With RAPTOR in service the RAF also honed its skills in deciphering the imagery by utilising the embryonic Tactical Intelligence Wing (TIW). They were responsible for gathering information as well as allocating targets. Significantly it was during this time that the Tornado force down-declared (withdrawal from service) the Tornado Infra Red Radar Recce (TIRRS) system, relying solely on the RAPTOR pod for intelligence gathering – an added bonus being that all GR4 aircraft could carry the large RAPTOR pod.

With a switch from ultra low-level missions to a more medium-level tasking the GR4 force wore a similar light grey paint scheme to that used by the F3s, again in washable alkaline paint. As in Gulf War 1 aircraft were adorned with nose art, although this time it was probably more tasteful. Of significance was ZA400 which became 'Scud Hunter' in tribute to its earlier fame during Gulf War 1 With the Marham Wing deployed to Kuwait and the Lossiemouth Wing in Qatar the conflict was almost as short as Gulf War 1, with aircraft returning to Britain by May 2003. Naturally, the RAF kept a small presence of aircraft in theatre for unforeseen eventualities.

December 2010 was officially the last month of RAF Harrier operations, with the Service now down to just two combat types – the Tornado GR4 and the Typhoon. Once more it fell to the Tornado to replace the Harrier in Afghanistan under Operation 'Herrick'. Since the war in Afghanistan had started the Harrier GR9 had been in theatre since 2004 and its continued commitment seemed assured until its demise from RAF service. History has proved (in my opinion) the choice of aircraft to withdraw was correct. Afghan Tornadoes have effectively gelled all the recent modifications into the GR4 Mid-Life Update to produce an airframe/weapons platform that is now superb at its role.

ABOVE A Tornado GR4 from RAF Marham takes off to join Operation Ellamy over Libya. *(RAF)*

In Afghanistan the Tornado GR4 standard fit is Paveway III/IV with Brimstone DMS missiles and of course the integral 27mm gun. The GR4 has a number of plus factors over the aircraft it replaced, which makes it more suitable for the job. The aircraft carries a formidable array of smart weapons but it also has the 27mm gun, which of course can be escalated to the use of deadly force should the need arise. Also, the GR4 has the ability to fly low and fast as a show of force using re-heat – something 'Pegasus power' lacks!

BELOW Two fully armed RAF Tornadoes from RAF Marham transit the Mediterranean Sea en-route to Libya as part of the UK's Operation Ellamy to enforce the UN no-fly zone in March 2011. *(RAF)*

ABOVE Ground crew complete pre-flight checks on a Tornado GR4 at Gioia Del Colle, Italy operating during Operation Ellamy in support of the no fly zone over Libya. The aircraft is armed with Paveway bombs and Brimstone missiles. *(RAF)*

Current plans are for Tornado Ground Reconnaissance Force (TGRF) to return to Britain in 2014 once operations are concluded.

Now some 7,000 words into a chapter on 'Tornado at War' and one might think the story is over, but like anything that involves the Tornado story this is far from the case. Operation 'Ellamy' over Libya in 2011 once more saw Tornado GR4s in action operating from their home base (initially) at RAF Marham. If 'Telic' was a precursor of what the GR4 could achieve, then perhaps 'Ellamy' will be the Tornado's finest hour. Alongside the RAF's newest asset the Typhoon, the Tornado GR4 really was in a class of its own during the Libyan operation.

Once again 9 Squadron was in on the action, with four GR4s loaded with a pair of Storm Shadow missiles leaving from RAF Marham on the night of 19 March 2011. Their mission was to launch eight MBDA Storm Shadow missiles against high value targets using a time-on-target mode, then returning to Britain. A second strike was called off by AWACS due to a risk of civilian casualties – the air war was getting smart. In total the mission clocked up some 3,000 miles, which was no mean feat in an aircraft approaching its third decade of service.

With a rationalisation of weapons fits the RAF was able to pre-load designated aircraft into representative war fits. While all GR4s are mission-capable, some are obviously more suited to war tasks than others – aircraft that have been involved in Operation 'Herrick' as an example are optimised for that theatre. The wing stations/pylons of the GR4 are pretty much in the standard fit of Storm Shadow, 2,250-litre fuel tanks (war missions) and BOZ pod; added to this is the option to attach ASRAAM and BOL pods, depending on the threat. This simplifies the engineers' task as they have only to load Storm Shadow, RAPTOR or a combination of Brimstone and Paveway underneath the aircraft with a suitable targeting pod.

With RAF Marham designated as the main TGRF (Tornado Ground Reconnaissance Force)

RIGHT Preparing for launch, the first operational mission by an RAF Tornado GR4 from Gioia Dell Colle. *(RAF)*

base for the conflict, station personnel needed to adapt to the fact that for the first time in 60 years the RAF was going to launch live missions from British soil. Like Gulf War 1, 20 years earlier, crews had little time to assimilate all the information required against a threat that had not been considered high risk up to that time. Intelligence officers worked quickly gathering as much information on the capabilities of the Libyan Air Force. At the time of 'Ellamy' the RAF TGRF was also actively engaged on Operation 'Herrick' as well as on exercises around the world. To achieve the task crews from the Lossiemouth Wing worked together with those from Marham.

With the Harrier and Tornado F3 (almost) withdrawn from service by this time, this was the first chance the RAF had to show how the mix of Typhoon and Tornado force would work together. Typhoon is an undisputed air combat aircraft bristling with technology and the ability to data-link information between aircraft. The Tornado on the other hand is a master of dropping weapons, both guided and un-guided, and the two aircraft worked together extremely well as a team, learning from each other's experience.

Libya became a high profile televised war and the emphasis and responsibility to avoid collateral damage lay firmly with the crews. Utilising Dual Mode Brimstone, Paveway and Storm Shadow, Tornado crews achieved outstanding results and have once again shown the aircraft is now at the top of its game. Operation 'Ellamy' may have lasted just five months but the Tornado force clocked up over 4,600 hours as well as engaging over 650 targets. Unlike earlier conflicts the targets were not heavily defended airfields, but this time were politically sensitive targets often deep inside cities and towns where civilians lived. Once again Operation 'Ellamy' showed that the GR4 was able to deploy worldwide at short notice and successfully carry out the tasks it had been given.

Since 1990 the Tornado has been in action constantly, but with the end of its service life drawing near the prospect of it slipping quietly into retirement is slim. Despite its age, the Tornado of 2013 is still perhaps the most capable ground-attack combat aircraft anywhere in the world.

ABOVE A still image taken from footage provided by a Tornado GR4, which destroyed a number of Gaddafi-regime rocket launchers and missiles in May 2011 as part of the NATO mission Operation Unified Protector, to protect Libyan civilians from attack. Two GR4s struck the weapons at a location south of Sirte in a coordinated attack based on intelligence gathered earlier by other RAF aircraft. Video taken from the Tornado's Litening III targeting pod clearly shows a number of large secondary explosions after Paveway bombs struck the targets. *(RAF)*

BELOW This image is from footage taken by an RAF Tornado GR4, showing the aircraft using Brimstone Missiles to destroy a Main Battle Tank in Libya during Operation Ellamy in 2011. *(RAF)*

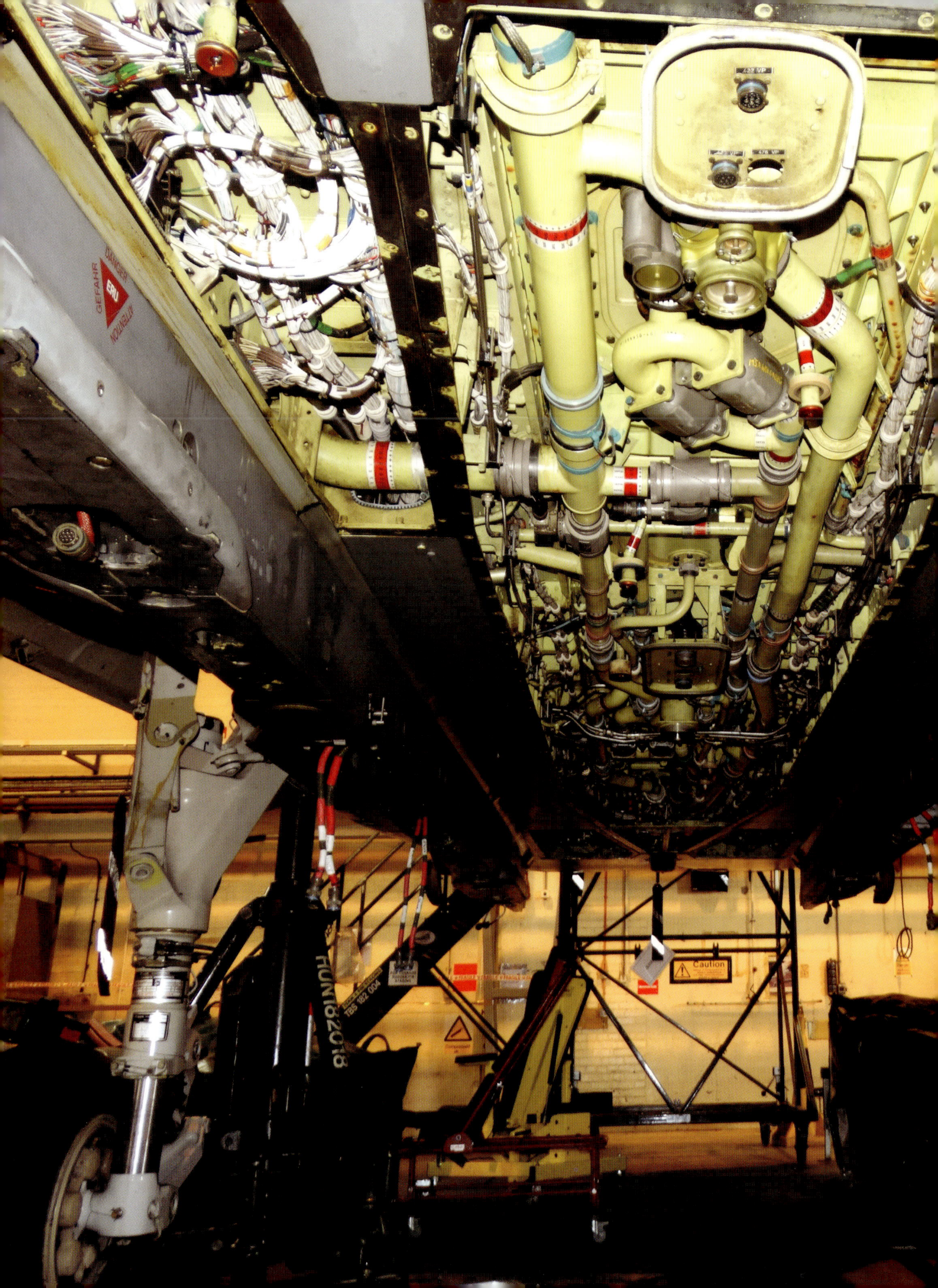
DANGER
GEFAHR
ERU
Caution
HUN182018
TBS 182 004

Chapter Four

Anatomy of the Tornado

━━━━●━━━━

The Tornado is a twin-engine, two-seat, shoulder-wing multi-role aircraft employing integrated all-weather navigation and weapon delivery avionics, variable geometry wings and fly-by-wire control system. The airframe uses 72% aluminium alloys, 17% titanium alloys, 6% steel and 5% non-metallic materials. Front and rear fuselage manufacture is by BAE Systems, Warton; wings by Aeritalia, Turin; and centre fuselage by Messerschmitt-Bölkow-Blohm, Augsburg.

OPPOSITE With access panels removed this is the complex underbelly of the Tornado.

ABOVE Refuelling panel and CMP.

Airframe structure

Designed from the outset to be used in the punishing role of high-speed low-level flight the Tornado is from an era before composite was the material of choice. With hindsight the construction of the Tornado has been another undivided success story. Constructed mainly of aluminum and titanium the manufacture relied on traditional machining methods to produce an aircraft that was built to last. Each host nation had its own production and final assembly line. All the British/RAF Tornados were 'final' assembled at the British Aerospace plant at Warton in Lancashire.

Unlike the first generation of jet fighters like the Meteor and Hunter, the Tornado has a plethora of maintenance and access panels – in fact 45% of the fuselage can be removed for maintenance. From the outset the designers had decided that the airframe should be built to remain in service far longer than any previous fighter-bomber. For this reason all three partner nations agreed that everything about the aircraft would be state-of-the-art and no pre-existing major system should be incorporated.

As early as 1970 wooden mockups of the Tornado displayed a shape that would change little from the airframes we see in service today. With the focus on the swing-wing design of the time, the General Dynamics F-111, the Tornado would also be swing-wing but with a very different design approach. All three nations agreed what they wanted from the airframe and so its design features fell naturally into place.

Most of the fuselage is made up of closely spaced, integrally machined frames, longerons and skins. Care was taken to 'hide' delicate items within the structure to protect them from ground fire. However, the emphasis was on accessibility so most of the fuselage can be opened up, with lightweight panels allowing ground crews easy access to change line units. Panels that require frequent opening are hinged and have quick release fasteners, while others are secured by screws and anchor nuts.

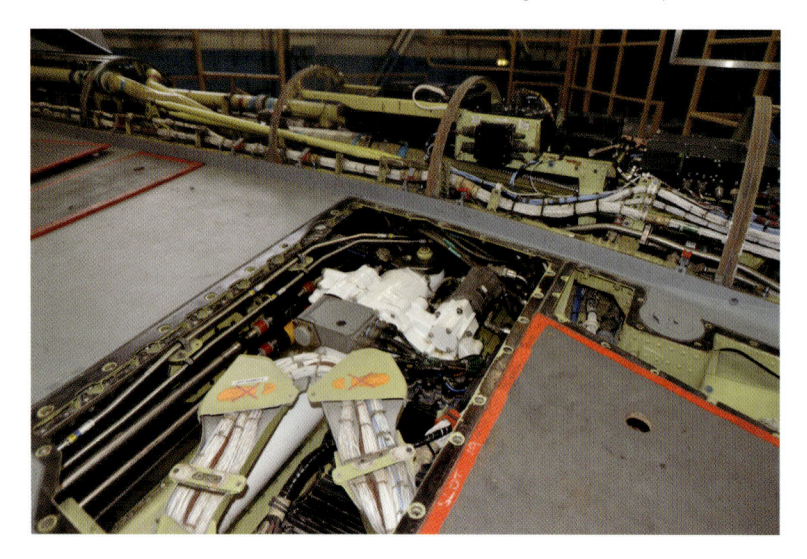

ABOVE Access panels removed on the upper wing surface and spine of the fuselage. Note how the cables containing miles of wiring are held in movable harnesses that allow the swing wing to sweep freely.

RIGHT F3 with panels removed.

Front nose section

From the front, the nose section (built by BAe in Britain) is used to house the two-man crew and the important radar and avionics. On the IDS version the radome (manufactured in Germany by AEG Telefunken) can be unlatched and opened to the starboard. The GR radome is in two parts, both of which are openable. The IDS version has both a Ground Mapping Radar (GMR) and a Terrain Following Radar (TFR). The nose landing gear is housed centrally beneath the cockpit floor. The rear of the front fuselage houses the pressure bulkhead. Contained within the front fuselage section is the gun, spent cartridge cases compartment, crew oxygen system and nitrogen accumulator bottle. The crew oxygen is a single container for rapid replacement and has a capacity of 10 litres

RIGHT Canopy controls.

BELOW Canopy.

Canopy

The cockpit canopy has the function of protecting the crew, while giving them adequate protection from high-speed bird strikes and keeping internal noise levels low during flight. The main canopy is of German manufacture but the front windscreen and side panels are made by Lucas Aerospace. Although the cockpit canopy cannot be opened while the aircraft is taxying (due to its weight) the internal air conditioning is more than adequate

ABOVE Unlike the GR4 (which has a two-part radar section) the ADV radome has a single hinge.

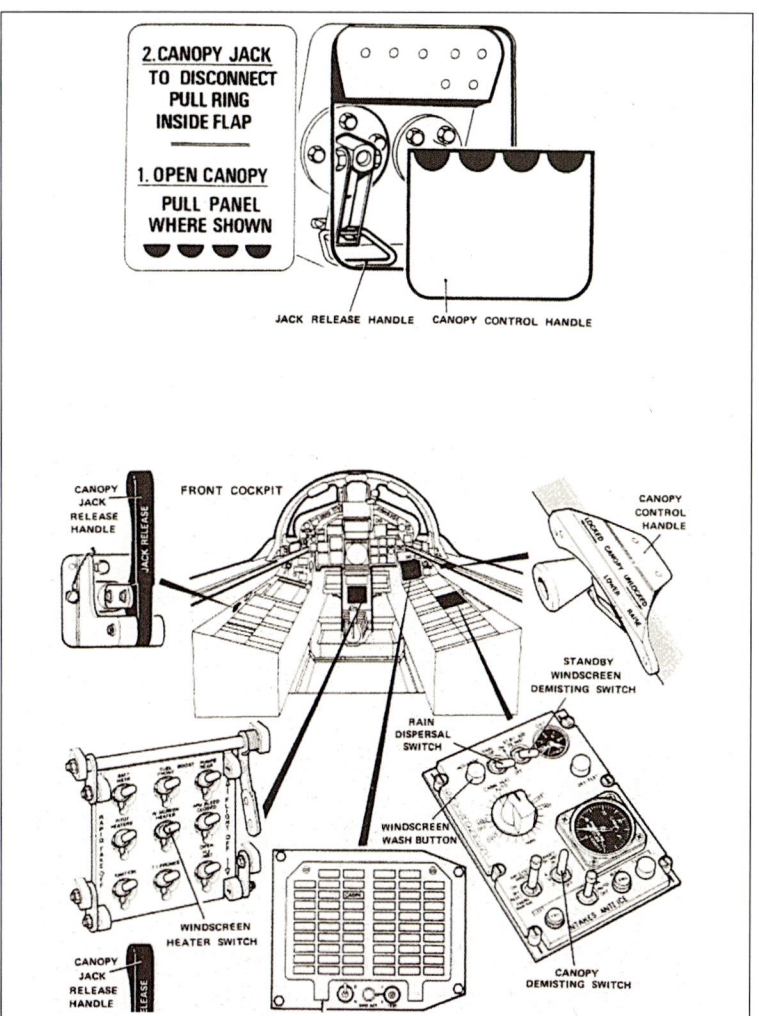

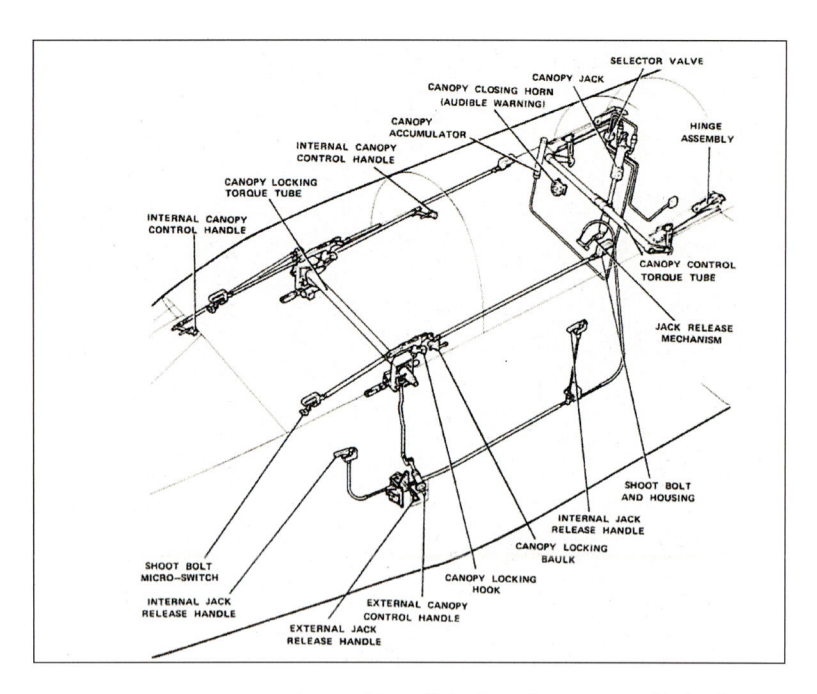

ABOVE Canopy mechanism.

ABOVE RIGHT Canopy Miniature Detonating Cord (MDC).

BELOW Canopy open.

to provide sufficient cooling even on the hottest days. Indeed, the first task of operating a Tornado in the Middle East is to shut the canopy and let the environmental control system cool you down. The canopy is designed to jettison in an emergency but also has Miniature Detonating Cord (MDC) should this fail. Should the crew be incapacitated, an external handle can be used to fire the MDC in an emergency. The canopy is electrically controlled, hydraulically operated and mechanically locked.

Another smart idea during construction was allowing the front windscreen section to hinge forwards allowing the ground engineers to access avionics more easily than removing the pilot's instrument panel. From an operator's viewpoint the Tornado canopy is a far cry from the goldfish bowl 360 vision enjoyed by the likes of the F-15 Eagle. In particular the front windscreen has a low strake, which, combined with the wide Head-Up Display (HUD) can make forward vision difficult, especially at low altitude during winter operations when the sun is low in the sky. It is, however, extremely strong and to the best of my knowledge has never caused problems due to bird strikes. It also needs to be born in mind that from the outset the Tornado was not designed as a fighter and thus canopy view was not as important as high-speed bird strike protection.

Cockpit

The design and layout of the cockpit could have been a contentious issue among different national aircrew, but it proved surprisingly simple. Internally the Tornado cockpit is well laid out and a far cry from the cramped confines of previous generations of fighter-bombers, with lessons having been learned from US Century-series fighters and emphasis given to roominess. The cockpit is pressurised from 5,000ft with cooled air fed from both engines and its internal temperature can be set from 5 to 30 degrees Centigrade. The canopy has a large inflatable rubber seal, which helps to reduce wind noise at high speed and low level.

Inside the cockpit, designers used the latest Martin-Baker Mk 10A seats that were rocket-assisted. Similar to those used on the RAF's Hawk trainers, they brought a new level of comfort and survivability to front line units.

Tornado GR4 front cockpit

1. Left and right throttles.
1A. Airbrake selector back and forward, and manoeuvre flap up and down.
2. Mount for wander lamp.
3. Frequency card, radios.
4. Pilot's weapon aiming/laser designator.
5. 100% oxygen selector switch.
6. Ejector seat oxygen contents gauge.
7. Seat go forward lever.
8. Wing sweep lever.
9. Combined trim gauge – pitch, roll and yaw.
11. Stores jettison switch.
10. Undercarriage lever.
12. Combined flap, slat and wing sweep position indicator.
13. Fuel LP (Low Pressure) cocks guarded ON.
14. Thrust reverse indication including emergency override.
15. Hook light.
16. Master armament switch.
17. Autopilot indications.
18. TFR (Terrain Following Radar) front display.
20. VSI (Vertical Speed Indicator).
21. Combined Mach/ASI (Air Speed Indicator).
22. Standby artificial horizon.
23. Altimeter.
24. HSI (Horizontal Situation Indicator).
25. Rudder pedal adjust.
26. HUD (Head-Up Display), wide field.
27. AOA (Angle of Attack) gauge.
28. Late arm switch – guarded OFF.
29. Left-hand attention getter.
30. Right-hand attention getter.
31. G meter.
32. Pilot's Multi Function Display Screen.
33. F-18 style stick with HOTAS (Hands on Throttle and Stick).
34. Rapid start gang bar.
35. Pilot's lower ejector seat handle.
36. Ejector seat safety pin.
37. Martin Baker QRB (Quick Release Box).
38. Arm restraints, white.
39. Leg restraints, blue.
40. RHWR (Radar Homing Warning Receiver).
41. Left and right RB199 RPM gauges.
42. Left and right RB199 temperature gauges.
43. Left and right RB199 nozzle gauges.
44. Fuel flow meter.
45. Fuel contents gauge.
46. Individual fuel cell group's selector.
48. Emergency power switch, guarded and safety pin in OFF position.
47. Left and right hydraulic gauges.
49. Stop watch.
50. Secure comms radio.
51. CWP (Central Warning Panel).
52. Stowage for cockpit pins, four in total – seat, EPS (xxxxxxxxxxx), canopy, MDC (Miniature Detonation Cord).
53. Standby compass.
54. Radio frequency card.
55. Flight refuel panel.
56. ILS (Instrument Landing System) selector.
57. Comms box.
58. Fuel selector panel.
59. Engine control panel.
60. Left and right generator switches.
61. TACAN (Tactical Air Navigation System) selector.

Tornado ADV front cockpit.

1. F-18 stick top with HOTAS (Hands on Throttle and Stick) including AOA (Angle of Attack) override and weapons selection and trigger press.
2. Martin Baker Mk10 seat oxygen contents.
3. Martin Baker Mk10 seat, go forward lever, also locks harness.
4. Wing sweep lever – fully forward 25 degrees, aft 67 degrees.
5. Flap/slat and wing sweep gauge.
6. Rudder pedal adjust.
7. Undercarriage lever.
8. Fuel LP (Low Pressure) cocks.
9. Hook light – GREEN for deployed.
10. Master armament safety key.
11. Combined ASI (Air Speed Indicator), Mach and indicated air speed gauge.
12. MMS (Missile Management System) panel.
13. Standby artificial horizon.
14. Altimeter.
15. HSI (Horizontal Situation Indicator) compass and TACAN (Tactical Air Navigation System) read-out.
16. Rudder pedals – left.
17. AOA gauge, orange flag showing power OFF.
18. Final arm switch guarded OFF.
19. HUD (Head-Up Display).
20. G meter.
21. Right-hand warning panel attention getters.
22. Trim switch, triple axis – all except rudder.
23. Pilot's TV display radar and plan display.
24. Flight refuel light.
25. Standby compass.
26. Left and right engine RPM gauges.
27. Left and right engine temperature gauges.
28. Left and right reheat nozzles position indicators
29. Fuel flow gauges.
30. Fuel quantity gauge.
31. Fuel tank contents selection
32. RAT (Ram Air Turbine) switch, safety pin installed and off.
33. Left and right hydraulics – OFF.
34. CWP (Central Warning Panel).
35. Brake pressure gauge.
36. ILS (Instrument Landing System) selector.
37. TACAN (Tactical Air Navigation System) selector.
38. RHWR (Radar Homing Warning Receiver) controls.
39. RHWR display.
40. Rapid start gang bar.
41. Fuel sequence selector, above shows probe IN/OUT, and guarded yellow and black emergency probe OUT switch.
42. Canopy unlock handle.
43. Front radio box.
44. Left and right generators.
45. Main oxygen panel.
46. Manual seat release.
47. Map/FRC (xxxxxxxxxxxxx) stowage.
48. PEC (Personal Equipment Connector) cover.
49. HUD glass.
50. ????????

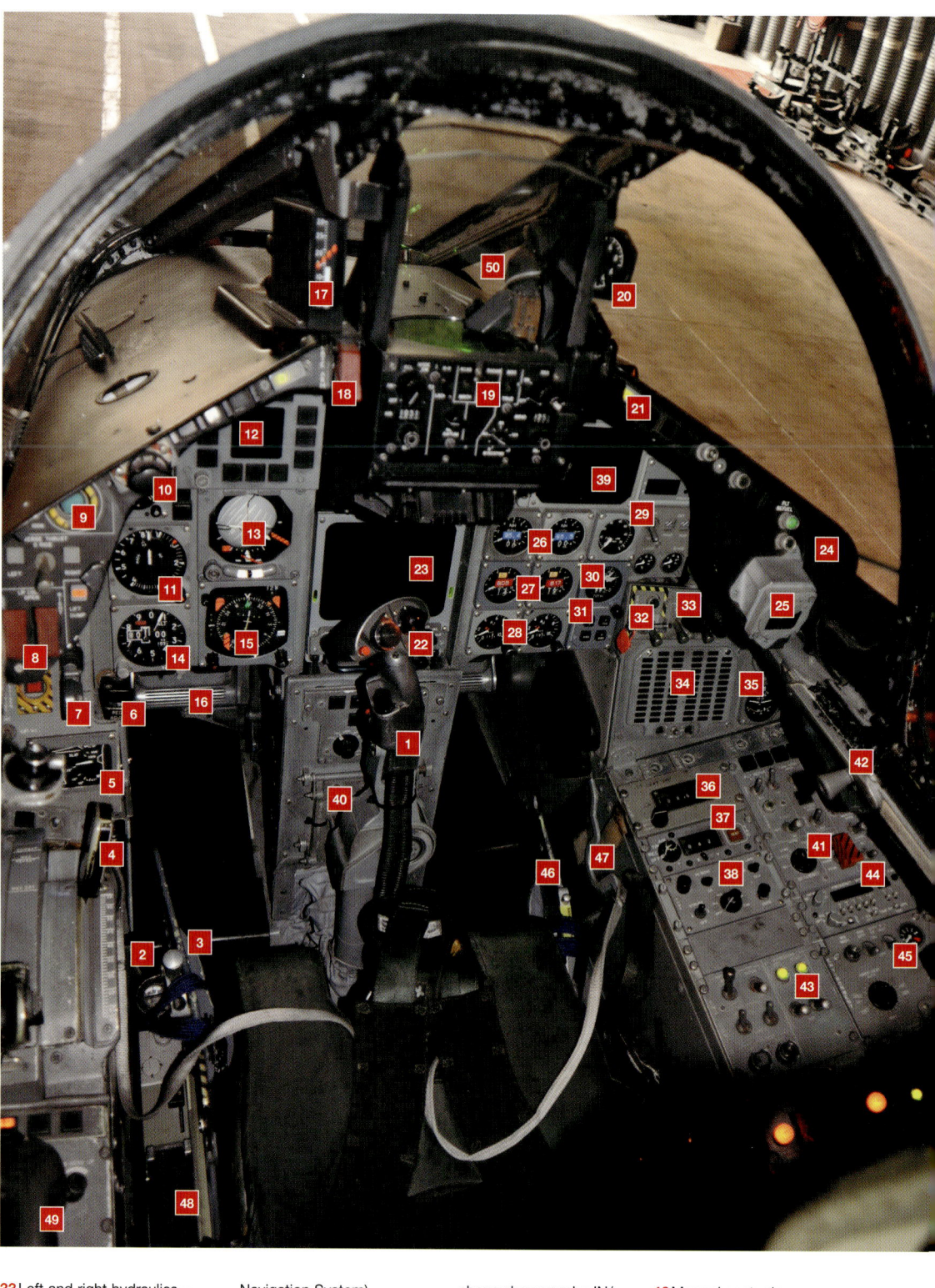

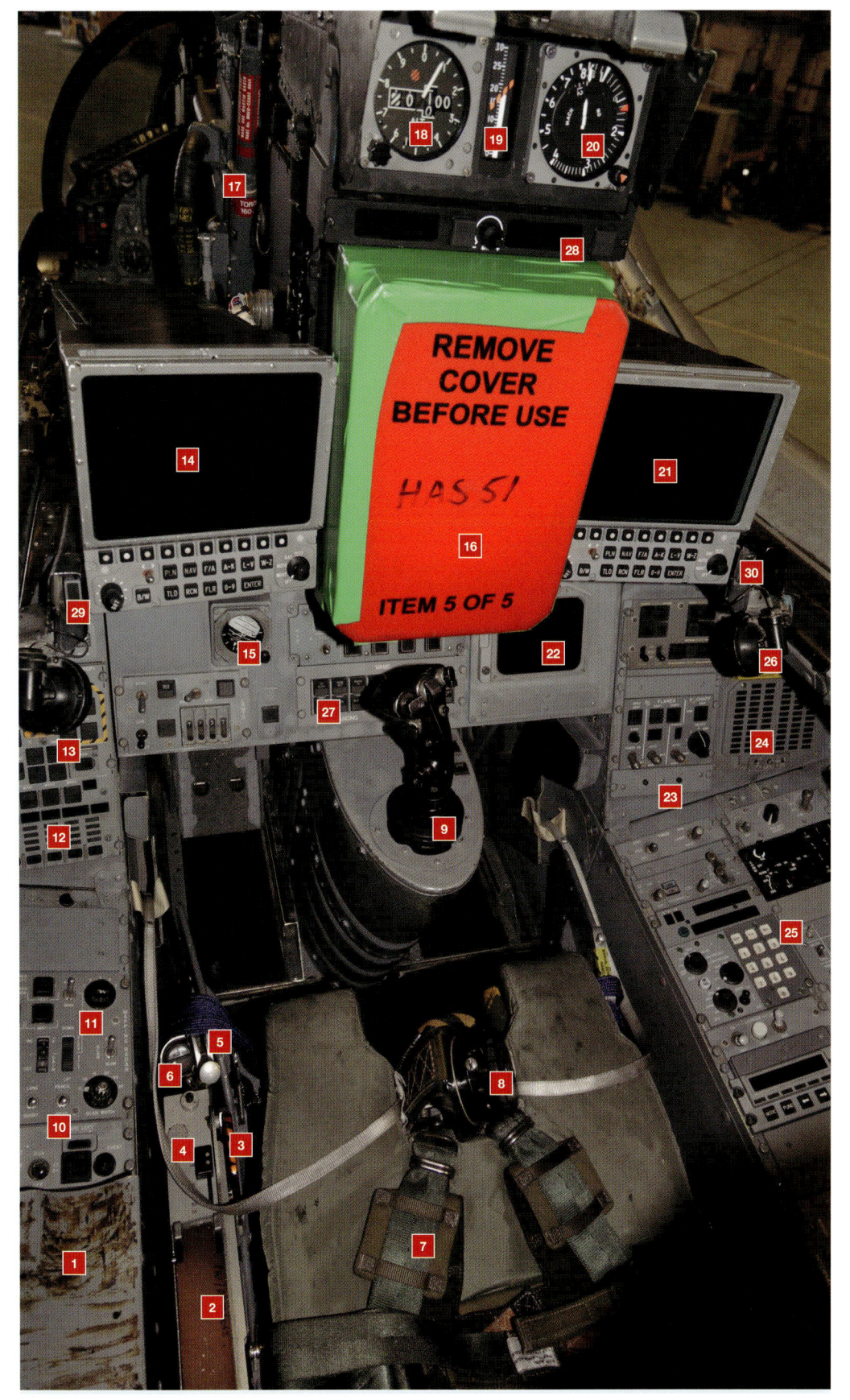

Tornado GR4 rear cockpit.

1. Arm rest.
2. PEC (Personal Equipment Connector) – oxygen, anti-G and intercom.
3. Emergency oxygen selector.
4. 100% oxygen selector.
5. Go forward lever.
6. Martin Baker Mk10 seat oxygen contents gauge.
7. Seat harness.
8. QRB (Quick Release Box).
9. WSO's (Weapon System Officer's) hand controller, multi-function.
10. Tape recording.
11. GMR (Ground Mapping Radar) controls.
12. Weapons control panel.
13. Weapon control panel.
14. Left-hand TV display.
15. Standby artificial horizon.
16. TARDIS (Tornado Advanced Radar Display) cover.
17. Rocket pack from front seat ejection seat.
18. Altimeter.
19. AOA (Angle of Attack) gauge.
20. ASI (Air Speed Indicator).
21. Right-hand TV display.
22. TFR (Terrain Following Radar) display.
23. Chaff and flare control panel.
24. CWP (Central Warning Panel).
25. Data input switches.
26. Wander lamp.
27. Weapons aiming switches.
28. Comms suite.
29. Attention getter left.
30. Attention getter right.

ANATOMY OF THE TORNADO

Panavia Tornado F3.

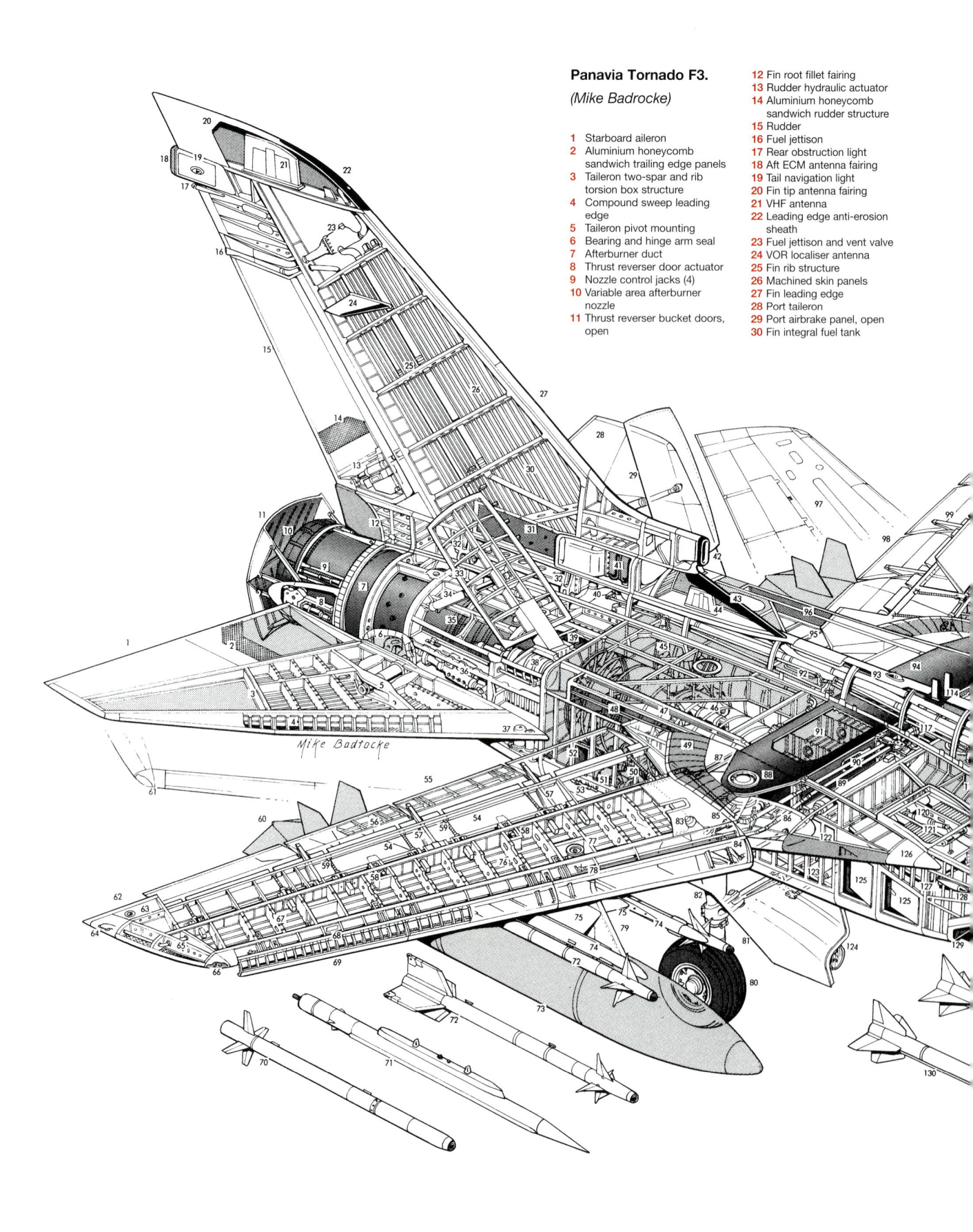

(Mike Badrocke)

1. Starboard aileron
2. Aluminium honeycomb sandwich trailing edge panels
3. Taileron two-spar and rib torsion box structure
4. Compound sweep leading edge
5. Taileron pivot mounting
6. Bearing and hinge arm seal
7. Afterburner duct
8. Thrust reverser door actuator
9. Nozzle control jacks (4)
10. Variable area afterburner nozzle
11. Thrust reverser bucket doors, open
12. Fin root fillet fairing
13. Rudder hydraulic actuator
14. Aluminium honeycomb sandwich rudder structure
15. Rudder
16. Fuel jettison
17. Rear obstruction light
18. Aft ECM antenna fairing
19. Tail navigation light
20. Fin tip antenna fairing
21. VHF antenna
22. Leading edge anti-erosion sheath
23. Fuel jettison and vent valve
24. VOR localiser antenna
25. Fin rib structure
26. Machined skin panels
27. Fin leading edge
28. Port taileron
29. Port airbrake panel, open
30. Fin integral fuel tank

88

RAF TORNADO MANUAL

31 Heat exchanger exhaust shield
32 Fin spar attachment joints
33 Starboard airbrake panel
34 Airbrake hydraulic jack
35 Turbo Union RB199-34R Mk 104 afterburning turbofan engine
36 Taileron hydraulic actuator
37 Hydraulic filters
38 Hydraulic system reservoir, port and starboard
39 Airbrake hinge mounting
40 Engine bleed-air ducting
41 Bleed-air primary heat exchanger
42 Primary heat exchanger air intake
43 Fin root antenna fairing
44 HF antenna
45 Rear fuselage integral fuel tank, total capacity 7,143 litres (1,571 Imp gal)
46 Port airframe mounted Secondary Power System (SPS) gearbox
47 Gear box interconnecting cross-shaft
48 Wing root pneumatic seal
49 Flexible wing glove sealing plates
50 Starboard SPS gearbox
51 Auxiliary Power Unit (APU)
52 APU exhaust
53 Ventral equipment bay access panel
54 Starboard wing spoiler panel housings
55 Starboard double-slotted flap
56 Flap rib structure
57 Flap guide rails
58 Spoiler hydraulic actuators
59 Flap operating screw jacks
60 External tank tail fins
61 Starboard wing fully swept, 67° position
62 Wing fully forward, 25° position
63 Starboard obstruction light
64 Fuel vent
65 Wingtip fairing structure
66 Starboard navigation light
67 Wing panel two-spar and rib torsion box structure
68 Leading edge slat rib structure
69 Starboard three-segment leading edge slat
70 BAe advanced short range air-to-air missile (ASRAAM)
71 Philips-Matra 'Phimat' chaff/flare dispenser, may be carried on starboard outer sidewinder pylon
72 AIM-9L Sidewinder air-to-air missile
73 2,250-litre (495 Imp gal) external fuel tank; 1,500-litre (330 Imp gal) tank alternative fit
74 Missile launch rail
75 Anhedral missile pylons
76 Starboard wing integral fuel tank
77 Wing pylon pivot mounting
78 Pylon angle control link and operating rod
79 Starboard wing swivelling pylon
80 Starboard main wheel
81 Main wheel door
82 Shock absorber leg strut
83 Main undercarriage pivot mounting
84 Leg swivelling link
85 Hydraulic retraction jack
86 Leading edge glove seal fairing
87 Telescopic fuel feed and vent lines from wing tank
88 Wing pivot bearing
89 Wing sweep control screw jack
90 Flap and slat actuating torque shafts
91 Wing pivot box integral fuel tank
92 Tailplane control rods
93 Anti-collision beacon
94 Electron beam-welded titanium wing pivot box structure
95 Wing root housing, swept position
96 Port pneumatic root seal
97 Port wing fully-swept position
98 Port double-slotted flap
99 Flap guide rails
100 Port spoiler panels, open
101 Port obstruction light
102 Port navigation light
103 Three-segment leading-edge slat
104 Port wing integral fuel tank
105 Leading edge slat operating torque shaft
106 Slat screw jacks
107 Port missile carriage
108 Swivelling pylon bearing mounting
109 Port wing pylon
110 Port external fuel tank
111 Port and forward oblique ECM antenna fairing
112 Intake by-pass air spill duct fairing
113 Port wing sweep operating screw jack
114 UHF antenna
115 Dorsal spine fairing
116 Air system ducting to port side environmental control system
117 Central flap/slat control unit and drive motor
118 Forward fuselage fuel tank
119 Boundary layer air spill duct
120 Intake ramp hydraulic actuator
121 Starboard intake by-pass air spill ducts
122 Starboard and forward oblique ECM antennae fairing
123 Main wheel door hydraulic jack
124 Door-mounted landing light, port and starboard
125 Intake suction relief doors
126 Fixed wing glove fairing
127 Two-dimensional variable area intake ramp doors
128 Starboard navigation light
129 Starboard engine air intake
130 AIM-120 advanced medium range air-to-air missile (AMRAAM)
131 BAe Skyflash medium range air-to-air missile, four carried semi-recessed beneath fuselage
132 Starboard equipment bay
133 Cartridge case and ammunition link collector box
134 Cockpit pressure section sidewall framing
135 Sloping rear pressure bulkhead
136 Canopy hinge point
137 Canopy hinge link and actuator
138 Tactical navigator's Martin-Baker Mk 10A 'zero-zero' ejection seat
139 Port engine intake lip
140 Tactical navigator's instrument and display console
141 Canopy centre arch
142 Radar hand controller
143 Under-floor transverse ammunition magazine, 180 rounds
144 Ammunition feed chute
145 Mauser 27mm cannon, starboard side only
146 Cannon barrel mounting
147 Pitot head, port and starboard
148 Cockpit starboard side console panels
149 Pilot's Martin-Baker Mk 10A ejection seat
150 Ejection seat head rest
151 Canopy-breaker miniature detonation cord (MDC)
152 Upward-hinging cockpit canopy
153 Canopy open position
154 Windscreen panel open position for instrument access
155 Retractable telescopic flight refuelling probe
156 Probe retraction link
157 Windscreen panels
158 Pilot's head-up display (HUD)
159 Port side console with engine throttles, wing sweep control and pilot's radar hand controller
160 Instrument panel
161 Instrument panel shroud
162 Control column, hands on throttle and stick (HOTAS) controls
163 Rudder pedals
164 Forward equipment bay, stability and control augmentation system equipment
165 Cannon blast suppressor and purging air intake
166 Nose wheel leg door
167 Nose undercarriage leg strut
168 Twin nose wheels, forward retracting
169 Torque scissors links
170 Nose wheel doors
171 Taxiing light
172 Cannon barrel
173 Lower UHF antenna
174 Cannon muzzle aperture
175 Incidence transmitter
176 Front pressure bulkhead
177 Forward avionics equipment bay
178 Windscreen rain dispersal air ducts
179 IFF antenna
180 Radar equipment module
181 Radome hinged, double-action radome and equipment module hinging to starboard
182 Scanner tracking mechanism
183 GEC-Marconi AI Mk 24 Foxhunter multi-mode, track-while-scan/pulse-Doppler radar scanner
184 Glass fibre radome
185 Air data probe

MARTIN-BAKER MK10 EJECTION SEAT – SURVIVAL EQUIPMENT

With over 5,500 Mk 10 seats in service worldwide, the Mk 10 ejector seat is used by all Tornado variants and has been installed since the first flight in 1974. At 2013, the lives of more than 80 aircrew have been saved using this seat, although not all of them on the Tornado. The seat takes Martin-Baker's long experience of designing aircrew escape systems and combines the best of previous designs to produce a seat that has given excellent service.

The seat has four main parts: catapult, main beam structure, seat pan and parachute assembly. By being modular the seat is easy to remove and to service, with its principal parts easily removable *in-situ*. Of great significance is the ability to remove the seat from the aircraft without any need to remove the cockpit canopy.

Designed to be used in the low-level high-speed environment the seat can be used safely at speeds of up to 630kts and altitudes as high as 50,000ft. The Mk 10A is a 'zero-zero' seat, which means that a crew can vacate the Tornado in an emergency while the aircraft is stationary and on the ground. The Tornado is equipped with a selectable command ejection system that allows either crewmember to eject the other, or both, in the event of incapacitation.

The seat has a rocket pack located under the seat pan and a single firing handle located between the crew member's legs. Improvements over older style ejection seats include the fitment of arm restraints and a double leg-restraint system designed to reduce injury caused by flailing limbs at high speed. Each seat is equipped with a Personal Equipment Connector (PEC). This provides the crew with main oxygen and emergency oxygen, as well as air for the anti-G suit and electrical connections for the pilot/navigator's helmet.

Unlike older seats, strapping into the unit is simple via a central Quick Release Box (QRB). This is permanently connected to the central crotch strap allowing the crew to simply buckle the two lap straps and two shoulder straps into the QRB to be secured to the seat. On the Tornado, crews wear special life jackets that have a woven mesh arm assembly with sewn-in lanyards to connect to the seat. During ejection these lanyards retract pulling your arms into the correct position, thereby preventing you from damaging them on the aircraft or in the high-speed airflow.

For simplicity the seat is made safe with only a single seat pan firing pin with three other pins used to arm the seat prior to strapping in. Current seats fitted to RAF GR4s have been upgraded with a 'comfort cushion' modification to reduce aircrew fatigue on increasingly lengthy sortie times during combat operations.

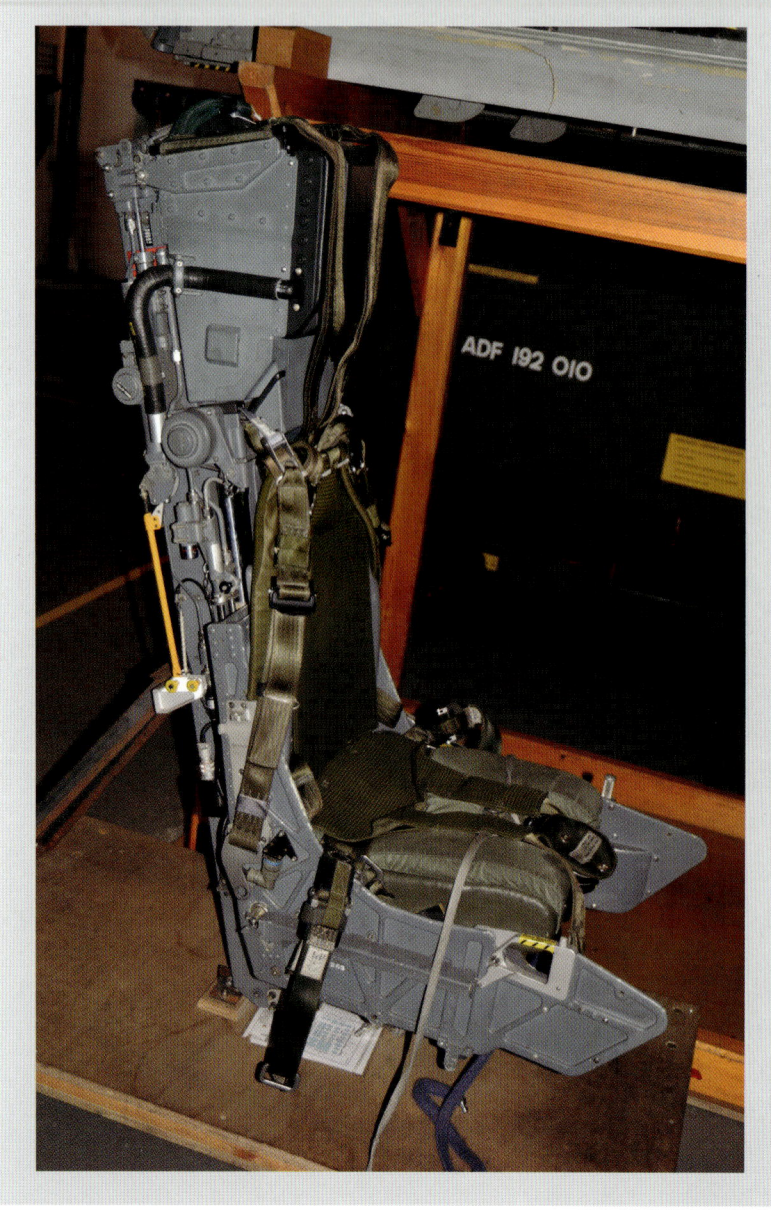

BELOW Mk 10 ejector seat.

Ground Mapping Radar (GMR)

Staying with the front fuselage, one part of the aircraft that seems to have escaped 'Europeanisation' is the RAF IDS version's radar. While everything else is European the Ground Mapping and Terrain Following Radar (TFR) is American. After much research the answer appears to have been a compromise between Germany and Britain. The RAF wanted a Ferranti radar, or its equivalent, but the Germans insisted that nothing existed which would suit the task and asked for an American-built device. Perhaps a knock-back from the abortive British F-111 radar, Britain finally agreed to a Texas Instruments radar so long as the aircraft had a Ferranti INAS (the Germans wanted an American Litton system). In the end another compromise was reached and that seems to be how a small part of the USA ended up in the MRCA!

The radar unit is located in the front of the Tornado and as mentioned the radome can be opened in two parts. In fact the Tornado has two radars, both made by Texas Instruments – a ground mapping radar and a TFR. The radar is optimised for blind navigation and weapon attack, mainly in the low altitude air-to-ground modes. The radar provides high resolution mapping as well as target acquisition and radar fixing. Once again, as a testament to the initial design phase, both units differ little today from what was installed nearly 40 years ago. Modern updates have included a small improvement to the GR force giving them a limited air-to-air capability – much to the annoyance of air defence crews. While not in the league of the Foxhunter it does allow the GR version the ability to find and track a tanker aircraft and then effect a join-up – something that happens on nearly every combat mission.

Centre section

Secondary Flying Controls System (SFCS)

The SFCS controls the following: wing sweep, flaps and slats, Kruger flaps (now disabled), and airbrakes.

While the front fuselage is fairly conventional, the centre section is (or was) revolutionary. Built by MBB in Germany the centre section would

ABOVE As well as allowing access to the front and rear of the radar, the double-hinged nose on the GR4 enables ground level servicing of the forward avionics bay. *(Mark Jones)*

LEFT Wing flaps seen from beneath, showing mechanism.

BELOW Leading edge slats deployed.

91

ANATOMY OF THE TORNADO

ABOVE GR4, ZD719, displays its slots and flaps on take-off from Nellis AFB. *(Chris Wood)*

BELOW Port wing leading edge slat, Sky Shadow and ASRAAM training round.

really be the make or break of the whole MRCA project. Swing-wing philosophy had been around in Britain for some time, but no-one had built an aircraft that flew with variable geometry wings, or indeed an aircraft that could sweep the wings to such extremes. In truth, early proposals were probably too far ahead of themselves to ever work. One problem of variable geometry wings is that as you move them fore and aft the whole dynamics of lift and centre of pressure change, so you really need a fly-by-wire or computer-controlled flight system for it to work effectively.

Experience gained from the problems encountered with the F-111 meant that Panavia opted to produce the centre box built from titanium, not held together by bolts, but using electron beam welding. For this revolutionary process Panavia turned to the US plane maker Grumman for help, which at the time was building the F-14 Tomcat. Located not far from New York City on Long Island, the Grumman aircraft factory at Bethpage had invested heavily in the new technique using beam welding. So confident was Panavia that this was the answer to the wing box that Grumman actually built the first two wing boxes under supervision of MBB. Meanwhile, MBB set up its own plant at Ottobrunn in Germany to perfect the process. The wing box is also designed as an integral fuel tank.

It cannot be emphasised enough just how crucial the wing design and its location on the fuselage is to the overall success of the Tornado. Panavia definitely got it right in placing the wing high on the fuselage, with the tailplane set low enough so as not to be disturbed by changing airflow. From an operator's point of view it became the most natural flying skill you could imagine to simply have one hand on the throttles and then simply move the wings forward and back as your speed increased or decreased. In the blink of an eye Panavia had developed 'seat of the pants wing sweeping' without any effort. The only fly in the ointment was the designers who wanted the wing sweep lever to be illogical – moving forward to move the wings back, and vice versa. Luckily, common sense and pilot input prevailed and the wing sweep lever is moved aft for the wings to move back!

It was in 1968 that designers at Warton designed what is probably the jewel in the Tornado's crown – the Teflon bearing, which has been used (virtually maintenance free) on every Tornado that has been built. The wing sweep is and can be swept from forward 25 degrees to aft 67 or 68 degrees. The wing sweep is hydro-mechanically operated and should take approximately 7 seconds to cover the full range, with each wing rotating around a special pivot in the fixed section of the wing. The wing is moved by re-circulating ball screw actuators powered by hydraulic motors. One is fitted to each side of the centre line and are interconnected by a synchronising shaft able to transmit the drive from one side to another should one hydraulic system fail. This is a fail-safe system to ensure it is impossible to have an asymmetric wing sweep position. Early F-14 trials resulted in an asymmetric wing sweep failure, which led to the loss of the aircraft on final approach.

ABOVE Wing sweep, left spoiler deployed, tailerons up and down, centre box section exposed.

Perhaps the most well-known acronym to both Tornado crews and engineers is the HLWSCU – the High Level Wing Sweep Control Unit. This is the unit that controls the wing sweep via the pilot moving the wing sweep lever just inboard of the throttles, beside his left leg. By moving the wing sweep lever (depressing the clutch) the HLWSCU converts this signal to a hydraulic pressure and the wings move to the desired position.

Outer wing sections

The outer wing sections are made of alloy and are produced in Italy. They are different from conventional wings in that the Tornado does not have ailerons. Instead it devotes the full span of the wing to lift enhancing devices, both at the front and the rear of the leading and trailing edges. The entire rear section of the wing has double-slotted fowler flaps. On the top surfaces of the wing are spoilers, which, together with the tailerons, provide roll control. The spoilers also have a function of deploying immediately on touchdown, thus killing any lift and preventing the aircraft from bouncing. On the RAF GR versions Krueger Flaps were fitted to the forward leading edge of the inner wing nibs, but these are no longer used (it was deemed that the

RIGHT Wing sweep lever internal mechanism.

ABOVE Upper wing sweep skirts exposed.

LEFT Wing sweep/pivot.

LEFT Wing sweep ram.

93

ANATOMY OF THE TORNADO

ABOVE Wings swept 67 degrees fighter-style.

ABOVE RIGHT Wings forward.

BELOW Secondary Flight Controls. Note the defunct Kruger flaps indicator on the left.

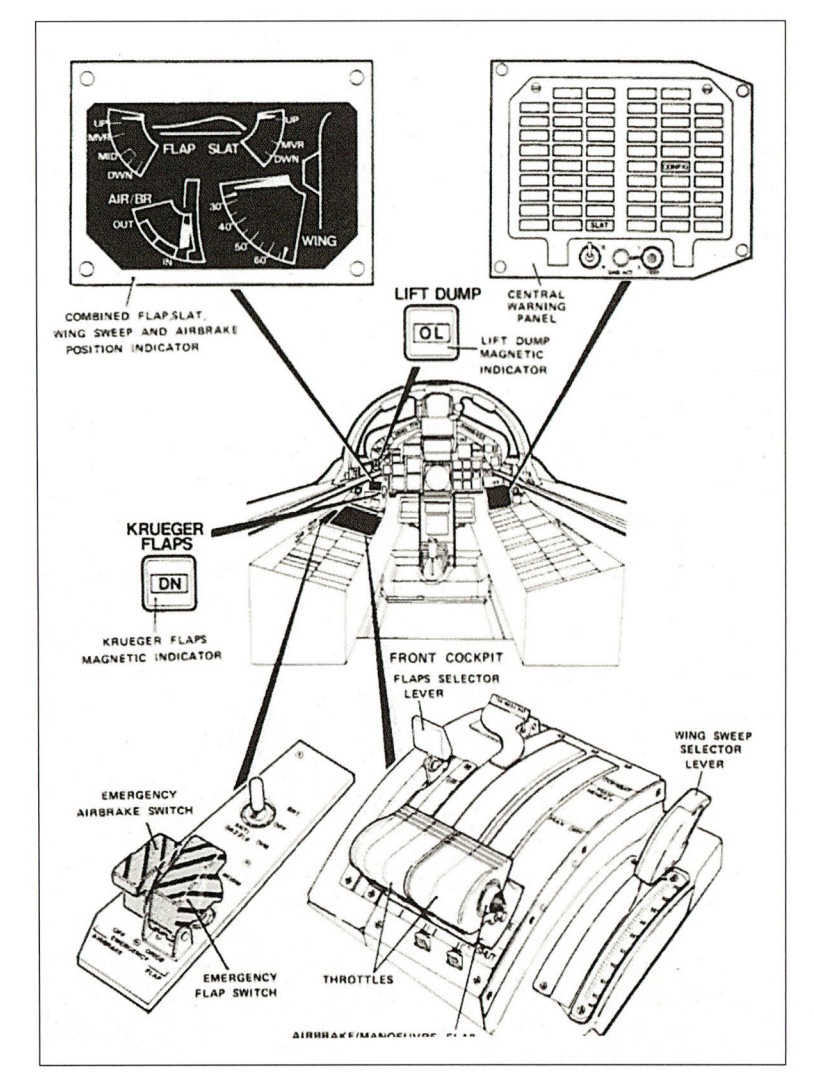

reduction in landing speed was insignificant so they were immobilised).

Generally the wings are left in 25-degree sweep up to speeds of 450kts, and then swept progressively aft as speed increases. Only in the forward 25-degree sweep are full slats and flaps available. In 45-degree sweep some manoeuvre flap for improved turn performance is available. With variable geometry wings one problem that arises is solved by a simple system of rods and levers.

Secondary Flight Controls (SFC)

The secondary flight controls are the wing sweep, flaps, slats and airbrakes. Controls for the SFCs are all well located on and around the throttles.

Wing sweep

The wing sweep lever is inboard of the twin throttles and is marked from 25 to 68°. To move the wings the pilot presses the detent on the trigger and selects the desired sweep – a detent is set at 45 degrees. On the forward left front coaming is a combined flaps, airbrake and wing sweep position indicator.

BELOW Wing-sweep lever fully forward at 25 degrees.

94
RAF TORNADO MANUAL

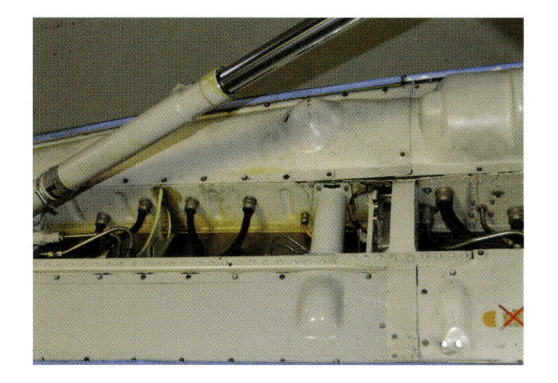

LEFT The airbrakes are raised by actuators.

Wing sweep has three main positions:
- 25° – fully forward slow-speed flight below 450kts and used for take-off and landing, allowing full slat and flap deployment.
- 45° – mid-position, often used by the GR force for low-level flight and weapon delivery.
- 67° – fully rearward, high-speed low-level dash, or in the GR4/F3 for high speed/supersonic flight.

Flaps and slats

Flaps can be selected from up, mid or down, with the wings fully forward in 25°. With the wings in 45°, manoeuvre flap is available – indicated by the MNVR indication. In an emergency flaps and airbrakes can be selected using the black and yellow covered switches outboard of the throttles.

Airbrakes

The spade-type airbrakes are located on the shoulders of the rear fuselage. Airbrakes are selected 'in' or 'out' using the switch located on the right throttle. The airbrakes are opened by actuators are opened proportionately in relation to the forward speed of the aircraft.

Wing pylons

The Tornado has two (four in total) under-wing hard points – outer and inner – and these are always aligned to the fore and aft axis of the aircraft irrespective of wing sweep angle. Wing pylons are not jettisonable, but the stores are.

Air intakes are covered in detail in the RB199 section but the two wedge shaped intakes also provide a point for the forward anti collision lights to be fitted.

Rear fuselage

The rear of the fuselage is made by BAE Systems and mainly devoted to housing the engines and APU. With a Titanium firewall the rear fuselage has a Graviner fire detection and suppression system. While the older fighters like the F-104, Hunter and F-4 had the engines removed by withdrawing them directly from the fuselage, the

LEFT Taxi nozzle open with reverse thrust stowed.

SPIN PREVENTION AND INCIDENCE LIMITING SYSTEM (SPILS)

Another first for RAF fighter-bomber aircraft was the introduction of the Spin Prevention and Incidence Limiting System (SPILS), which effectively gave pilots greater freedom to mishandle the aircraft and not end up losing control. SPILS has a basic ON/OFF switch so is very simple for the operator. Taking its signals from the CSAS and the two Angle of Attack (AOA) probes, all the inputs are processed within the SPILS computer, which in turn feeds back to the CSAS to limit the maximum AOA attainable. The Tornado was probably also the first RAF fighter not to have a sideslip indicator as SPILS took care of this moment. When the pilot reaches high AOA (19.2 units or greater) SPILS will reduce the amount of pitch and roll and yaw authority. SPILS is turned off for landing and for air-to-air gun firing. Initially pilots were sceptical about SPILS, feeling it was restricting their ability to fly the aircraft to the limits. However, after a short time it was soon realised the benefits of carefree handling outweighed the risk of turning off SPILS and losing control. What SPILS achieves brilliantly is a simple system that covers all handling in any wing sweep or weapon configuration.

ABOVE Taileron position indicator.

ABOVE RIGHT Taileron internal mechanisms.

BELOW Tornado fly-by-wire schematic. *(Panavia)*

BELOW RIGHT ADV CWP panel.

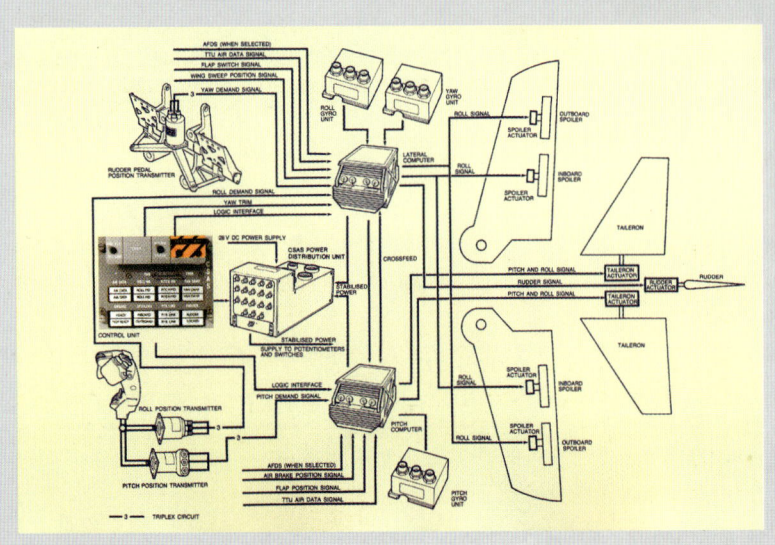

PRIMARY FLIGHT CONTROL SYSTEM (PFCS)

The Primary Flight Control System (PFCS) on the Tornado include the tailerons, rudder and the spoilers – the primary flying control surfaces. These are controlled by the Command and Stability Augmentation System (CSAS). These surfaces are controlled by the pilot's control column, which interconnects with the rudder. When the tailerons move symmetrically this allows the aircraft to pitch and dive; when the tailerons are moved differentially this rolls the aircraft. Rudders can be moved using the pilot's foot-mounted rudder pedals. The wing-mounted spoilers augment roll control but are inhibited once the wings are swept aft of 50°.

CSAS is an integral part of the PFCS giving the aircraft 'fly-by-wire' in two modes – firstly in full CSAS (which is known as Manoeuvre Demand – MD); or in Direct Link (DL – which is an electrical reversionary mode). On the top of the spine are traditional mechanical control rods. These allow the aircraft to by flown using conventional hydraulically-powered control via the tailerons in certain multiple failure situations of the CSAS. The system is normally disengaged.

The CSAS uses a mode and failure logic system to continuously monitor the fly-by-wire and displays faults on the Central Warning Panel (CWP) or on the main CSAS panel on the left side of the cockpit behind the throttles. Should any failures occur, the system automatically reconfigures using faders to ensure a smooth transition. Should the pilot wish he can engage a training mode to enable him to simulate certain failures for practice.

In full CSAS the system is triplex for safety, and incorporates the three axis of pitch, roll and yaw. Inputs are added to a Triplex Transducer Unit (TTU), which gives wing sweep, flap and airbrake positions. CSAS can be used with or without autopilot. If the pilot moves the stick the CSAS sends an electrical signal to the tailerons' power-actuated servos, which in turn produce a movement. If it is a roll input and the wings are less than 50°, the spoilers will also move. Likewise, any yaw input is fed to the rudders for controlled smooth balanced flight.

In normal flight the roll-rate is limited to 150°/sec; with the flaps down this reduces to 40°/sec. Due to the size of the fin (the Tornado is nicknamed 'the fin' due to its size) the amount of yaw is limited to reduce structural overloading. Should a failure occur and the CSAS defaults to Direct Law (DL), the pilot's signals are fed directly to the control surface and authority is reduced.

In Mechanical Mode the aircraft's flight characteristics change completely. When used in training the pilot can place the aircraft into 'Mech Mode' and the aircraft becomes much less stable. A fair amount of skill is then needed to fly the aircraft smoothly. Initially, it feels like stirring porridge but after a few minutes it actually

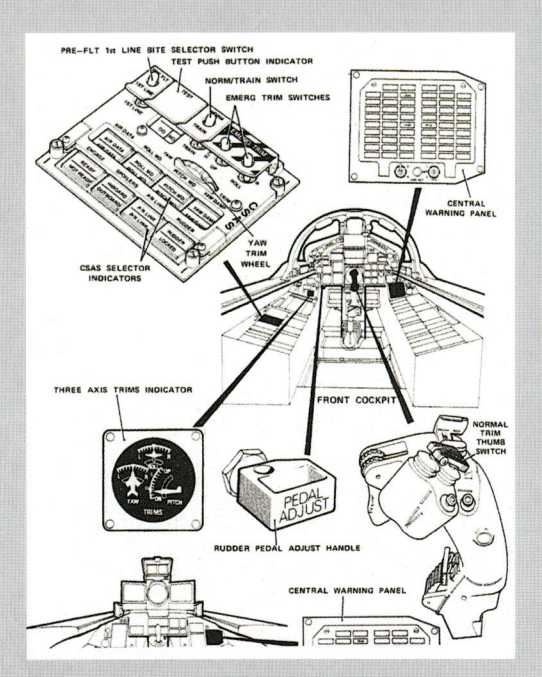

FAR LEFT CSAS panel. *(Panavia)*

LEFT CSAS panel and cockpit layout. *(Panavia)*

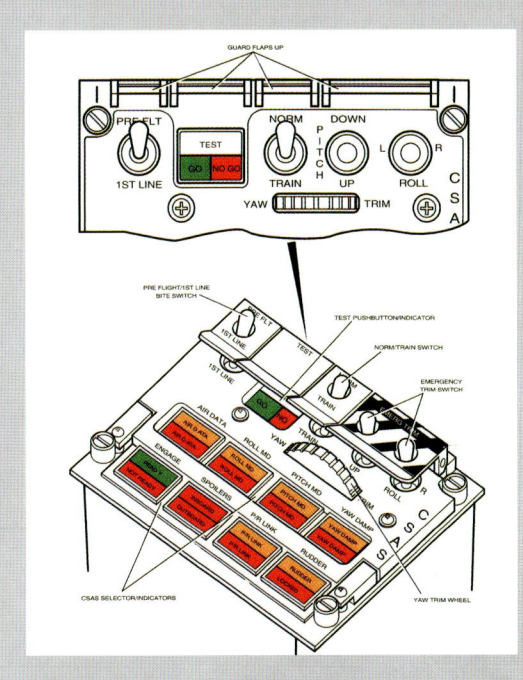

becomes quite controllable, although it is not a failure you would want to go to war with.

CSAS is another feature of the Tornado story that has proved a winner. While more modern aircraft use advanced fly-by-wire systems, the Tornado still retains the original CSAS pretty much unchanged since its inception – quite remarkable for an aircraft nearly 40 years old and that has undergone so many role changes.

Spoilers

Two pairs of spoilers inboard and outboard are fitted to the upper surfaces of both wings. The inboard spoilers take their power from the left and the outboard spoilers take their power from the right utility system. The spoilers operate in pairs to augment roll control at wing sweeps less than 50 degrees. Once the wings are swept back the spoilers are inhibited. The amount of spoiler deployment is relative to the amount of roll demand generated by the CSAS to the tailerons. When the Tornado lands all four spoilers deploy fully when thrust reverse is selected to kill any residual lift, although lift dump is not a function of the CSAS. Should there be a hydraulic failure the spoilers will blow shut under aerodynamic air pressure.

Tailerons

One of defining recognition features of the Tornado is its large rear tailerons. Fitted under the fin and around the engine compartment these are controlled by individual power control units (PCUs). Each PCU is powered hydraulically from both hydraulic systems. Should one hydraulic system fail this allows the tailerons to continue moving, albeit at a reduced rate. Paint is often left off the leading edges of the tailerons because the firing of wing-mounted stores tends to scorch the tailerons' leading edges. Forward of the taileron, painted on the fuselage, are the markings that allow the ground crew to check the correct operation of the fly-by-wire system on the ground during the flying control functional check.

Rudder

The rudder PCU operates in a similar way to the tailerons: in the event of a failure the rudder is centered. From a pilot's point of view whereas conventional aircraft required coordination with rudder and aileron, the Tornado can be flown pretty much balanced with your feet off the rudders.

LEFT With tailerons and air brakes in full view, ZA606 is pictured early in her life with the original serial markings under the tailerons. At the time of writing this aircraft was still in service as a GR4.

97

ANATOMY OF THE TORNADO

RIGHT Engine bay empty.

RIGHT ADV left hand engine door.

FAR RIGHT Arrester hook.

Tornado incorporates a novel approach of engine removal. Taking up no bigger footprint than the airframe itself, the engines can be changed in the confined space of a HAS with comparative ease. Two large load-carrying doors are mounted under the rear fuselage that simply unlatch and drop down exposing the entire lower portion of the RB199 engines.

As an added bonus to engine removal Rolls-Royce produced a tailor-made hoist that allows the ground crew to raise and lower the engine with relative ease using the fuselage-mounted attachment points. Above each engine on either side of the fuselage are the spade-type hydraulically operated airbrakes.

Centrally mounted beneath the rear fuselage is the arrestor hook which, by American standards, appears flimsy (it is not designed for carrier ops!).

Tailplane

Attached to the rear of the fuselage is the all-moving tailplane, also produced by BAe. The tailplane can move differentially providing roll, or symmetrically to provide pitch. Unlike the F-14 and F-15 the Tornado adopted a single large fin which, on some British aircraft, can be filled with fuel (indeed, all ADV Tornadoes had a 'wet' fin). It also acts as a convenient place to mount the Radar Homing and Warning Receiver (RHWR) aerials. At the base of the fin is a scoop allowing ram air in to a heat exchanger. The reason the Tornado fin is so large is primarily due to the air defence version having a Mach 2.0 capability

BELOW The GR Tornado fin (right) has a forward-mounted RHWR aerial, while that for the ADV (left) is in the forward wing nib.

98
RAF TORNADO MANUAL

TOP Undercarriage detailing.

FAR LEFT ADV right undercarriage bay.

LEFT Undercarriage door jack.

BELOW Landing gear controls inside cockpit.

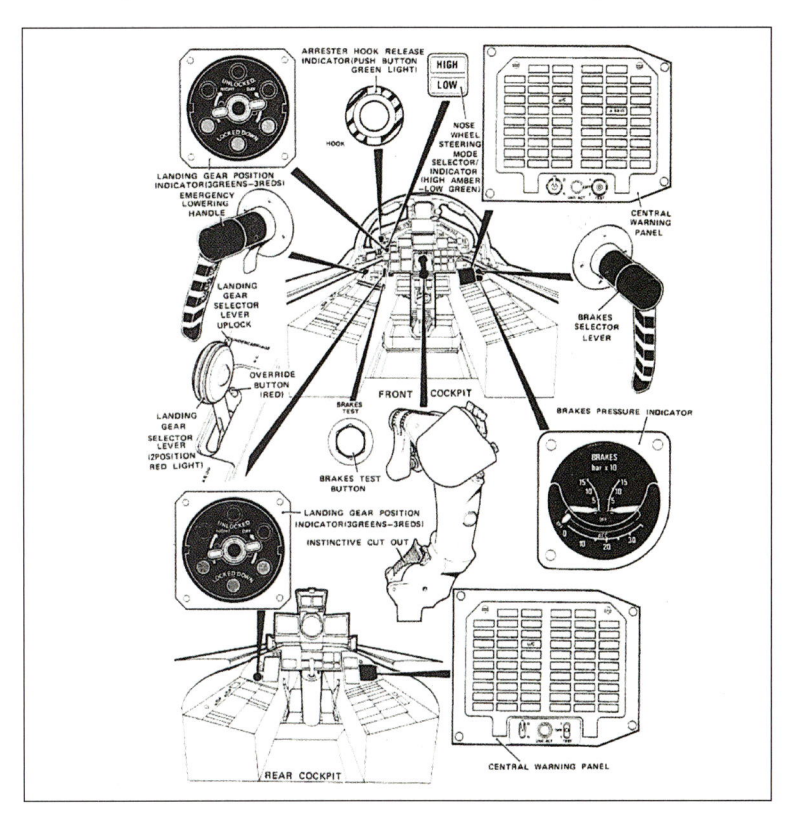

and needing the extra size for controllability. Indeed it was not only Britain that wanted a Mach 2.0 aircraft – the Italians also wanted this twice-the-speed-of-sound ability in the nuclear strike role; the other option would have been to put a double vertical fin (smaller) in the style of the F-14/-15/-18.

Undercarriage

Designed to operate from semi-prepared strips (though never used in practice) the Tornado's undercarriage is excellent and poses few problems. Although the design concept of operating from semi-prepared strips may have been Cold War fantasy, the Tornado has normally flown its war missions at maximum take-off weight where in reality the limiting factor has always been tyre speeds as rotation occurs at nearly 200kts. In an effort to overcome this special Dunlop high speed tyres are used in hot and high areas.

As with most aircraft the undercarriage is manufacture by Dowty-Rotol, wheels brakes and tyres by Dunlop and the anti-skid system is made by Goodyear. The nose-wheel, which has two tyres, retracts forward into its bay. One minor design fault is the location of the circuit breaker box in the same bay – if the door is not shut properly the nose gear will fail to retract. The main wheels are mounted under the fuselage, but sufficiently widely spaced to allow for the under-fuselage area to be free for stores (the F-111 adopted a central mid-gear position). The main undercarriage is a single-wheel assembly that retracts forwards then upwards. It is hydraulically lowered and raised but in an emergency it can be lowered by use of an accumulator.

Systems

Hydraulic

Both the ADV and IDS have identical independent dual hydraulic systems supplying pressure from two hydraulic pumps mounted on each of the engine-driven accessory gearboxes. Being independent of one another, each hydraulic system has its own hydraulic reservoirs. The hydraulics can be pressurised by either the engines or the APU via a cross-drive system. Normally each engine will drive its own gearbox and hydraulic system, but should the need arise the left hydraulic system can also be pressurised by means of a hand pump located in the left accessory gearbox compartment. When you open the door the handle is conveniently stowed inside the door.

Each system has two separate sides – a 'control' and a 'utility' system, both of which are protected in the event of a leak. In the cockpit the pilot has two hydraulic switches (left and right) with three positions: 'OFF – AUTO – ON'. The hydraulic reservoirs are located in the rear fuselage and have a capacity of 16.2 litres pressurised to 8 bar. (If there was ever a re-design it might have been better to locate the reservoirs away from the hot engine areas, but this has never been done because it is deemed an acceptable risk.)

The reservoirs have level indicators as well as temperature sensors and pressure relief valves, and finally a low level sensor. To ease maintenance the fluid levels are shown on the aircraft skin gauges. Just aft of where the aircraft serial number is painted are two small gauges, forward of the APU exhaust opening. Each gauge is marked with either 'LH' or 'RH Reservoir' and the revised LED displays also have a traffic light system of red, yellow and green to show fluid levels. On the ADV the left gauge is on the left side and the right hydraulics is logically on the right rear fuselage. Around the exterior of the airframe are various "skin" gauges, which allow both the air and ground crew the ability to check the Tornado's various hydraulic pressures and contents.

Each hydraulic circuit has accumulators that smooth out pressure surges when the system is under heavy loading, for example when selecting landing gear down while moving the wings and flaps.

Canopy operation

The canopy is opened by hydraulic pressure, the gauge being situated below the canopy. The canopy handle is located flush to the fuselage

RIGHT Manual hydraulic pump.

HYDRAULIC SYSTEM

The hydraulic system is divided into a left and right circuit. The left utilities circuit controls the following:
- Flight Control System – tailerons.
- The Utility System – rudder flaps, slats, inboard spoilers, wing sweep, intake ramps, pitch feel, canopy, wheel brakes, probe emergency extension.
- A protected circuit covers the tailerons.

The Right Utilities hydraulic system controls:
- tailerons and rudder

The Utilities Circuit controls:
- Flaps and slats as well as airbrakes, outboard spoilers, wing sweep, right intake ramps, pitch feel normal AAR probe extension, landing gear, nose wheel steering, radar stabilisation and scanner.
- A Protected Circuit covers the tailerons and rudder

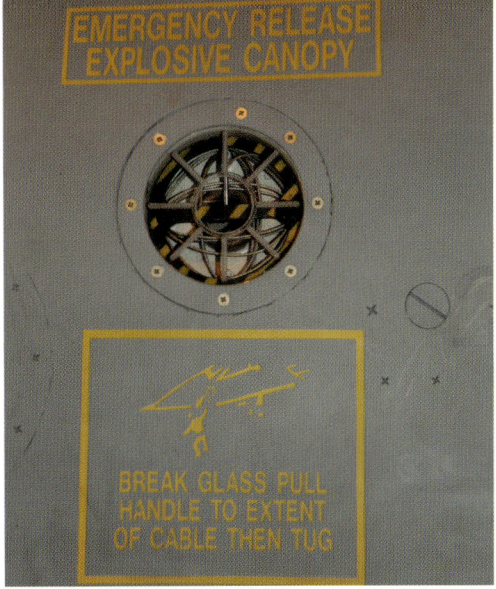

FAR LEFT Normal canopy opening handle.

LEFT ADV emergency canopy release.

just beneath the sill. The canopy can be pressurised via the hand pump on the ground if access is required.

The hydraulic system is fairly robust but the biggest problems occur in the harsh environments where the Tornado has to operate, ranging from Alaska to Afghanistan to the damp of Britain. The aircraft operates in some fairly extreme weather, which can play havoc on rubber seals until aircraft have acclimatised.

Emergency Power System (EPS)

In the event of a double engine failure emergency hydraulic power is provided on the GR4 by the Emergency Power System (EPS), a large 28V silver zinc battery located in the rear left of the fuselage. For a short time it will allow emergency operation of the tailerons via a small DC motor that drives a hydraulic pump. The EPS is a one-shot battery activated by an integral electro-optical explosive device. Once

BELOW The EPS is the large battery-shaped object in the forward part of the bay.

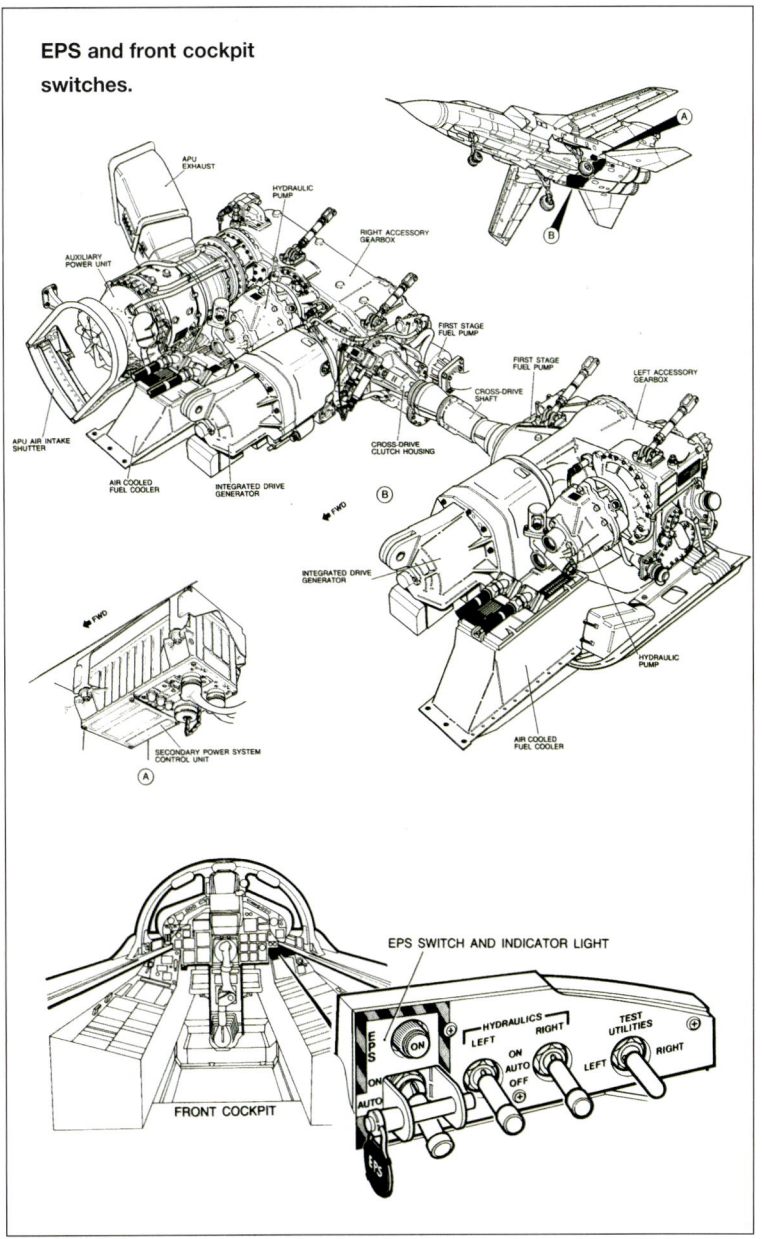

EPS and front cockpit switches.

101

ANATOMY OF THE TORNADO

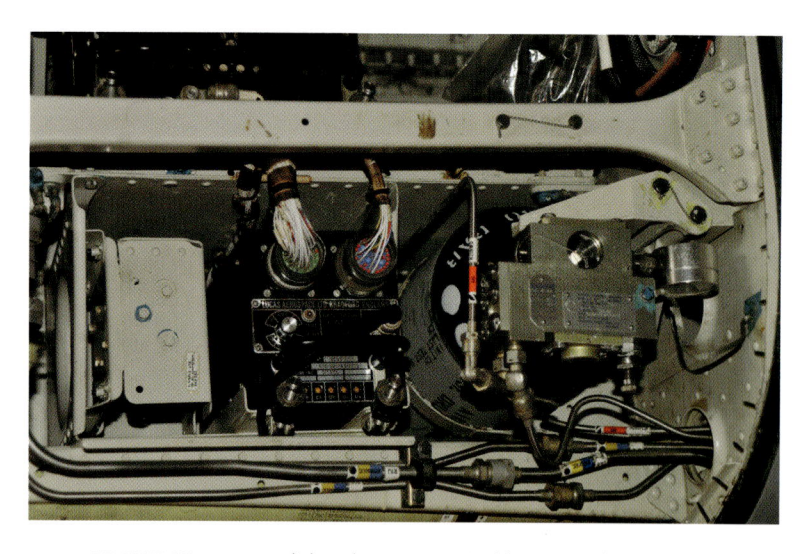

ABOVE Nitrogen bottle for emergency gear lowering.

BELOW Undercarriage lever and indicator.

it has been operated it cannot be turned off, hence the reason why a safety pin is fitted when the aircraft is on the ground.

Ram Air Turbine (RAT)

On the ADV version the hydraulic emergency power is provided by a pop-out Ram Air Turbine (RAT). The EPS/RAT switch is guarded with a safety pin and normally left in the AUTO position. Due to its small size (the RAT is like a small four-bladed propeller) the speed limit for operating the RAT on the ADV is less than 600kts, or Mach 2.0.

Undercarriage operation

The undercarriage on the Tornado is standard to all variants and is operated by the hydraulic system. It is a typical tricycle-type assembly that retracts forward into three distinct bays. The gear retracts symmetrically – that is to say both main gears and nose (in theory) all extend and retract in unison. The nose-wheel has a twin-tyre assembly while the main gear has a single tyre of sturdy size. While the gear is raised and lowered hydraulically the control is done electrically. In the event of an emergency the gear can be 'blown' down using a nitrogen accumulator.

On the ground the aircraft is steered by the nose-wheel, which incorporates a 'high' and 'low' setting for turning. Low ratio gives up to 30 degrees of movement and is used at higher ground speeds (during take-off, for example). The 'high' setting is used for taxying and can give up to +/- 60 degrees of movement. Differential braking can also be used but it is not as effective.

On the forward left side of the instrument panel the pilot has the landing gear lever (lollipop). While the gear is prevented from being raised on the ground by a weight-on-wheels switch, in an emergency this can be overridden by pressing a red button to raise the gear should it be deemed necessary. To raise the gear requires the lever to be pushed in/out as a double safety measure to prevent the lever being knocked inadvertently. To raise and lower the gear takes about 5 seconds.

The nose gear is retracted forward into the nose-wheel well. On the main oleo is a heavy-duty spring to aid retraction as well as the nose-wheel steering motor. To sequence raising and lowering, the nose gear doors are all mechanically linked.

The crew are alerted to the undercarriage position by a standard gear indicator panel – three greens for all down; three reds for unlocked or travelling; lights out for gear up. The six lights have two bulbs as a safety feature and are checked prior to each sortie. Should a light remain red, or the undercarriage handle flashes red, the crew would need to diagnose whether they have a gear unlocked or a landing gear door not shut.

The main landing gear is fitted with hydraulically operated multiple disc brakes, which are effective (but not startlingly so) in stopping the aircraft. When landing the Tornado relies on a combination of lift dump and aerodynamic braking, but primarily on reverse thrust to bring the aircraft to a stop.

The aircraft is fitted with both an anti-skid system and an emergency braking system. The brakes are modulated by the pilot pressing his two foot-pedals, which in turn apply hydraulic pressure to the brakes. Tornado is also fitted with a parking brake (for use when the aircraft is parked), but in a dire emergency it could be used. However when the lever is operated it sets the wheels to park (ie, full pressure), so if the aircraft was moving both tyres would lock or, worse still, burst. Consequently the parking brake lever is painted with black and yellow stripes to warn the crew of its potential to be applied incorrectly. On the right-hand lower panel is the emergency gear-lowering handle, also painted black and yellow.
- Hydraulic fluid (mineral oil): OM-15 MSDS (NATO H-515)
- Hydraulic system reservoirs (left and right fuselage forward of fin) : 16.2 litres (3.6 Imp gals)

Electrical

As the RAFs first 'electric jet' the Tornado's electrical system forms a significant part of the aircraft's make-up. As the aircraft has evolved the added capability has made the aircraft power hungry, but the original concept of electrical generation has stood the test of time.

The Tornado has two Integrated Drive Generators (IDG), which produce 115V/200V 400 Hertz AC power as well as DC power produced by two Transformer Rectifier Units (TRU). Importantly, the aircraft is fitted with a heavy duty Varta battery in the forward left fuselage. This supplies 24V power, which can be used to start the APU and power essential systems in the event of a total electrical failure. The battery/APU combination was a major step forward in giving the RAF's front line combat aircraft a method of self-sufficiency without the need to rely on complex external power sources.

Designers build aircraft with a cascading redundancy system when it comes to failures, as electrics are crucial to the Tornado. With two generators the aircraft can afford to lose one with no significant systems failures, while a double generator failure is a more serious emergency with the aircraft relying on either the battery or the emergency power supply to get it home. The generators can be turned on and off by the pilot and the corresponding light above the switch will show if either has failed. The battery is selected 'ON' with the rapid take-off panel being lifted up, or by simply selecting the battery master 'ON', which is the switch at top left. The battery is charged by the generators when online and cooled by air from the equipment cooling systems. The battery voltmeter is located in the rear cockpit.

On the ground the aircraft can be connected to external ground power for maintenance or pre-starting. The large green 3-ton Houchin ground power units are seen next to Tornado aircraft at their home base on the flight lines, or in HASs. Powered by a diesel engine they can provide the aircraft with all its needs in terms of AC and DC power. They are used primarily to start the APU and preserve battery life, or when the ground crews need to work on the aircraft.

ABOVE Nickel cadmium Varta battery.

BELOW ADV APU starter panel.

103
ANATOMY OF THE TORNADO

Due to the nature of the Tornado with its electric fly-by-wire and associated systems, the early days of GR1 flying was surrounded by myths of it being prone to electrical faults. Indeed, an early RAF Tornado loss (ZA586) was due to a complete electrical system failure that caused the engines to 'run away' to destruction. The Tornado's designers thought that a total electrical failure would be an extremely unlikely occurrence, and consequently the engines were designed (in a total failure) to be powered by DC (battery power). In the event of a total DC failure the engines would be supplied with full fuel flow to cater for the worst case failure – that is, one on take-off. But in the case of ZA586 the battery was also at low charge and the engines accelerated to destruction. Although this was not the sole cause of the accident, it illustrates how the Tornado relies on the generation of electrical power and how the system copes in the event of failures.

At the back left of the front cockpit each Tornado is fitted with a crash panel which, when lifted, effectively isolates the aircraft's electrical system except for the battery. One of the few differences between the GR version and the retired F3 version is how electrical power is generated in an emergency. On the F3, on the left-hand side by the taileron is a small door marked with a warning sign; on the F3 and on the GR4 a fire access panel. Behind the door is the Emergency Power Supply (EPS) on the GR and the Ram Air Turbine (RAT) on the F3. On the GR version the EPS (a very large battery) will provide up to 2 minutes of power to the hydraulically driven taileron actuators, or 20 minutes of power should there be a total electrical failure. Should both engines flame out, the system also allows the crew time to relight while keeping control of the aircraft.

During the design phase the system was optimised for the GR version but incorporated a RAT for the Air Defence version, which (supposedly) would be operating at long range over the sea and may need a longer time to recover to base in event of electrical failures. In the cockpit the EPS has a three-position switch: 'OFF – AUTO – ON'. The switch has a safety pin to prevent it being switched on inadvertently. In the AUTO position, should a double flame-out occur, the EPS would start up automatically. In the GR version the EPS is a one-shot battery (OSB) giving enough power to keep the fuel pumps running and a small electro-hydraulic pump for the flying controls. Generally, electrical faults in the Tornado are rare but spurious electrical warnings are often the first signs of a rear fuselage fire so electrical failures are not taken lightly.

Fuel

Tornado was designed from the outset to have a good range with the emphasis on internal fuel capacity (wings and fuselage), as well as the ability to carry under-wing and under-fuselage fuel tanks. The addition of an in-flight refueling probe seems to have been an afterthought. One can only assume the original design specification had the GR1 flying a high-low profile into the former Soviet Union/Warsaw Pact area, and the chance of air-to-air refuelling was a pretty remote possibility.

In the fuselage fuel is carried in two tank groups, while under the wings both the ADV and GR can carry the 1,500-litre (small tanks) and 2,250-litre (large tanks). Each tank has limitations on speed and 'G'. The British Tornado has a 'wet' fin (ie, fuel is carried inside the fin) as well as the ADV having an 'O' (overload) tank behind the rear cockpit for extra range. Only the British Tornado force had the fuel in the fin option. On the negative side the fin fuel is not kept in a bag-type arrangement, but is an integral part of the fin structure. This does cause problems if the fin leaks, which

BELOW ADV fuel tank locations. *(Panavia)*

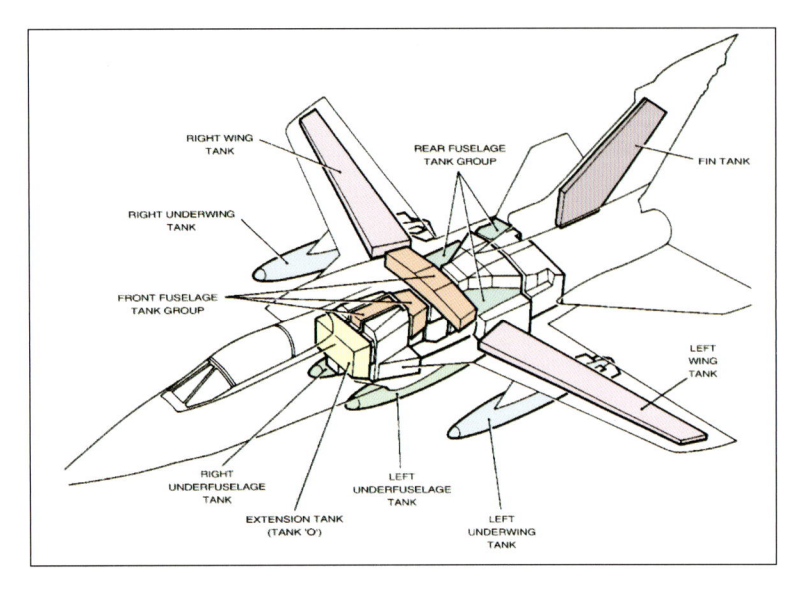

generally requires removal of the entire fin and in this case it is only done at major servicing intervals. Often ground crew will mark inside the refuel panel door 'Fin Fuel', telling them that the aircraft can be filled to full. Should a leak occur (as the fin fuel is directly above the engines) the fin is often left empty.

Unlike the F3, the slightly shorter GR version has a tendency to sit on its tail in various configurations when the wings are swept back and the fin is full of fuel. One worry that crews had initially was small arms fire hitting the fin, which may have been full of fuel or vapour. The original specification allowed crews to purge the fin with nitrogen if required.

Normally the fuel will feed to the engines in the order wings and external tanks into the internal tanks, and this feed in turn into the engines – front group to the left engine and rear group to the right engine and APU. The fuel feed is automatic but has a manual back-up should the pilot wish to feed tanks in a specific order. The fuel is transferred by air pressure from the engine bleed air into the external tanks and dual transfer pumps from the wings. Any of the external fuel tanks can be jettisoned and fuel can also be dumped from the vent mast in the top of the fin. The fuel also serves to cool hydraulic oil and engine oil by way of recirculation.

The Tornado is refuelled via a standard NATO connector on the right hand side of the aircraft adjacent to the Central Maintenance Panel. Via the panel ground crew can pre-programme the amount of fuel and where it goes inside the aircraft. On the right side of the IDS is a bolt-on retractable refuelling probe, seldom seen on the GR force until 1990 when the Gulf War made it an almost permanent fixture. The probe is hydraulically extended and to assist in night refuelling it has a red lamp located near the tip. The ADV has a simple stowable probe on the left-hand side of the aircraft, which can be folded away flush when not in use.

Fuel is kept in the wings as part of the structure. Normally, with the system in automatic, fuel will transfer from the tanks in the following order: the fin fuel would be used first (normally enough to get you airborne), next the under-wing tanks, and then the under fuselage tanks. Often the IDS can be seen in a ferry fit of two wing tanks and one or two ferry tanks on the under-fuselage pylons. The ADV only carried the under-fuselage tanks during development (aircraft A01–3); operational F3s did not carry under-fuselage tanks due to the Skyflash missile fitment.

Each engine is fed by fuel booster pumps. Should they fail the pilot will receive a F/R (Front, Rear) PUMP caption on the CWP. Fuel can be dumped via the fin and although the system has safety measures to prevent you dumping ALL your fuel, a wise pilot keeps his hand on the fuel dump switch until he reaches the required level! The low pressure (LP) fuel cocks are guarded by two red plastic covers and are located on the top left side of the pilot's coaming, while the high pressure (HP) cocks are opened and closed when the throttles are moved forward of the shut-off gate.

In general the Tornado fuel system works well and the aircraft does not suffer the same problems of the older aircraft where fuel pipes were routed around hot parts of the engine, which led to in-flight fires should leaks occur – which on the Tornado have been rare.

ABOVE The fuel refuel cap/connector is NATO standard. Note the handwritten markings telling the groundcrew the aircraft is capable of taking fin fuel.

FUEL LOAD

- 4,000kg in the internal tanks;
- 800kg in the wings;
- additional fuel in the fin and 'O' tank for the ADV;
- Tornado can use AVTUR, AVTAG or AVCAT fuels;
- Total fuel approx. 5,100kg.

(Note: these figures are approximate.)

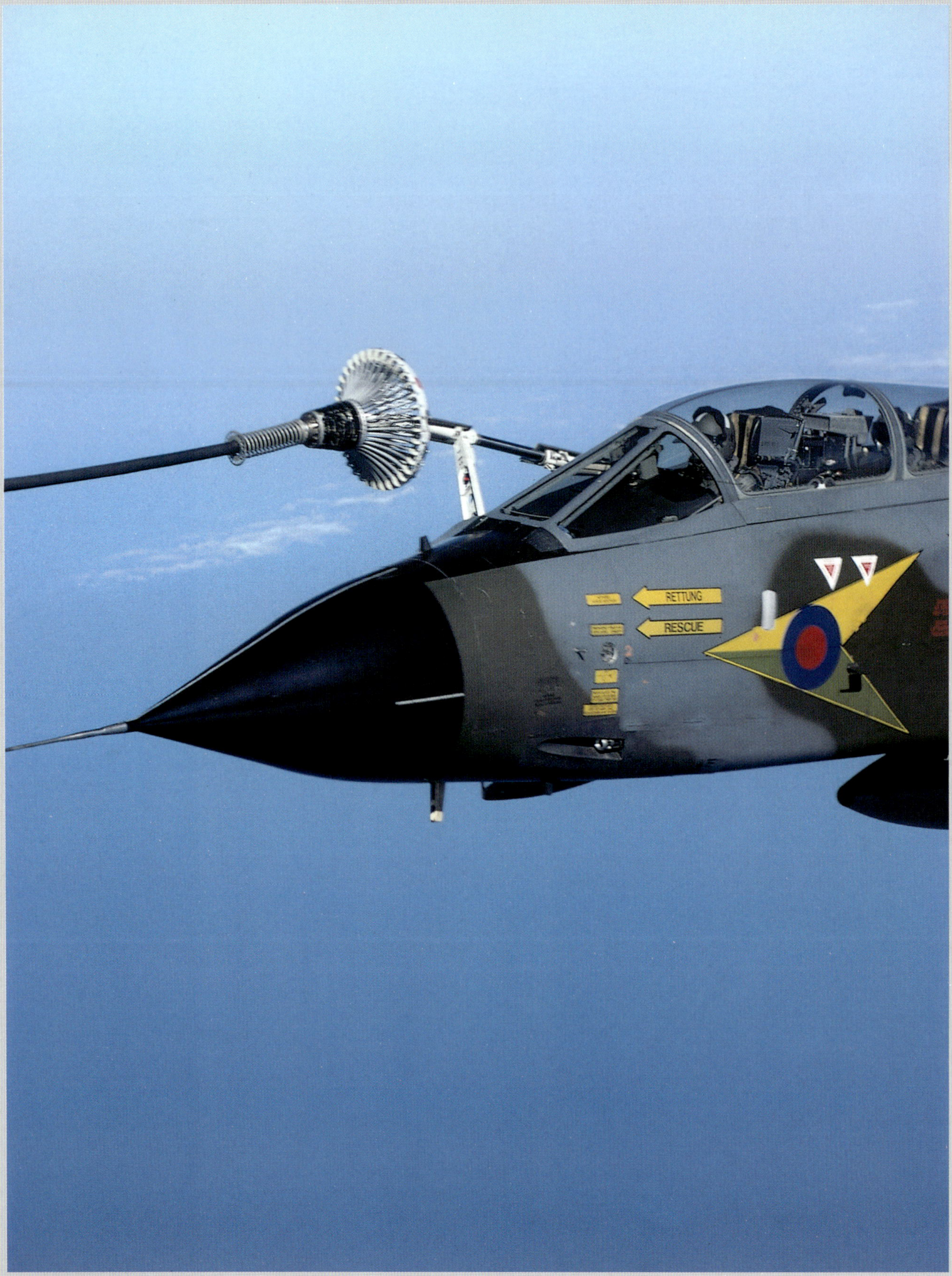
RETTUNG
RESCUE

AIR-TO-AIR REFUELLING (AAR)

Sitting in the comfort of my armchair it is pretty glib to say re-fuelling the Tornado is easy. It is definitely an art.

Initially IDS crews did very little air-to-air refueling (AAR). In fact RAF Germany squadrons never did it as their aircraft at first were not fitted with the bolt-on probe. Air Defence squadrons tend to sit on CAP for long periods, the boredom broken only by trips back and forth to the tanker aircraft, while the GR4 crews usually plan their missions with pinpoint accuracy, including fuel burn, and take on fuel from tanker aircraft. Air Defence crews tend to work to a different set of criteria. They normally take-off full, sit on CAP, and then head to a tanker to top up. Obviously you cannot sit on CAP until your fuel state is critical, just in case that's the moment when GCI vector you off to a target. It's a fine balance.

As mentioned the Tornado refuel probe is operated hydraulically (No 2 system), although in the event of a failure it can be selected 'OUT' on a different system (No 1 System), but it cannot then be retracted. This is important should an aircraft be returning from a mission with a hydraulic failure, but still needs to refuel. On the ADV the probe extension switch is just under the CW on the main fuel panel. Below a certain speed the pilot simply selects probe 'OUT'. The probe extends and a small green light on the right-hand coaming illuminates, telling you that the tanks have de-pressurised and are ready to take on more fuel.

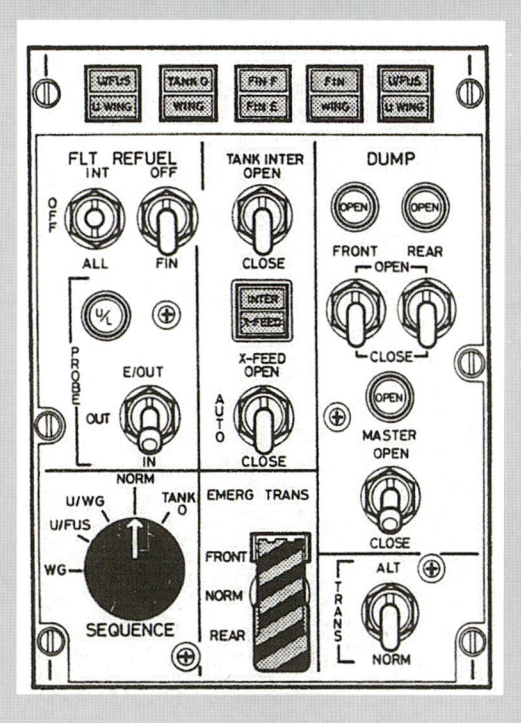

OPPOSITE A No 31 Squadron Tornado GR1 on Tow Line 4 takes on fuel over the North Sea from a VC10 tanker just prior to Gulf War 1. Note the UK-style probe and drogue system.

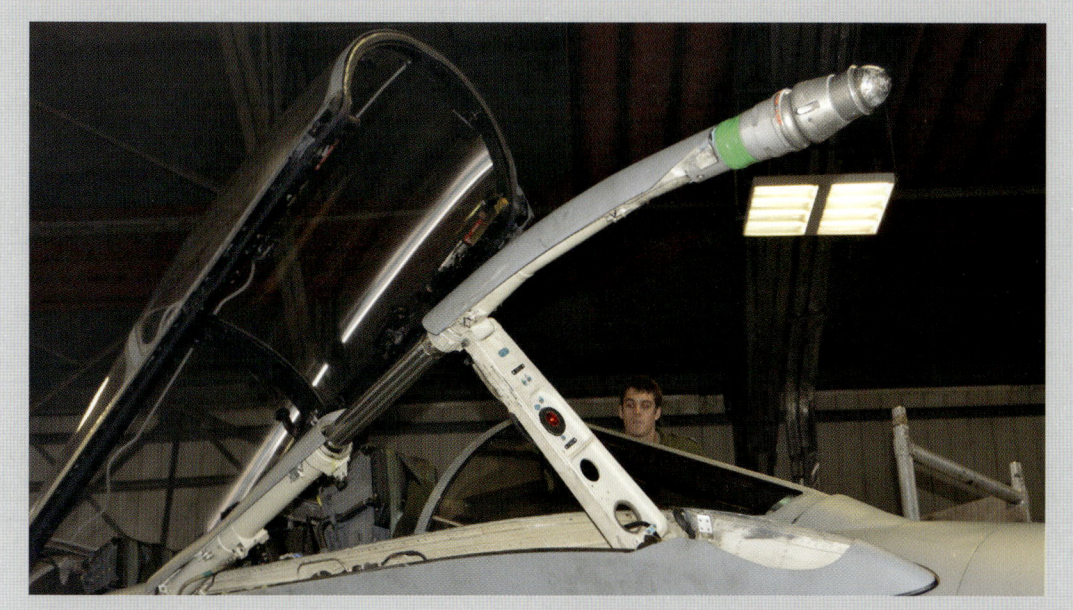

LEFT A well-worn refueling probe on a Tornado GR4. This 41 Squadron aircraft had just completed the heavyweight trials in 2012 with the RAF's newest tanker, the A330 Voyager.

LEFT ADV cockpit fuel control panel.

107
ANATOMY OF THE TORNADO

RIGHT Positioned behind the basket. *(RAF)*

BELOW AAR view from Tornado cockpit.

Having extended the probe and positioned yourself behind the basket, the Tornado is pretty stable in terms of basket movement. Normally, pilots either get the back-seater to help with guidance or simply use a visual reference point in the HUD (the speed symbol) to fly up the hose and hopefully into the basket. At light weight, the ADV is very simple to refuel but at similar weights to a GR4 with missiles and 2,250-litre tanks it can run out of power at height. The trick is then to select one engine in burner (carefully) while ensuring you are not burning more fuel than you're taking on!

Having got yourself behind the tanker one of the vital actions performed by all Tornado crews is 'lookout'. With the possibility of large numbers of aircraft in a small space of sky all jostling for position behind the tanker (and often in darkness), it requires a strict adherence to standard operating procedures to avoid accidents. The Tornado is cleared to tank off a variety of different types, all of which have slight nuances as to how best to make contact. Most European tankers operate the drogue system where the refuelling basket is trailed behind a long fuel pipe, but the French operate an American-style boom and basket, which is considerably harder to tank off.

With his aircraft now just a couple of feet behind the basket the pilot smoothly applies a small amount of power to ease forward and make contact. The trick is smooth flying as you

FAR LEFT Night refuelling. *(RAF)*

LEFT Flight refuelling night light.

are now extremely close to the tanker's tail and wings – too much power and you run the risk of damaging the basket, or worse still moving too far forwards. Pilots try not to use the airbrakes. They produce so much drag the Tornado will simply drop too far back and then the whole procedure will have to start again. With a maximum of two hoses on most tanker types, filling up formations of four or more aircraft, it requires some degree of planning as ideally you all want to leave the tanker full of fuel. Even though the GR Tornado did not feature a refuelling probe at first, AAR has since become one of the essential skill sets learned by all Tornado crews.

BELOW ADV Tornadoes take on fuel.

109

ANATOMY OF THE TORNADO

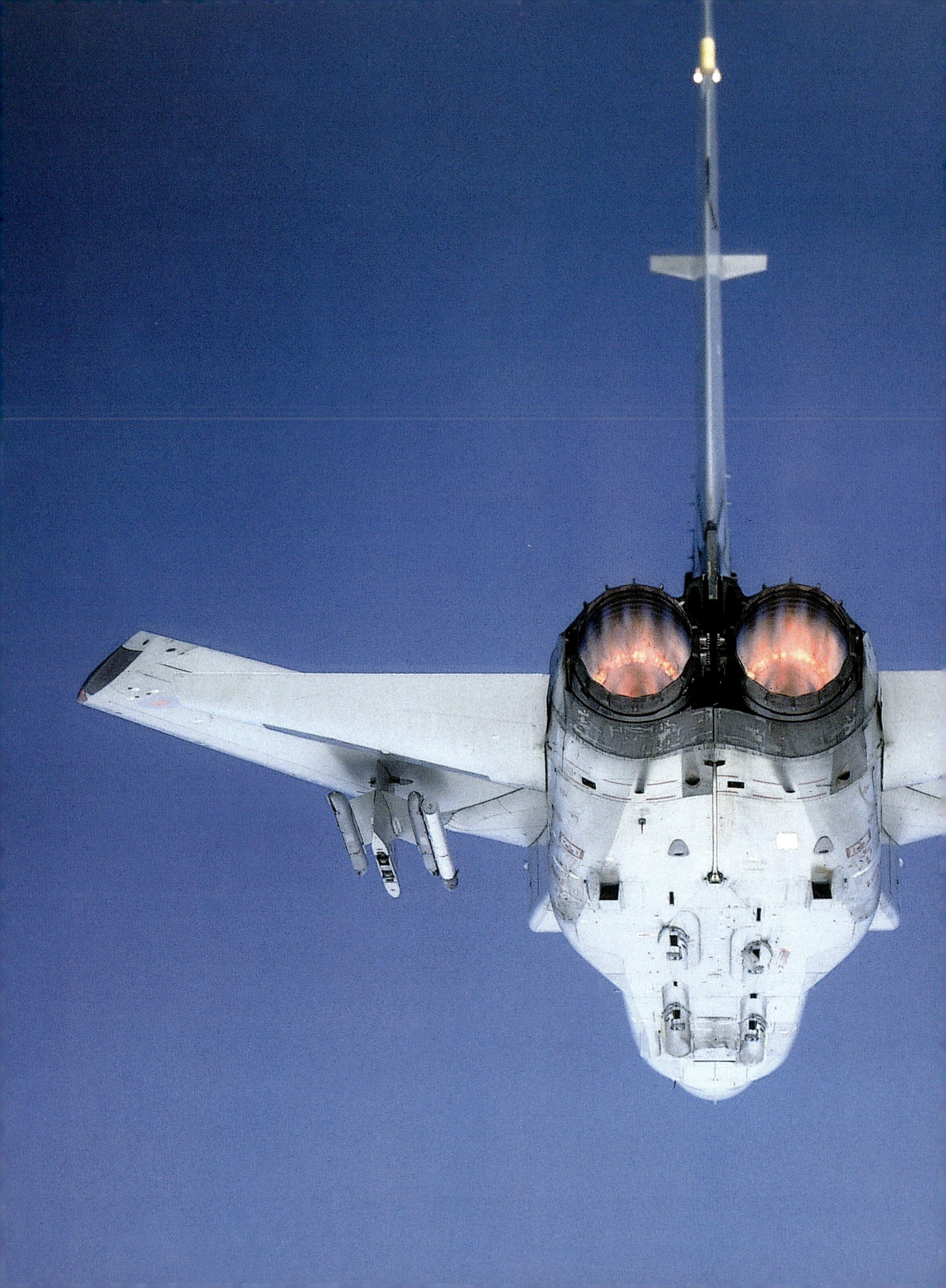

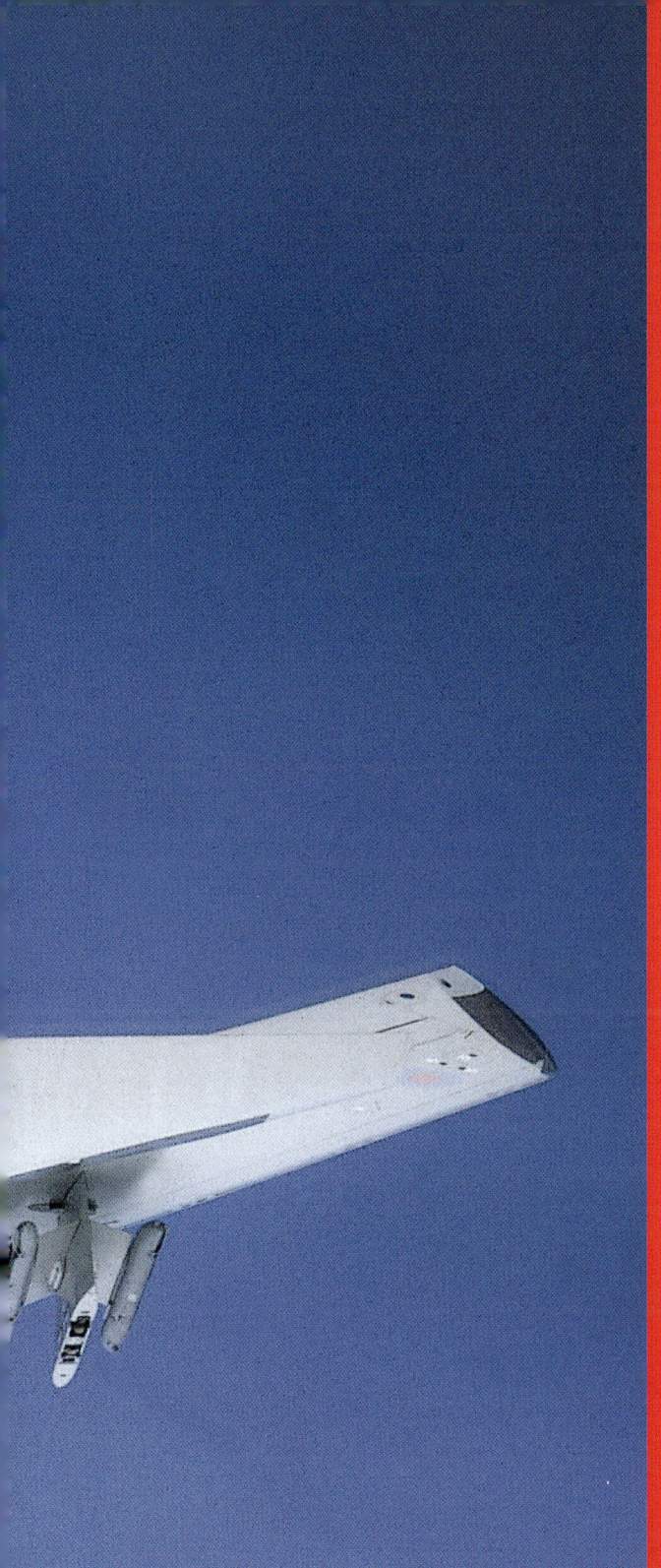

Chapter Five

The RB199 engine

The RB199 turbofan is the power behind the Tornado's success. Rolls-Royce built an engine that has stood the test of time, giving the Tornado an edge over its contemporaries in available thrust versus size, reliability and ease of maintenance – an engine change on a Tornado no longer takes up huge amounts of time and manpower. RB199 is the engine that put the Tornado on the map.

OPPOSITE Sitting in line-astern I called 'burner go!' The leader selected full combat power as we held position. You could almost feel the heat rise to 800 degrees as the RB199s lit.

ABOVE **The RB199 has excelled as an engine.**

Background to the RB199

Perhaps the most significant single factor in the Tornado's success was the choice of the Turbo-Union RB199 as the main power plant. In a myriad of ways the RB199 has excelled as the engine for both the ADV and the GR versions in RAF service.

From an operator and engineer's viewpoint the engine fitted to the Tornado has been nothing short of outstanding. While a Lightning could have sat in a hangar for three days having a troublesome Avon engine changed, a Tornado could have an RB199 changed in a matter of hours, not days. With the onboard APU the Tornado could be started autonomously – no more dangerous Avpin or cartridges to start jet engines.

Early jet engines needed to be handled with kid gloves. From a pilot's perspective the RAF now operated an aircraft that was truly care-free: moving the throttles from 'Idle' to 'Combat' could be done with complete confidence.

When the Tornado was still at the design stage no 'off-the-shelf' engine was available that could simply be adapted to suit the new aircraft's needs. Coupled to this, the Bristol Olympus engine planned to be fitted to the TSR2 was a major reason the entire programme failed. Although it worked well in the Vulcan and on Concorde, its adaptation for the TSR2 was nothing short of a disaster. By taking on the RB199 (an unproven and untried engine) it was a massive risk to the entire MRCA programme. From a testing point of view minor design errors can normally be overcome relatively quickly, but choosing the wrong engine can often make or break a programme.

Turning the clock back 50 years the prospect of the new MRCA having a European engine was not good. The Americans had developed the General Electric J79 turbojet in the F-4, which was working extremely well, but Britain was still using the obsolete Rolls-Royce Avon and Spey, the latter having major problems in its re-heated version as fitted to the RAF's Phantom fleet. Fortuitously, work undertaken on the stillborn Anglo-French AFVG had produced the M45G after-burning turbofan, which Bristol Siddeley (now Rolls-Royce) was working on when the programme was cancelled.

Design

With Rolls-Royce taking up the reins they decided on a design that used a three-shaft layout similar to that used on the civilian RB211 engine. This led to the three-spool turbo-fan, which initially looks complex but actually makes the engine smaller (in particular, shorter) and importantly allows the engine to have fewer moving parts than most engines. Each of the three spools can run at its own optimum speed, resulting in fewer stages to achieve the optimum pressure ratio. As work progressed, by 1968 the three-stage concept looked like a world-beater, exceeding any American proposals and thus Rolls-Royce was awarded the contract to produce the RB199 for the MRCA in late September 1969, beating off proposals from both General Electric and Pratt & Whitney.

Turbo-Union is formed

With the selection procedure complete it now needed one final 'Europeanisation' – the forming of a consortium. Rolls-Royce can justifiably claim the lion's share of the success of the RB199, but the consortium is made up of MTU (West Germany) and Fiat (Italy), split in the ratio of MTU 40%, Fiat 20% and the rest being Rolls-Royce, known as Turbo-Union, with its head office in Bristol. Rolls-Royce was the majority shareholder.

Development

At this stage the MRCA was still five years away from its maiden flight and designers had not yet agreed on its final configuration. Similarly, in 1970 the RAF's desire for a fighter version of the MRCA was still a dream. The demands of the RB199 would be severely tested if it was to fulfill the roles of low level strike/attack as well as high level air defence interceptor.

In many respects the MRCA was a pocket-sized bomber that was designed to punch well above its weight. Initial plans were for an engine that could produce 7,800lb of thrust in 'cold power' and 15,700lb in reheat. Compared to the J79, which powered the American F-104 and F-4, this was going to be ambitious for an engine whose size would be just 10ft 8in (3.3m) long, this compared to the J79 at 17ft 3in (5.25m). In terms of weight the RB199-34R was targeted at just 1,980lb (or just under 900kg). Fuel consumption would also need to exceed that of the J79 by a considerable margin.

From the outset Turbo-Union had a difficult task on their hands, mainly due to the fact that the MRCA itself had yet to be built, so developing the engine was going to be a real challenge for the technology of the late 1960s. To counter this the consortium came up with the ingenious (yet slightly British) solution of mounting the new engine under a Vulcan bomber. The aircraft in question was the RAF's last airworthy B1 (XA903) and had been engaged previously on trials with the Bristol Olympus destined for Concorde. To accurately replicate the MRCA a full scale fuselage (starboard side only) was built and fitted underneath the Vulcan along with the new 27mm gun. The gun fitment was important as this would allow Turbo-Union to conduct airborne gun firing to determine the effect of gas ingestion into a running engine.

The idea of grafting half a Tornado onto an obsolete Vulcan had merit, but there was one important drawback: its lack of supersonic speed. Avro's big delta wing bomber was limited to Mach 0.92 so other methods were needed to test the RB199's top speed capability. For this the new RB199 was taken to the National Gas Turbine Establishment at Pyestock (part of the Royal Aircraft Establishment, Farnborough) for development trials.

Combat aircraft were in the thick of a number of wars during the late 1960s and early 1970s, but one major requirement seemed to be missing from the RB199's design spec – the matter of exhaust smoke. The F-104 and

ABOVE AND BELOW A Vulcan test-bed was used for flight trials of the Turbo Union RB199-34R, beginning in April 1973. The installation beneath the Vulcan comprised of the starboard half of a Tornado fuselage complete with an intake, reheat and thrust reverser fairing. *(Rolls-Royce)*

F-4 were renowned as being 'Smokey Joes', visible to the enemy at long range trailing a huge plume of black smoke. To counter this a pilot would engage reheat, which (often) would be a tactically unsound way just to get rid of your smoke. However, from an early stage in its development the RB199 benefitted from an almost smoke-free exhaust plume.

The design is finalised

The engine design was finalised as a low-pressure axial fan without inlet guide vanes (more of this later), an intermediate stage, and finally a high pressure stage. The three-stage fan was aerodynamically derived from Rolls-Royce's world-beating Pegasus engine and would be assembled by precision electron beam welding (EBW). Built for a specific flight regime (high speed low level flight), the role demanded of the RB199 was both demanding and prone to risk, predominantly that of bird strikes or bird ingestion. While older engines have Inlet Guide Vanes (IGV) the RB199 was designed without them. The reason was vanes would not be strong enough to withstand bird ingestion at 700kts and still keep running. (The RB199 works on the principle that should it hit a bird, the first stage compressor would be strong enough to simply 'mince' the unfortunate fellow flyer and continue running, something it does and has been proven to do on many occasions.)

[As mentioned earlier, in an ideal world aircraft manufacturers try to marry an existing engine to a new airframe to reduce development costs and risks.]

First flight and trials

Once Turbo-Union was given the go-ahead, they built 16 development engines and had them up and running at their Patchway site north of Bristol, with the first run taking place on 27 September 1971. The pace of the programme was electric and within a year the new RB199 was being bench-run on all three nation's development sites. The first 'flight' took place on 19 April 1973, albeit under-slung beneath its Vulcan airframe.

Initial problems were restricted to the shedding of turbine blades, but the robust construction of the engine meant this was often only noticed on post-flight inspection. Despite these minor setbacks the three-stage concept was obviously a winner and all that was need was refinement of the model. By tweaking various parameters Turbo-Union was achieving increasingly positive performance results.

RB199 engine trials were not always 'a bed of roses', but when compared to the problems that beset other new aircraft and their engines in their infancy the RB199 was coping well. On the MRCA's first flight in 1974 the engines gave no cause for concern. This was remarkable, given that the team had just four years to produce an engine pretty much from scratch and had no dedicated test-bed to trial the new power plant under operational conditions. As the flight programme got underway perhaps the biggest cause for concern was engine surging and unreliable reheat lighting.

Although the Vulcan was useful, Turbo-Union lacked a representative aircraft type with which to explore the full performance envelope. In a way the RB199 was a victim of its own success, being tailor-made for the Tornado, so it would have been difficult to have fitted it into an existing airframe as a test-bed. One reason for this lies in the thrust reverse system which, in 1974, was a pretty revolutionary feature on a military aircraft. One only has to study in detail the rear fuselage of the Tornado and it soon becomes apparent that the back end is simply two tightly packed engines onto which the tailerons, air brakes and reverse thrust buckets are placed.

BELOW This rear view shows how the Tornado's heritage (an F3 is depicted) can be traced to the TSR2's arrangement of a single large fin, tailerons and parallel mounting of twin engines.

Production version

Turbo-Union produced the final production standard RB199 in November 1978, known as the RB199 Mk101, with service delivery in July 1980. With the need for an air defence version of the Tornado specific to the RAF's needs the choice of power plant was always going to be the RB199, but obviously with its role the thrust would need to be increased. With a limited budget the team at Turbo-Union produced the Mk104 series by putting a 14in (36cm) plug into the rear of the engine module, increasing the thrust in the re-heat range to 17,000lb. As a bonus to the increased thrust, fuel consumption was also improved. Whilst the Mk104 was standard to the F3 the original batch of F2s retained the original Mk103s and hence have a shorter fuselage.

RB199 MK103 (GR4) and MK104 (F3) in detail

GENERAL DESCRIPTION

The Tornado GR4 is powered by two RB199 Mk103 engines made up of twelve compressors in a three-spool axial flow turbofan. The RB199 has re-heat (including a 'combat power' setting) and is equipped with thrust reversers. Both engines are mounted at the rear of the airframe and are interchangeable, although 'dressed' to be a left or right unit.

Engine starting is accomplished by the APU mounted on the lower right side of the fuselage.

The APU is known as the KHD-312 (the manufacturer is Kloeckner-Humboldt Deutz, who also make the starter) and powers the right-hand gearbox via a friction clutch.

The APU is a miniature gas turbine taking its fuel supply from the right-hand engine fuel supply. It also has the primary function of allowing the Tornado to operate autonomously without need for external ground units, and as a method of allowing servicing to be carried out remotely on the hydraulic and electrical systems.

ABOVE In September 1980 F2, ZA254, made the ADV's first public appearance was at the SBAC display, Farnborough.

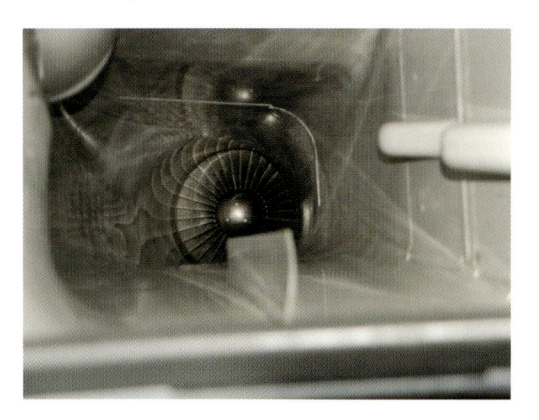

LEFT ADV engine air intake.

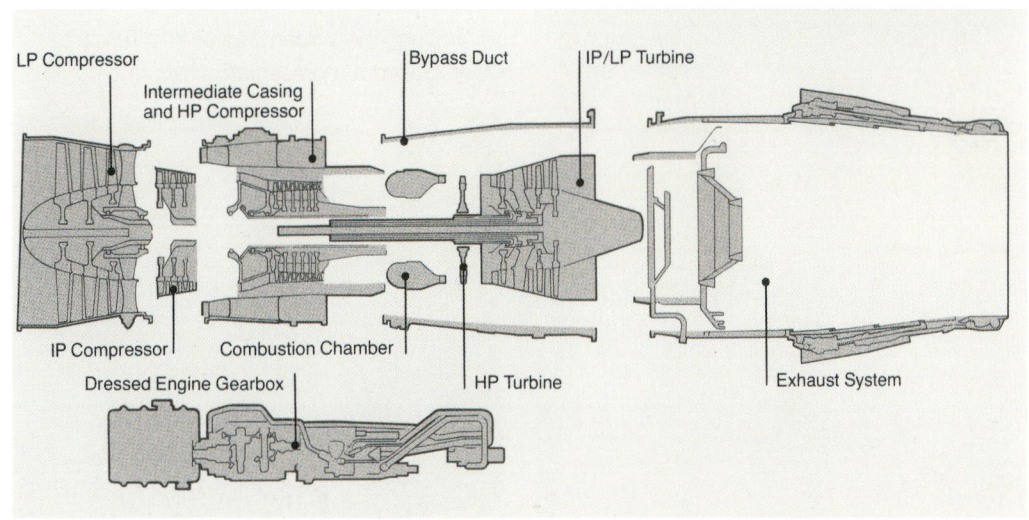

LEFT RB199 engine cutaway. *(Panavia)*

ABOVE Afterburner nozzle and exhaust diffuser (inside).

BELOW A pair of 'dressed' RB199s in RAF Marham's maintenance hangar ready to install in a Tornado.

BELOW RIGHT Thrust reverser mechanism.

Engine starting is accomplished with two high energy igniter units. Airflow for each engine is via two shoulder-mounted air intakes just forward of the wing sweep and behind the rear cockpit. Whilst each intake is separate, air is fed into the fuselage under the wing sweep mechanism prior to entering the engines. An automatically controlled moveable ramp is used in each inlet duct to control airflow to the engines at various speeds and altitudes. On the ground the intakes have side-mounted 'flapper' doors that allow extra air to be drawn in. These also allow extra air to be drawn in at low speed and high power settings. These combined intakes allow optimum air flow under all flight conditions for both the ground attack and air defence versions.

Air is then passed into the engine to both the basic engine and the fan section. The air is then divided into two streams – hot main stream and the cold bypass flow. The bypass flow passes through the annular duct, through the IP and HP area, and rejoins the main flow in the jet pipe. The main airflow passes the IP and HP compressor area into the annular combustion chamber where metered fuel is added to the compressed air, which is then ignited by the two igniter plugs. The hot gas then expands through the turbine into the jet pipe where it meets the cold bypass stream again.

Exhaust

The exhaust system is mounted off the rear of the bypass duct and includes the after-burning casing, a fire-proof bulkhead, the rear jet pipe, the variable nozzle assembly and the thrust reverser mechanism. The rear nozzle is fully variable in re-heat and held in a nominal position when dry power is used.

Additionally, to kill excess thrust while on the ground the pilot can raise the lever outboard of the left throttle and select 'Taxy Nozzle'. This opens the nozzle fully to reduce thrust. The maximum thrust the pilot can now select is approximately 72%. With the Taxy Nozzle open reverse thrust is inhibited.

Reverse thrust buckets

At the rear of each engine is a bucket-style thrust reverser used to reduce landing distance (as well as removing the need to employ a brake parachute, which needs specialist packing and storage facilities and is far less effective in stopping the aircraft). The reverse thrust buckets will only deploy once the aircraft is on the ground and a weight-on-wheels switch signals that the aircraft is not airborne. Interlocks also prevent the pilot from selecting re-heat while the buckets are deployed for obvious reasons.

Bleed air

The primary purpose of any jet engine is to provide thrust to achieve flight, but a number of other by-products the engines when running can be used in normal aircraft operations. Bleed air, which can be considered in most cases as an excess of air needed, is used for various functions. In no particular order bleed air is used for fuel tank pressurisation and outer fuel tank transfer; it is also used to move the jet pipe nozzles. Importantly bleed air is taken off for Environmental Control Systems (ECS).

Bleed air is a delicate balance between maintaining sufficient air for the requirements of the engine and not taking too much, thereby upsetting the stability of the airflow which could result in a stall or engine surges. In normal circumstances each engine will provide half the required air need for the ECS. The maximum amount of bleed air taken from one engine is approx. 4.5% of the total air flow.

Intake ramps

The GR4 version is unlikely to exceed supersonic flight due to its low altitude role, but the air defence variant definitely needs a method of controlling airflow in flight at speeds ranging from 160kts to Mach 2.2.

This is achieved with use of the engine air intakes' moveable ramps, which are operated by the Air Intake Control System (AICS) as well as the side-mounted 'flapper' doors at low speed. These ramps are electro-hydraulically controlled and receive inputs from various devices – primarily from the pitot probe, static side vents and the Angle of Attack gauge (AOA). Should the ramps fail they freeze in the last position they were in. In the cockpit the pilot has two ramp position indicators (although I've never actually seen them move). If required, after engine start a test of the ramps can be performed by the pilot with an amber caption 'RAMP' displayed on the CWP should a failure occur. Generally the ramps are held in the fully open position and only start to close (F3) once the aircraft accelerates past Mach 1.3.

FUEL SYSTEM

Each engine fuel control system provides optimum fuel flow for any throttle setting. The system comprises a HP engine driven pump, a fuel metering valve to meter fuel to the burners, and a pressure valve to maintain constant pressure. The fuel to the engine is controlled by an HP shut-off cock. This shuts down the engine post-flight by lifting the latch behind the throttle and also allows the engine to start, opening the high pressure fuel cock.

ABOVE LEFT Air intake with low speed ramps.

ABOVE Low speed air intakes.

BELOW Engine running with low speed intakes open.

ABOVE DECU and electronic replacable 'black boxes'. To the left is the space where normally the O2 bottle is fitted.

ABOVE RIGHT Engine oil drains.

MECU/DECU Control System

Being a new generation of jet engine the RB199 was far more advanced than anything previously used in RAF combat aircraft. Regulating the amount of fuel flow to the engines as well as monitoring the response of the six spools was down to a unit known as the Main Engine Control Unit (MECU) or Digital Electronic Control Unit (DECU) on the F3 Mk104. Produced by Lucas Aerospace it also allowed for in-flight recording of any faults, which could then be decoded and diagnosed post-flight.

The purpose of the unit is to provide full authority engine control and improved engine response, or carefree handling. Each engine has two 'lanes' that basically control the acceleration and deceleration of the engines, both on the ground and in the air. In brief, on the ground the engines will accelerate more slowly than when the aircraft is, say, at 30,000f. The lane control will also vary the ground idle speed based on various parameters such as pressure and temperature. The RB199 is also equipped with a turbine blade temperature limiter. The pilot can select the switch to either datum – allowing normal operation or 'Low' (decreasing the limit but improving engine life), or 'Combat' to increase thrust by increasing the blade temperature upper limit by 15 degrees Centigrade. Temperature is measured by optical pyrometers. Should one of the lane controls fail the pilot is alerted by a 'L' or 'R THROT' caption on the CWP and the other serviceable lane takes over. Various tests of the lane function can be performed on the ground by both air and ground crews.

ENGINE VIBRATION DETECTION

Each engine can detect abnormal vibration triggering either a 'L' or 'R Vib' caption on the CWP. Normal procedure is to retard the throttle to check the caption goes out. Vibration data is recorded on the Central Maintenance Panel (CMP) for the engineers to decode post-flight.

OIL

The RB199 engine oil system is self-contained and provides lubrication for the main bearings, engine gearbox and fuel pump bearings. Oil pressure is maintained by accumulators in the event of negative 'G' flight. Some oil is vented overboard via a breather pipe, which gives the aircraft its normal smoky look prior to take-off. In the event of a malfunction the pilot is presented with a red coloured caption on the CWP – 'L OIL P' or 'R OIL P' should the pressure drop. Equally, should the engine oil temperature rise above 165 degrees Centigrade the 'OIL T' light will illuminate in amber for each engine.

REHEAT

Reheat increases the engine dry power thrust by injecting fuel into the engine exhaust stream by means of the hot streak ignition system. To select reheat the throttle is moved beyond the maximum dry range detent and in the reheat zone. Once reheat is engaged a timing device then begins a sequence of events – selecting the nozzle position depending on throttle position as well as metering the correct amount of fuel to the reheat zone. Bench figures state that selecting 'MAX' reheat from 'MAX' dry should take 3.5sec. Selecting the throttle from reheat to max dry or less cancels the flame and

ABOVE Afterburner nozzle petals on the RB199.

ABOVE Full combat reheat.

LEFT Full reheat checks at night.

BELOW LEFT APU exhaust and wing glove.

BELOW APU and engine oil drains.

returns the nozzle to the correct position. Safety functions prevent the engine (in theory) from opening the nozzle but not engaging reheat. This would have the same effect of having the taxy nozzle open and drastically reducing thrust. Should the reheat fail the nozzle remains closed. A 'REHEAT' caption will illuminate on the CWP, which can be cleared by pressing the relevant throttle relight button. Other safety features will not allow reheat to engage from a low RPM setting, or if the thrust reverse is deployed. The rear nozzle is made up of 14 moveable petals on rollers that allow the nozzle to open and close.

THE APU AND ENGINE STARTING

The APU is located on the right-hand side of the fuselage behind the wing and is visible by its exhaust opening as well as the marking 'DANGER HOT GASES'. As well as providing torque to start both engines it has a secondary function of powering the aircraft generators or hydraulics without the need to start the engines. This function was deemed essential for F3 operations in times of war with the aircraft deployed to remote bases without ground support. The APU drives the right-hand gear box. The Secondary Power System (SPS) provides facilities for starting the engines and then mechanical power from the engines to various accessories, as well as the hydraulic pumps.

119

THE RB199 ENGINE

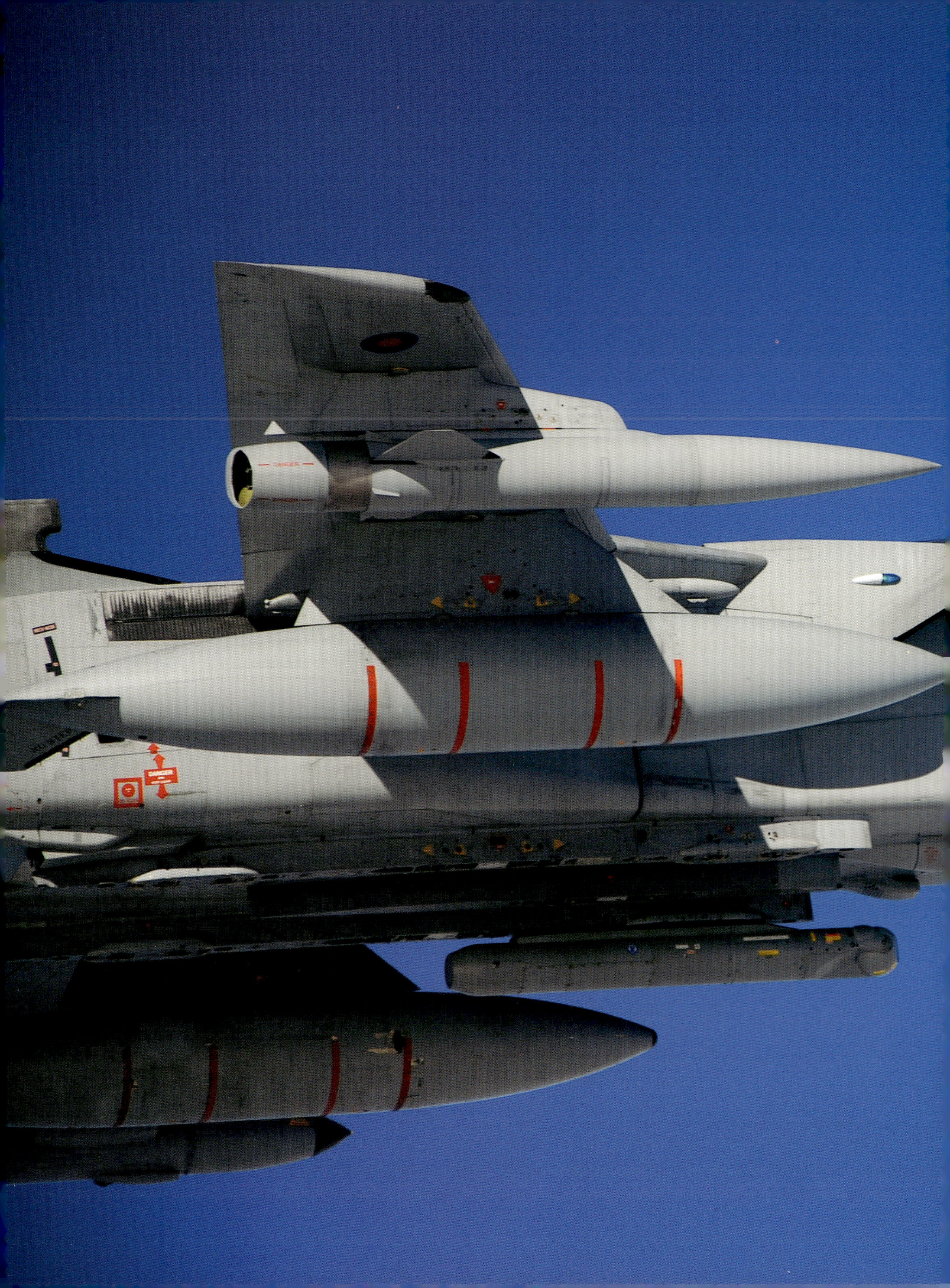

Chapter Six

Tornado weaponry

The Tornado ADV has had some serious weapons upgrades throughout its life – extra Sidewinders, then ASRAAM and AMRAAM; while the GR force has been totally transformed from old-style iron bombs to modern smart weapons. More than ever before the GR4 is a weapons delivery platform par excellence. Fitted with the Goodrich RAPTOR pod the Tornado GR has become an airborne recce platform without equal.

OPPOSITE Weapons platform par excellence – Tornado GR4 fitted with TIALD pod, BOZ pod and Sky Shadow ECM pod, with two 1,500 litre under-wing fuel tanks. *(RAF)*

ABOVE A weapons technician fits an ALARM (Air Launched Anti Radiation Missile) to a Tornado GR4 at an airbase in the Gulf. (RAF)

BELOW This GR4 from 15 Squadron carries Brimstone, Paveway and the more compact Litening targeting pod. (RAF)

Current weapons

(Reproduced with acknowledgement to Crown Copyright.)

Air-to-ground

ALAARM (Tornado F3, GR4, trialled on the EF 3 for possible use)

The Air Launched Anti-Radiation Missile (ALARM) is designed to destroy or suppress the use of enemy ground-based air-defence systems. ALARM operates by homing onto the radar energy being emitted by the target radar and can loiter in the area if the radar is switched off. It can also be pre-programmed to box-search for specific hostile radars after launch and then attack the highest priority threat.

Brimstone (Tornado GR4)

This advanced radar-guided weapon is derived from the US Army Hellfire AGM-114F missile and is deployed in RAF service on a pylon-mounted launching rack that contains three missiles.

It is powered by a rocket motor and can seek and destroy targets at long range.

Ground acquisition and target recognition are achieved by a millimetric wave radar seeker. The weapon locks onto a target after launch and is designed for the attack and destruction of armoured targets. Steerable fins guide the missile towards the target with final impact causing a tandem charge warhead to detonate. The first, smaller warhead nullifies reactive armour, allowing the follow-through charge to penetrate the main armour. It is designed to be carried by the Tornado GR4 and Typhoon F2.

The weapon can be used in Indirect and Direct modes. For Indirect attack weapons are launched when the targets and their position are not visible to the attacking aircraft. In Direct mode the pilot can use an onboard sighting system to select the target, which can lie off the aircraft's track, so that pilots do not need to manoeuvre to release weapons.

Paveway II and III (Tornado GR4)

The original version of the Paveway II laser-guided bomb entered service with the RAF in the 1970s and is composed of a standard UK 450kg bomb with a computer control group fitted to the nose, supporting a laser seeker head and steerable fins. A tail unit is fitted with fins that deploy after launch from the aircraft. Laser designation of targets can be provided by the Thermal Imaging Airborne Laser Designation (TIALD) pod, or from troops on the ground using a laser target designator. During the Gulf War 1 Tornadoes dropped weapons on targets designated by Tornadoes carrying TIALD pods and by Buccaneers carrying the Pave Spike pod. Paveway III is an upgraded LGB and is designed specifically to defeat hardened targets, such as protected underground command posts. 128 make 100

Enhanced Paveway II and III (Tornado GR4)

Both Enhanced Paveway II and Enhanced Paveway III (EPW) are based on Paveway II and Paveway III respectively, and use the same warheads and fin sections. However, EPW has a modified guidance section and wiring to accommodate a Global Positioning System Aided Inertial Navigation System (GAINS). Once released from the launch aircraft, EPW is fully autonomous in cases where there is cloud cover over the target, which may obstruct the laser and prevent weapon guidance. In these instances, it is steered to the target using Global Positioning System (GPS) information as well as guidance from its on-board inertial navigation unit.

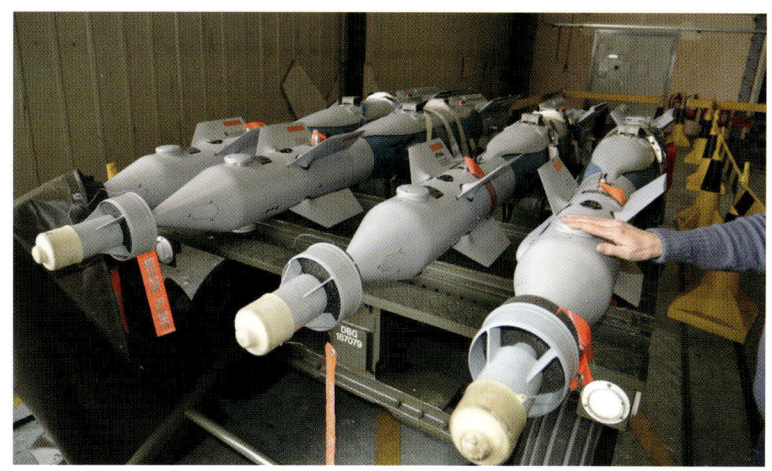

Paveway IV (Tornado GR4)

Paveway IV replaces the Paveway II and Enhanced Paveway II weapon systems as well as the 1,000lb unguided 'iron' bomb. It is an advanced and highly accurate weapon that provides the RAF's strike force with a state-of-the-art precision guided bombing capability against a variety of targets. Introduced in 2008 Paveway IV is equipped with the latest Inertial Navigation and Global Positioning System technology and a 500lb warhead.

Storm Shadow (Tornado GR4)

This long-range air-launched and conventionally-armed missile equips RAF Tornado GR4 squadrons and first saw operational service

ABOVE LEFT Brimstone launcher.

ABOVE Paveway munitions.

BELOW GR4 with two Storm Shadow missiles. *(RAF)*

ABOVE GR4 with TIALD targeting pod, BOZ pod on outer wing, Skyshadow on port outer. *(RAF)*

RIGHT Litening pod. *(Author)*

BELOW Litening pod and ASRAAM. *(Author)*

in 2003 with 617 Squadron during combat in Iraq, before entering full service in 2004. Post-deployment analysis demonstrated the missile's exceptional accuracy, and the effect on targets was described as devastating.

Storm Shadow is equipped with a powerful British-developed warhead and is designed to attack important hardened targets and infrastructure, such as buried and protected command centres.

Mission data, including target details, is loaded into the weapon's main computer before the aircraft leaves on its mission. After release, the wings deploy and the weapon navigates its way to the target at low level using terrain profile matching and an integrated Global Positioning System.

On final approach to the target the missile climbs, discards its nose cone and uses an advanced IR seeker to match the target area with stored imagery. This process is repeated as the missile dives onto the target, using higher-resolution imagery, to ensure maximum accuracy.

Laser targetting and reconnaissance pods

TIALD (Tornado GR4)

TIALD is a second-generation laser designator pod designed to be operable 24-hours a day and comprises a high-resolution FLIR (forward-looking infrared), a laser designator and a tracking system. The TIALD pod is pointed at the target by the aircraft's navigation system and once the pilot or WSO has identified the target on his cockpit display the aiming cross is positioned over the target and the pod is switched into automatic tracking mode. At the appropriate moment during the attack, the TIALD laser is turned on, which provides the bomb's guidance system with the required information to complete the attack. The whole process is recorded and can be replayed after landing to assess the success of the mission.

Litening III (GR4)

The Litening III laser targeting and reconnaissance pod provides a vital air-to-ground targeting capability, including the ability to laser-designate ground targets for attack by other assets, and a ground reconnaissance and scanning capability, even when the aircraft is flying at maximum speed at low altitudes and undertaking combat manoeuvres. The pod has additional operating modes including air-to-air targeting and is equipped with third-generation FLIR sensors, the images from which can be fed into the pilot's HUD to assist low-altitude supersonic night flying.

Reconnaissance Airborne Pod for Tornado (RAPTOR)

(See description on page 50–51.)

Defensive aids
SkyShadow 2 ECM pod

BOZ-107 chaff and flare dispenser pod

Bol-IR decoy chaff dispenser pod
TERMA AIRCM pod

For self-protection the Tornado GR4 is normally armed with two AIM-9L Sidewinder AAMs together with a choice of four different defensive

ABOVE Raptor pod. *(RAF)*

LEFT Skyshadow ECM pod. *(Author)*

LEFT The back end of BOZ pod chaff dispensers. *(Author)*

FAR LEFT BOZ pod. *(Author)*

LEFT Two BOZ pods and Litening targeting pod. *(RAF)*

BELOW TERMA ECM pod.

125

TORNADO WEAPONRY

ABOVE LEFT F3 flare dispenser.

ABOVE F3 releasing flare over the desert.

LEFT Live Skyflash firing.

aids pods: BOZ-107 pod to dispense chaff and flares; Sky Shadow-2 ECM; Bol-IR ; and TERMA AIRCM pods.

Air-to-air

Skyflash (Tornado F3)

Skyflash is a medium-range all-weather air-to-air missile able to engage targets at ultra-high or low level in a variety of countermeasures environments. The missile uses semi-active homing, where the launch aircraft illuminates the target and the missile uses its own radar receiver to home on the reflected energy. Skyflash is a BVR missile but it can also be used at shorter range to ensure quick reaction times and maximum manoeuvrability after it has been launched.

AIM-9L Sidewinder (Tornado F3, GR4)

Sidewinder is a 'fire and forget' supersonic, heat seeking short range air-to-air missile with an infra red (IR) seeker that guides the missile to impact by homing on the engine exhaust of the target aircraft. IR homing allows ther missile to be used by day or night and in electronic countermeasures conditions.

LEFT Sidewinder AIM-9M. *(Author)*

AIM-120 AMRAAM (Tornado F3)

The AIM-120 AMRAAM incorporates an active radar with an inertial reference unit and a datalink microcomputer system. In a typical BVR engagement, the AMRAAM is launched from a range of 20 nm and is then guided by its own inertial navigation system, while receiving guidance updates from the launch aircraft via the data link. The missiles own monopulse radar then detects the target and guides it to impact.

ASRAAM (Tornado F3, GR4)

The AIM-132 ASRAAM is a highly manoeuvrable heat seeking air to air missile able to counter sophisticated IR countermeasures. The missile is the world's first IR missile to use a sapphire domed staring array detector, which detects the whole target aircraft. The missile has a fire-and-forget capability, which means the pilot can engage multiple targets with several missiles simultaneously. Following release the missile accelerates to more than Mach 3 while being guided to the target using its IR seeker.

ABOVE LEFT No 43 Squadron F3 carrying AMRAAM. *(RAF)*

ABOVE F3 and AMRAAM.

LEFT F3 with ASRAAM.

FAR LEFT ASRAAM training round.

LEFT An armourer points out the ASRAAM's coolant bottle.

RIGHT Mauser cannon barrel.

RIGHT Rear of Mauser cannon with spent shell collector case.

RIGHT JP233.

Mauser Cannon (Tornado F3, GR4)

The Mauser 27mm cannon is a single-barrel, high performance breech cylinder gun operated by an electrically fired gas operated system at a selective rate of 1,000 or 1,700 rounds per minute. Targeting of the cannon is done through the aircraft's head-up display (HUD) by using either a pr4diction sight or, in the case of the F3, a radar designated sight. The cannon has a very high muzzle velocity and its high rate of fire, coupled with its ability to fire several different types of high-explosive shells, make it equally suitable for both interceptor-type aircraft and ground-attack aircraft alike. The system is relatively compact, extremely robust and its simple, rugged design makes it highly reliable.

Legacy weapons
JP233
Originally known as the LAAAS (Low-Altitude Airfield Attack System), the Hunting JP233 was a

RIGHT GR1 and JP233. *(Jonathan Falconer collection)*

128

RAF TORNADO MANUAL

submunition delivery system consisting of a large dispenser pod carrying several hundred explosive bomblets designed to disable runways. Each JP233 was fitted to the fuselage underside of a Tornado IDS and was divided into a rear section with 30 SG-357 runway cratering submunitions, and a front section carrying 215 HB-876 anti-personnel mines. Both types of submunitions were retarded by small parachutes.

1,000lb iron bomb

In addition the Tornado GR4 Force trains and maintains a capability with legacy weapons such as the 1,000lb unguided iron bomb or 'dumb' weapons.

BL755 Cluster Bombs

When BL755 releases it breaks open in the airflow and releases 147 high explosive bomblets into the target area, thus allowing multiple targets to be attacked with one weapon. The BL755 and upgraded IBL755 are used against vehicles and equipment and are delivered from low-level attacks.

WE177 thermonuclear weapon (A, B and C versions)

The WE177 was the last nuclear weapon in service with the RAF and the last tactical nuclear weapon to be deployed by the UK. There were three versions: WE177A (boosted fission weapon); and WE177B and WE177C (thermonuclear weapons). Several RAF Germany Tornado squadrons were assigned to SACEUR and equipped with WE177 to deter a major Soviet offensive. The weapon was retired in 1998.

The Armourers

Tornado weapons engineers

Often overlooked during peacetime the role of the RAF's armourers only really kicks in during times of conflict. The line engineers keep the jets in tip-top condition – replenishing, fuel, oils and hydraulic fluids as well as rectifying faults, but the armourers have the task of looking after anything that goes bang!

Owing to the versatility of the Tornado GR4 the task of the armourer should never be underestimated. In addition to the huge

ABOVE 1,000lb practice bombs. *(RAF)*

LEFT WE177 thermonuclear weapon.

LEFT The tailfins of an Enhanced Paveway III bomb are checked by a weapons technician during Operation Ellamy.

129

TORNADO WEAPONRY

RIGHT Missile containers. *(Author)*

BELOW Inventory checking in the weapons storage area. *(RAF)*

array of weapons carried by this aircraft there are explosives in drop-tank release fuses and aircraft ejector seats, not to mention infra-red decoy flares too. Their job is full-on. With three to four people on a team it is often thought that post-flight the armourers have little to do, but nothing could be further from the truth. Once the aircraft has been made 'safe' by the fitting of safety pins in weapons, the ordnance is either removed if it has not been used or reloaded if the aircraft has been re-tasked. Weapon safety in the RAF is paramount. Weapons are usually armed once the aircraft has left the HAS or is taxying. Some other air forces tend to taxy their aircraft to the 'last chance' point before take-off at which time the safety pins are removed.

With aircraft like the Tornado each mission might involve them in a different tasking. ADV Tornados generally flew in a standard war fit of fuel tanks, radar missiles, heat-seeking missiles, gun and self-defence chaff and flares, but the GR4 is altogether a different platform. It may be flying a recce sortie one day, then the next day it will need re-tasking for close air-support. Sometimes an aircraft will go unserviceable and will require all the weapons to be removed to allow engineers to work in safety; it may then require air-testing, which often will be flown 'clean' or just with auxiliary fuel tanks on.

A team of armourers would normally comprise two or three senior aircraftmen (SAC) led by a junior NCO (corporal). Once the Combined Operations centre has issued the tasking and the engineers have decided which aircraft are to be used for a specific mission, the armourers will set to work moving the munitions from a secure storage area to the allotted aircraft. Usually, the weapons are stored well away from the aircraft for safety reasons.

To move the weapons from the storage area to the aircraft a specialist tow truck is used. For loading the weapons onto the aircraft a variety of devices are employed, but perhaps the most commonly used (and the armourers' vehicle of choice) is the self-propelled Diesel External Weapons Loader, the Einsa VAP-

THIS PAGE Armourers prepare weapons for Tornado GR4 aircraft at an airbase in the Middle East during Operation Telic in 2003. *(RAF)*

60, which bears a passing resemblance to a 'go-faster' fork lift truck (but without the go-faster stripes). Built in Spain it is designed to transport, position, load and unload a wide range of external stores weighing up to 6,000lb. Also manufactured by EINSA is the unpowered Model Y manual weapon loader, which allows armourers to load weapons weighing up to 600kg. The VAP-60 is widely used by NATO forces so it should be available virtually anywhere the GR4 operates in Europe.

To the unenlightened it may look as though armourers simply collect the weapons, move them under the fuselage and load them onto the aircraft, but in reality there is an awful lot more to be done that includes function checks and safety procedures. With so much of the GR4's payload being 'smart' weapons it is vital that aircraft and weapons are 'talking to each other' prior to the aircrew arriving. Modern weapons are no longer 1,000lb concrete bombs, but have sophisticated GPS systems as well as delicate arming devices. More simple weapons like the gun need only to be connected to various leads, but complex weapons like Storm Shadow need a wide range of checks to be performed.

Once loaded, the aircraft is placed in the initial armed state awaiting the crew who, when they arrive, remove the pins and place the aircraft in its final armed state. If an aircraft is carrying weapons, ground crew place various

RIGHT Aircraft armed placard. *(RAF)*

FAR RIGHT Aircraft armed cockpit sign. *(RAF)*

BELOW Tornado F3, ZE729, wearing the markings of the RAF's Tornado Evaluation Unit (TOEU), carrying an AIM-9 Sidewinder round beneath its port wing.

red or yellow-coloured plaques on the ground in front of the aircraft that say 'Aircraft Armed – Danger'. This is to warn those people who are not working on the aircraft, as well as those who are, that the aircraft is live-armed. With the aircraft fully crewed, the safety pins removed and the covers or 'Noddy caps' (in the case of Sidewinder) removed just prior to the aircraft taxying (this protects delicate parts of the missile and also prevents damage to delicate items such as missile seeker heads, which often need electrical power to remain caged), the aircraft status passes to combat-armed. Indeed, ground crew could see this on the ADV when the pilot selected the MASS 'ON' and a small black and yellow flag disappeared from the cockpit coaming.

It is well-known that airframes have a specific 'life', but what is not so well known is that weapons are also 'lifed' and need very careful management by armourers and engineers. On the ADV, for example, the most critical-lifed item was the Skyflash missile. If a missile is only lifed for 500hrs then flying 5–6hr combat air patrol (CAP) sorties soon eats into its longevity. As an example, during Gulf War 1 ADVs were flying hundreds of hours of CAPs with four live Skyflash, which were never fired, but it still made them life-expired. With modern weapons becoming increasingly delicate and more expensive the RAF needs to get the maximum value out of each store. To that end, often as a conflict becomes less of a threat air defence aircraft might be seen flying with only one or two radar-guided missiles once air superiority has been achieved. In order to

ABOVE A Skyflash AAM is loaded onto a Tornado F3, which could carry four of these missiles semi-recessed underneath the fuselage.

even out weapon life, live rounds and stores are carefully monitored and as they approach life expiry they may be used for test firings or dropped on ranges as part of crew training. This also provides the RAF with valuable data as how missiles that have flown 500hrs or more on combat air patrol will perform when fired in anger. A good example of how the RAF manages its weapon resources is Operation 'Herrick'. On most sorties the GR4 carries no ASRAAM or AIM-9L as is there is no airborne threat, so therefore there is no need to carry self-defence missiles.

Perhaps the biggest problem for the ground armourers is flares. Apart from the fact they are extremely dangerous pyrotechnics they are also only used in self-defence or training and often the entire load is not used. This means bringing the aircraft home with a part load of flares, which is not ideal. Chaff on the other hand is pretty benign, but still not great if you breathe it in.

In order to support operations in Libya (Operation 'Ellamy') and Afghanistan (Operation 'Herrick') the RAF needed a certain level of Very High Readiness (VHR) weapons stockpiled. In 'Ellamy', a full-blown conflict, various munitions were being consumed quickly. MBDA for example did a brilliant job resupplying Brimstone, but the manufacture of a modern missile requires a long lead time. This also poses the problem of getting weapons to out-of-theatre bases as quickly and as safely as possible. Classed as Dangerous Air Cargo (DAC), moving Brimstone and Paveway around is not a straightforward task that can be left to regular cargo aircraft. These must be carried as air freight by RAF transport aircraft or in some cases, such as in Operation 'Ellamy', the weapons are moved by road.

As well as looking after the aircraft, armourers have perhaps the most important job of all – maintaining the safety of the two Martin-Baker Mk 10 ejector seats. While Martin-Baker have done a brilliant job in always keeping the seat as simple as possible, from an engineering point of view it still requires careful maintenance. Like any explosives the rocket packs need changing when they reach a certain age as well as any explosive cartridges.

No 93 (EA) Squadron ensures that any Forward Operating Base for the Tornado GR4 and Typhoon would also be able to accommodate the safe storage of weapons, and allow the safe loading of munitions in a high turnaround combat environment – something they successfully achieved.

LEFT 27mm Mauser cannon rounds are prepared by an armourer. *(RAF)*

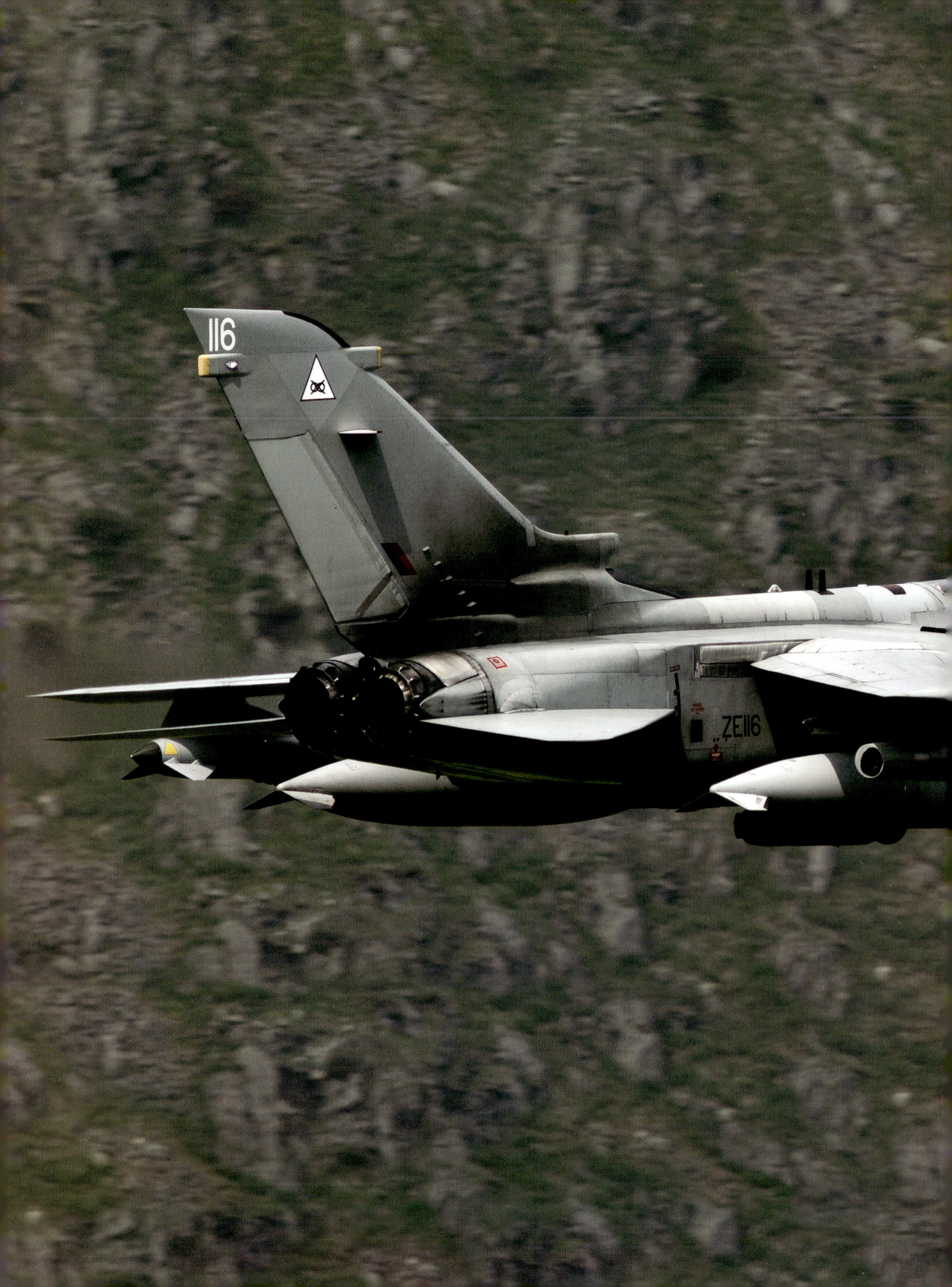
116
ZE116

Chapter Seven

Flying 'the Fin'

From a pilot's perspective the Tornado is a satisfying aircraft to handle. Whilst many fighters and fighter-bombers over the years have been described with varying degrees of praise, the Tornado simply does the job it was built for. As an interceptor it was extremely competent and as a bomber/recce aircraft it has been exceptional. Despite the continual upgrades the basic airframe remains the same and handles well, especially in the clean configuration.

OPPOSITE No 2 Squadron's GR4A, ZE116, thunders around Dunmail Rise in the Lake District.

ABOVE The Tornado is a two-crew aircraft.

BELOW Mission planning.

BELOW RIGHT Mission briefing.

Tornado from the cockpit

Having talked about the development of the Tornado, the ADV and the IDS, what is it like to fly? In an attempt to cover all versions and types I will describe from a pilot's perspective what it was like flying a heavy ADV (avoiding any reference to specific missions), Combat Air Patrol, Air Combat, air- to-ground etc.

I will describe in general terms how a Tornado flies. First of all, the Tornado is a two-crew aircraft and can only be operated on that basis. As such, both the crew rely on each other. Add to this the engineering support upon which a Tornado and its crew is reliant.

Ever since it entered service the Tornado has never been an aircraft that you fill with fuel and fly away without fault, trip after trip – ask any groundcrew engineer if the Tornado has a mind of its own! It never throws up the same problem twice, be it hydraulic leaks, wing sweep faults, electrical snags or the dreaded CSAS failures. The Tornado is like no other combat aircraft and keeps its engineers on their toes. Granted it's easy to get at most things behind the panels to fix them, but other items can be buried among pipes and wires and take an age to find and cure.

Briefing

For the crew every mission begins with a pre-flight briefing, even if it is to be flown singly. This then culminates in an 'out brief' given by a senior squadron aircrew member to check that everything has been briefed correctly – for example, you are aware of the weather and its trending pattern as well as diversion airfields. Particular emphasis is given to keeping crews aware of any Royal Flights active during the sortie as well as any areas NOTAMS (Notices to Airmen) danger areas that you may be flying close to. Very often the duty authorising officer will ask the crew an emergency question or drill which they are required to answer word perfectly. For example, again, what are your actions in the event of an engine fire?

Kitting up

Having signed to say they understand what mission they are going to fly the crew don the required flying clothing. In summer during peacetime this may be just a G-suit, life jacket and helmet. In winter this involves donning the cumbersome but vital immersion (exposure) suit. When the sea temperature drops below 10 degrees Centigrade the time of useful consciousness (should you end up in the water) is reduced to minutes. Wearing the suit might give you an hour.

Form 700

With all your flying kit gathered and donned it's time to walk to the engineer's office. Here the particular airframe (aircraft) you are allocated will have its Form 700 (logbook) left open ready for you to sign. Around the room are various boards used by the ground crew to keep track of the squadron's airframes. On a normal squadron of, say, 12 aircraft, 3 may be in deep maintenance while 2 may be undergoing routine servicing for minor faults, with the rest serviceable – in theory!

Often the engineers might have an aircraft – say, tail letter 'B' – down as 'U/S CSAS (Unserviceable Command and Stability Augmentation System) fault, estimate 4 hours', meaning aircraft 'B' has a problem with the CSAS that they hope to rectify in 4 hours. Scanning through the aircraft Form 700 gives the crew a good idea of the state of the aircraft and what fit it's in. It will detail every bit of work carried out on the aircraft and who performed it. It will show the crew how many hours it has flown, how much of its fatigue life has been used, how much oil has been replenished, who flew it last and a myriad of other facts. At first reading (and digesting) the Form 700 can be daunting with so much information to take in. Experienced crews learn what to look for and skim what's non-essential.

The pages at the front of the Form 700 are red and known as red line entries (or items

ABOVE Out briefing.

LEFT Kitting up.

BELOW Form 700.

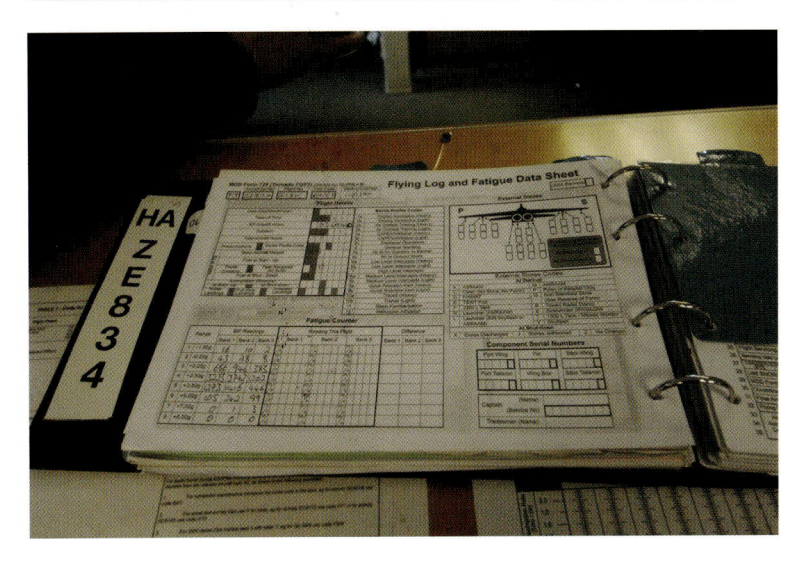

RIGHT Walk out to aircraft.

BELOW Inside the HAS.

BELOW Front-seater pre-start checks.

BELOW Back-seater pre-start checks.

that are safety critical). For example, an aircraft may be limited to 'no air-to-air refueling', 'not permitted due probe fault'. Obviously this is important just in case you were sent to a tanker. Reading the Form 700 and chatting with the engineers takes a couple of minutes and from there the crew walks either to their allocated HAS or to the aircraft parked on the flight line. By this stage the ground crew will have already performed their pre-flight checks and are waiting for the crew.

Pre-flight checks

Having spoken to the ground crew, the first task is to make sure both the front and rear seats are safe to enter as well as checking the aircraft is 'safe' should it be carrying live weapons. The front-seater checks the canopy accumulator pressure is 150 bar (pretty important if you want to open the canopy in a hurry) and makes sure his Martin-Baker ejector seat is safe for parking (that is, pins are fitted). On the left side he checks the crash bar is aft. Looking at the wing sweep and flap lever it needs to be set to the actual position of the wings and flaps. The x-drive clutch is set to 'open' and the landing gear lever is set to 'down'. The throttles are set to 'off' and the master arm selected to 'safe' as well as the late arm. Hydraulics are set to 'auto' and the parking brake set to 'park'. Finally the dump switch is confirmed 'off'. All of this is pretty much common

RIGHT The back-seater completes his safety checks and inputs mission data.

CENTRE Two-man engineer-type ladder.

sense to ensure the aircraft is in a safe condition prior to starting engines.

Once the back-seater has completed his checks the pilot can raise the rapid take-off panel gang bar putting all switches 'on' except for the pitot head heat, which would get too hot on the ground. With the throttles shut the two igniters are checked by pressing the relights (engine relight buttons) behind the throttles and listening to the faint 'click click' in the intakes. With both generators selected 'off' the APU is tested and then the signal is given to the ground crew to connect external power. While the front-seater performs his checks the back-seater is also completing safety checks, including alignment of the INS inserting mission data, while ensuring the radar is not selected 'on'.

Prior to entering the cockpit one thorny issue that has always plagued the Tornado is the lack of internal [integral??] ladders. Two types are normally used: the larger two-man/engineer-type ladders, or the smaller, individual clip-on type. The latter had a habit of falling off so crews are obliged to wear their flying helmets when climbing – health and safety!

Normally the ground crew consists of a 'see off' team comprising two or three men or women. One of these will normally connect himself to the aircraft by a wander-lead plugged in to his headset, allowing him to talk to the crew. If no headset is available then the crew communicates with hand signals.

Walk-around

Having checked the front cockpit is safe the pilot then does the aircraft walk-around in standard fashion. Working from the front left side to the rear and forward again. As the ground crew has already done this it's really only a final safety check. Checking all the skin gauges are at the correct pressure the pilot turns the AOA gauges on the front of the nose to confirm they move freely; the pitot probe is checked for obstructions

BELOW Walkround check.

RIGHT Look-down check inside engine intake.

BELOW Groundcrew help the front-seater to strap-in.

BELOW Back-seater does his comms check.

and a good look is performed inside the nose wheel bay to ensure the circuit breaker door is shut (otherwise it will get scrunched during gear retraction). For those of us who are tall enough, a look down inside the engine intake shows no loose articles or standing water and that the ramps move freely. Under the intake the ground crew will have opened the refuel panel, where banks of switches and lights are checked to be in the correct position. Moving aft the fuselage has various gauges for hydraulic accumulator pressure as well as indicators for fire extinguishers. All are confirmed correct. Depending on the weapon fit all safety pins are checked either in or out as required.

Strap-in and final checks

Back in the cockpit a detailed check of each crewmember's ejector seat is made – this is the one thing that will save your life and crews do this religiously without deviation. There are over 30 individual checks to be done, all from memory. Finally, having been helped by the ground crew to strap in, the crew remove the ejector seat pins and stow them within view of the ground crew. Local procedures may differ if you are parked in a HAS, although in theory the seat won't fire with the canopy open.

First task now is to turn the radio on and check in with the tower – vital because should you catch fire on start you need to know you can call ATC for fire cover. Having signalled to the ground crew to connect the external power, permission is asked to start the APU. With no headset the pilot clenches his fist in a circular motion, which the ground crew mirrors. Thumbs up as the APU winds up with a reassuring whine.

While the APU is running up the fuel contents are checked. After one minute the x-drive is selected to 'auto' and the left and right hydraulics selected to 'on' and then in turn both generators are switched 'on'. The CWP should now be clear of electrical captions. From the back seat the battery can be checked as charging. To close the canopy the left hydraulics are selected 'on' and the crew place masks on and slip their visors down. The ground crew turn their backs to the aircraft just in case the canopy MDC detonates. The pilot closes the canopy then checks all the switches from left to right prior to engine start and confirms with the ground team they are clear to do so.

Engine start

Starting the RB199 is a very simple affair. Beginning with the right engine the pilot selects the engine start switch to 'right'; as the RPM (NH) reaches 21% he simply opens the throttle and leaves it at idle. As the engine winds up a check is made that the 'OIL P' caption goes out on the CWP as well as looking to see that the temperature stays below 675° C. The engine start light should then go out as well as the APU run light. If the engine fails to start it is a case of selecting the 'start cancel' to 'cancel' while shutting off the throttle, lifting the gate and selecting 'HP off'.

After the first engine is started the pilot ensures the x-drive is in 'auto' and removes the external power (via the ground crew on headset) then checks the utilities system, ensures the wings are at 25° and the flaps are cycled; the manoeuvre flaps are cycled as well as the airbrakes and the stick is set at neutral with 2° nose-up trim. The CSAS and SPILS are then selected 'on'.

Control check

Next the pilot performs the control check with the help of the ground crew who are watching the controls move in the correct sense. With flaps up the controls are checked in 'Mech Mode' in the order: fly down–fly up–fly left–fly right. The control column is moved slowly trying to feel for any restrictions, which might indicate a crushable strut failure.

Should the pilot have any CSAS problems he has a couple of options: if the weather's cold, then moving the controls will warm up the hydraulic fluid; or performing a lengthy CSAS bite may cure the problem. If all else fails he can ask the ground crew to call an avionics expert for more advice. Once the controls are checked the left engine is started. After left engine start the x-drive is pushed open and the CWP tested again, ensuring the 'VIB' (engine vibrations) captions illuminate. Once the aircraft has both engines under power, the crew runs through another 20 checks to ensure the aircraft is safe to taxi.

Time to taxi

With the chocks waved away the ground crew gives the traditional salute and the aircraft moves forward with little need to increase power unless you are on an upslope or the aircraft is very heavy.

ABOVE LEFT AND ABOVE Canopy close.

BELOW Controls checks with the help of groundcrew.

ABOVE Chocks away.

BELOW Taxying.

Once on the move the brakes are checked as well as the nose-wheel steering. With the forward speed rising the pilot can select the taxi nozzle open to kill excess thrust. The back-seater can now read out the pre-take-off checklist in the style of challenge and response. In all there are 25 checks. For example the back-seater will read: 'wing sweep' and the pilot replies '25 degrees'; 'airbrakes', and the reply follows 'in and locked; 'flaps' to which he responds 'mid and indicating' – up until the final check, which is the take-off brief performed on every sortie or replaced perhaps on a scramble with SOP.

Final check

A typical brief would include a check of acceleration at 100kts after which abort decisions are as follows: below Vgo (calculated prior to walk) – abort for any emergency; above Vgo and below Vstop – abort for any serious emergency. Decision speed is Vstop. Above Vstop continue with the take-off unless it's dangerous or impossible, in which case the pilot will stop using maximum braking and full thrust reverse and use the overrun cable if available. Depending on how experienced the crew is, they will also talk through what they will do should they leave the runway and who will pull the handle and how the command ejection will be set up.

Lined up on the runway the back-seater reads a final check list and most pilots then perform their own last chance checks – for me it was 'wings 25, flaps in mid, captions out, canopy closed and locked'. That should cover you for any glaring omission. A final check that you're pointing straight down the runway and the nose wheel steering is set to low gearing – now you can slowly increase the power.

Take-off

The Tornado is from a generation where it's a simple procedure to move the throttles to a point where maximum dry thrust is reached – check the indications then push them smoothly forward into minimum reheat. Holding on the brakes the nozzle position is again checked and the throttles advanced fully to full reheat or combat power. Looking straight through the HUD (Head-Up Display) everything you need is clearly displayed before you in plain green writing.

At maximum all-up weight the aircraft lifts off the runway at over 150kts and has no tendency to sink with a firm back pressure on the stick. Pilots who have flown the Hawk immediately notice the controls feel heavy – it is after all a giant Hawk! The undercarriage is raised and a check is made; the lights go out by 250kts. At heavy weight and providing there are no noise limitations the reheat is left in until 300 or even 350kts.

Flaps are retracted at 5 AOA and the aircraft is accelerated to climb speed. Again the Tornado is from a generation where the pilot needs to trim the aircraft, but accurate flying by reference to the HUD is a very simple affair. Tornado crews have a range of skill sets that require constant practice, for example: heavy-weight single-engine flying simulating an engine failure just after take-off, which will require the crew to return to base and fly a heavy-weight instrument approach. Other emergencies might

RIGHT F3 close-formation take-off.

involve wing sweep failures, so approaches are flown with the wings simulated stuck back, though always to a low overshoot in training. The Tornado adopts a very high nose attitude when flying low-speed swept-wing, and with approach speeds in excess of 200kts a touch-and-go would be too hazardous.

Pilots practice instrument flying regularly but the HUD display makes what was once a challenging activity relatively easy. In terms of handling the Tornado performs well even at high weights, but care is needed not to allow the

BELOW F3 rotate.

RIGHT F3 gear up.

RIGHT AND BELOW GR4 take-off.

143

FLYING 'THE FIN'

ABOVE No XV Squadron GR1. *(Jonathan Falconer collection)*

nose to fall too far below the horizon at both high and low speeds. At maximum weights care is needed in hot conditions as the aircraft mass is high and speed reduction is rapid. At low level the aircraft is in its element with a superbly smooth ride even in gusty conditions. As mentioned earlier wing-sweeping is a non-event and a skill that quickly becomes second nature.

As a flying machine the Tornado is vice-less. Common sense and airmanship cater for flying at different all-up weights. Instrument flying is a joy as well as circuits and landings. Formation is also easy, though once again stick force movements are higher than most other fighter-type aircraft.

Tornado training 2013

XV (R) Squadron, RAF Lossiemouth

With the modern RAF pilot having only two combat aircraft types to choose from it would seem that most pilots would choose the Typhoon. Whilst this may be the case the chance to fly a 'legacy' aircraft is always high on any budding pilot/navigator's wish list. With the RAF having already trained its last true fast jet navigator, they are soon to be a dying breed.

No 15 Squadron is pretty much synonymous with anything to do with the Tornado. Thirty years ago in 1983 the squadron transferred from the Buccaneer to the Tornado GR1 at its RAF Germany base in Laarbruch. Escaping the cull of Tornado number plates it took on the role of the Tornado Weapons and Conversion Unit (TWCU) in 1992 when the TWCU badge of 45 Squadron was removed. Having moved from RAF Honington to RAF Lossiemouth, at the time of writing the unit is the largest Tornado user by a considerable margin.

When the TTTE closed down the most loved course in the RAF (TTTE had a reputation as being the only course in the RAF where no-one shouted at you!) was amalgamated into the 15 Squadron syllabus and the Tornado OCU taught students how to fly the Tornado and to operate it. Now fully established with 24 GR4s the transformation from GR1 to GR4 was rapid; beginning in 2000 it was complete by 2001.

The role of Tornado has been transformed since the early days at sleepy RAF Cottesmore. Perhaps Gulf War 1 was a benchmark in how the future would pan out for the Tornado. Now its mission is no longer deep penetration and strike, but more focused on Combat Intelligence, Surveillance, Target and Acquisition (CISTAR). Now the RAF talks about a weapons platform that is able to deliver both a 'kinetic' and 'non-kinetic' show of force.

Today's Tornado crews (pilots and weapon system operators) are selected for the Tornado and initially undergo ground school, which is carried out under civilian contract by staff from Thales.

This takes around six weeks, teaching students all aspects of the technical side of the Tornado – less time, in fact, than it took me to write this book! The staff are normally ex-fast jet crews, preferably with a Tornado background. Traditional classroom lectures are supplemented by modern synthetic aids. With ground school complete the next phase is a two-week simulator phase. This can prove daunting for *ab initio* crews. For pilots it's often the first time they will have flown with a back-seater, and for a back-seater it may be the first time (if they've not flown the Hawk) they get to operate anything remotely complex.

For front-seaters the first nine sorties are flown in twin-stick GR4s with an instructor pilot in the rear. This phase culminates in the pilot being awarded an Instrument Rating. Now the fledgling pilot is allowed to fly with a Weapon System Operator (WSO).

Prior to each mission crews use a system known as Tornado Advanced Mission Planning Aid (TAMPA). This truly is a 'magic piece of kit' in RAF parlance. My thanks go to 41 (F) Squadron who gave me a demonstration of this computer-driven device. Long gone are the days when Tornado WSOs would need to be skilled in Origami and be able to wallpaper the planning room in low level charts and Ordnance Survey maps. Now crews can do rapid mission planning with full colour displays. Data can be input that works out timings for routes, tracks, distances and even fuel calculations depending on what the aircraft fit is. Once in the target area Google-style maps can give you a God's-eye view of the target area and run the whole attack profile at real-time speed. The amount of information available prior to the sortie is stunning. TAMPA supports mission planning with smart weapons such as RAPTOR, Storm Shadow and DMS Brimstone as well as integrating with current targeting pods and LGBs.

Once planning is complete the WSO can download the mission data onto a Transportable Data Module (TDM) to load into the aircraft's main computer. For mission debriefing the aircraft are fitted with video recorders or the aircraft can carry the Rangeless Airborne Instrumentation And Debriefing System (RAIDS) pods which allow the entire mission to be recorded. With each aircraft in a formation carrying a RAIDS pod the post-mission debrief can put together all the formation displaying who was where and when. As well as staff pilots and WSOs the squadron also has a cadre of Qualified Weapons Instructors (QWI) on hand for the finer detail of weapon employment.

In a short space of time the student crew has a lot to learn to fly and fight the modern Tornado effectively. Students will be honed in the arts of low level flying, close formation, night flying, air combat as well as sorties to the nearby ranges. Amazingly students also perform Night TFR sorties whilst on the OCU, as well as an introduction to NVG flying. Previously many of these skill sets would be taught on the squadron or when the crews had more experience on type. Missions are flown to teach crews the level of confidence they need to fly night TFR using a combination of NVGs, TFR and FLIR. With the learning curve steeper than an Austrian Black run, air-to-air refuelling (AAR) is added to the syllabus when tanker assets are available. Now a cast iron certainty that any combat mission will involve AAR, it is vital the front-seater can master the art quickly. While the Tornado is not a difficult aircraft to learn to air-to air-refuel, heavy weight does require some care as the aircraft is often in reheat on one engine while the tanks fill.

With the basic phase complete students progress to the advanced part of the course where more operational aspects of modern warfare are added – EW, SAM threats as well as being given no notice re-tasking whilst airborne. Finally, like any OCU course the students are given a final sortie that encompasses any of the skill sets they have learned during the past few months. In the early days of RAF Tornado development crews would leave the OCU in a pretty raw state, most of the complex operational sorties would be performed by the front line squadrons. This meant that valuable sorties were being wasted on the front line often re-teaching students what they had already learnt on the OCU. Now Tornado GR4 crews leave XV Squadron as Combat Ready 1 – this means they deploy pretty much straight away to theatre – currently Afghanistan. This is quite remarkable considering the amount of knowledge a crew needs to absorb. As well as teaching *ab initio* crews XV Squadron has the task of teaching QWI Course Instrument Rating examiners and returning aircrew. The year 2012 also saw XV provide the hugely popular Tornado GR4 role demo (the RAF Tornado GR4 display team, which is a pair of aircraft as opposed to the old singleton aerobatics).

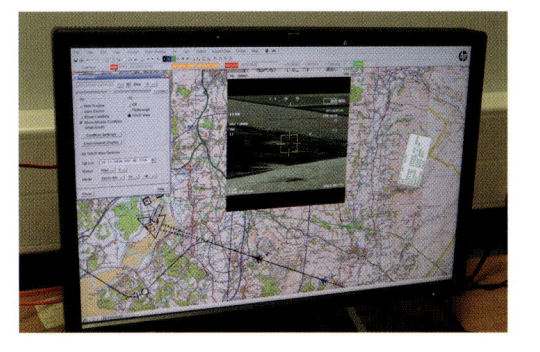

LEFT 'Google' map display.

BELOW Air-to-air refuelling as seen from the back seat. *(Jamie Hunter)*

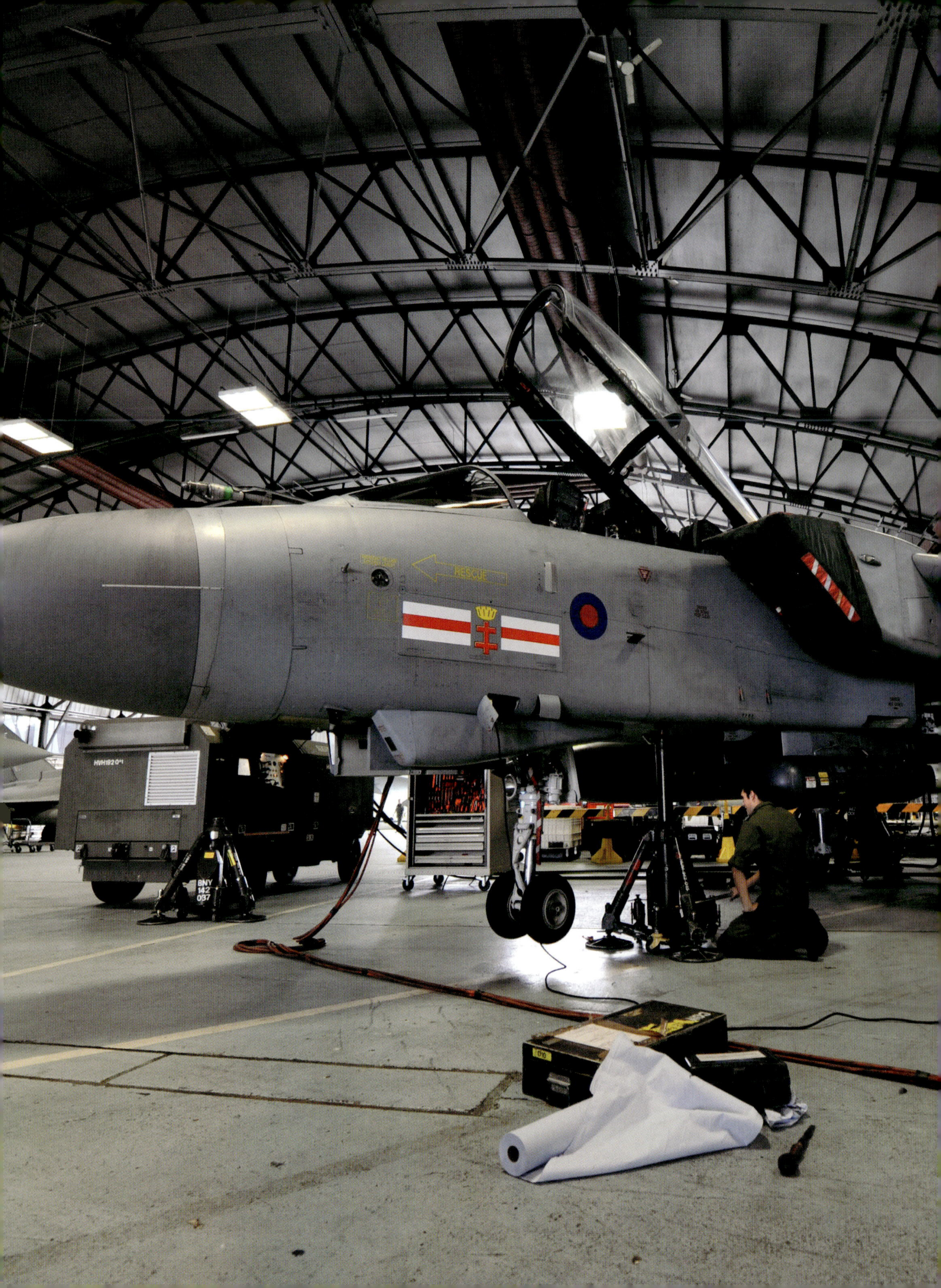
RESCUE
BNY
142
037

Chapter Eight

Maintaining the Tornado

Designed to be easily maintained the Tornado has proved a reliable workhorse to the RAF for over 30 years. Although it still requires a large amount of ground support equipment, it represents a quantum leap in maintainability over other legacy fighters. With its myriad of eye-level access panels the Tornado has also benefited from a wealth of engineering experience built up over its long service life.

OPPOSITE Tornado GR4 of 41 Squadron undergoes maintenance inside a hangar at RAF Leeming.

ABOVE A Tornado F3 receives attention from groundcrew outside on the apron.

BELOW Major servicing is usually carried out inside a hangar.

Tornado maintenance

On a front-line Tornado unit there are more than 800 ground-based personnel whose sole task is to keep the aircraft flying. Added to this are other support teams who play their part in the bigger picture. Designed from the outset to be easily maintainable the Tornado is kept serviceable through scheduled maintenance, either on a daily basis or via deep servicing. Servicing of the Tornado is accomplished by a specialist team of ground-based engineers and tradesmen. In no specific order the various trade groups are propulsion (engines), electricians, airframes and avionics. Added to this are the armourers whose work is described in a separate chapter. Accompanying the various technical trades are administrative staff who are directly involved in keeping maintenance records up to date and servicing manuals in good order, as well as ordering and supplying any replacement parts when required.

In an ideal world the Tornado would fly its mission, land, refuel and be rearmed and fly its next mission. The Tornado's maintenance concept required that no scheduled maintenance is allotted to any one component and that many individual parts are not given a set life expectancy, except of course where it would be justified on the grounds of flight safety. Nearly every system on the Tornado incorporates an Onboard Checkout And Monitoring facility (OCAM), or with crew-initiated or continuously operated Built-In Test Equipment (BITE). Faults in a Line Replacement Unit (LRU)

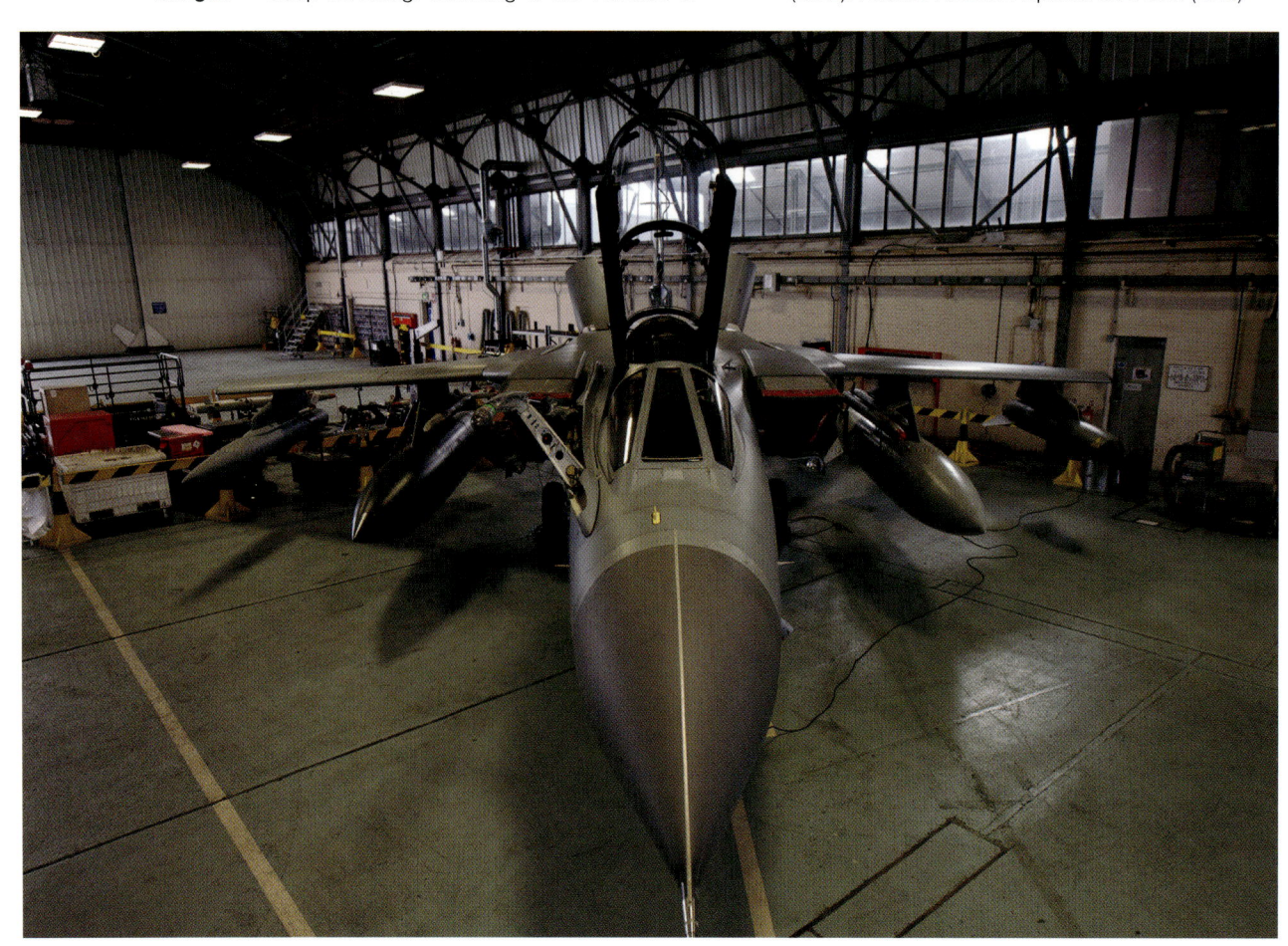

are indicated to the ground crew on the Central Maintenance Panel (CMP) on the right hand side of the fuselage. Once the defective LRU is identified it can be replaced in the HAS, normally without specialist tools.

One major benefit of the Tornado is that most access panels can be opened at ground level without tradesmen requiring ladders or specialist ramps.

Originally, the British Tornadoes were flown to RAF St Athan in South Wales for major servicing but this task has now been moved to RAF Marham where BAE Systems undertakes all major work on the airframes. Under a contract known as Availability Transformation Tornado Aircraft Contract (ATTAC), BAE was awarded a £1.3 billion contract in 2006 to carry out in-depth maintenance of the RAF Tornado fleet as well as provide spares support and technical support. The programme has been a great success. Due to expire in 2016, ATTAC will ensure the Tornado is well maintained until its projected out-of-service date.

While major servicing is carried out in one of the old-style large hangars at RAF Marham, day-to-day servicing is carried out inside hardened shelters. This has mixed benefits: the aircraft are kept covered from the elements allowing ground crews to work in comfort, but it does mean that each HAS needs its own dedicated servicing equipment. As previously mentioned the home of Tornado servicing was originally at RAF St Athan, which was responsible for preparing the aircraft for the Mid-Life Update. Prior to this, aircraft would be flown to St Athan for deep servicing that involved the total strip-down of the airframe as well as a complete repaint. Once in its 'bare' state the latest modifications to the airframe were embodied as well as any repair work that could not be completed at unit level. Over time the RAF became quite adept at in-house repairs, saving considerable sums on costly manufacturers' repairs. As a rough guide a major Tornado service took some five months and 20,000 man-hours to complete.

BELOW Groundcrew service a 43 Squadron Tornado F3 on the apron in a thunderstorm.

ABOVE Routine servicing inside the HAS.   **ABOVE** Plane wash!

Main undercarriage retraction test

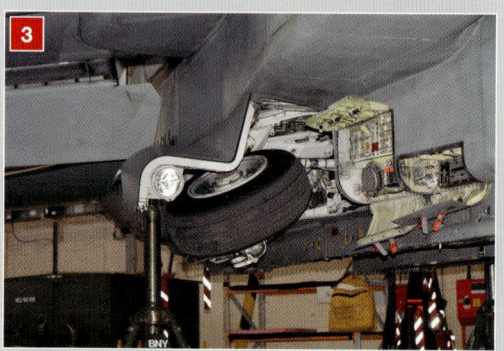

150
RAF TORNADO MANUAL

Routine servicing for normal operations

Aircraft operating on the frontline are subject to routine servicing comprising:

- Turnaround Checks – valid for 8hrs
- After-Flight Checks – valid for 72hrs after flight
- Before-Flight Checks – valid for 8hrs before flight

Though not comprehensive, the ground crew will check the following after each flight:

- Ensure the aircraft is safe. Master Arm Safety Key – 'SAFE'.
- If a mission involved AAR, check the probe for damage.
- Read the CMP note codes.
- Check tyres and liquid oxygen (LOX) contents.
- Ensure the aircraft is safely chocked.
- Prepare aircraft for refueling, noting shutdown contents.
- Clean the windscreen, canopy and HUD. Ensure the canopy is not damaged and pins are in place. Check ejector seats – 15 individual items.
- Check external and internal lighting.

1 and 2 Tornado Groundcrew, Operation Telic.
3 Tornado F3 beneath aircraft shelter in the Gulf. *(RAF)*
4 Shading the cockpits from the noonday sun.
5 Central maintenance panel.
6 Oxygen cylinders.
7 Stowage for liquid oxygen (LOX).

151
MAINTAINING THE TORNADO

8 Ground earthing.

9 External ground power.

10 Aircraft prepared for refuelling.

11 Refuelling bowser.

12 Refuelling ground earthing point.

13 Refuelling hose attached to aircraft.

14 Ground refuelling panel on aircraft.

- Ensure aircraft is ground-earthed. Pull any relevant circuit breakers.
- Check oil levels for gearbox, APU and engines. Replenish if required. Engine oils need checking within 30mins of shutting down.
- Refuel the aircraft, check external skin gauges and fit any warning flags if aircraft is parked.
- Check the fire extinguisher has not been fired and that no filters have popped.
- Finally, the ground crew checks the fatigue readings and transfers the data to the aircraft log.

External inspection

This pretty much mirrors what the pilot performs on his walk around checks:

- Parking Brake – Check 'ON'.
- General check for leaks. Check tyres for any damage and cuts, and any fluid leaks.
- Front fuselage – check that ADD probes move freely (Angle of Attack).
- Gun check – after the last flight of the day carry out a detailed gun check.
- Check radar coolant.
- Check intakes and engines for damage.
- Check main undercarriage as per nose wheel.
- Check hydraulic contents on LEDs and that no filters have popped.

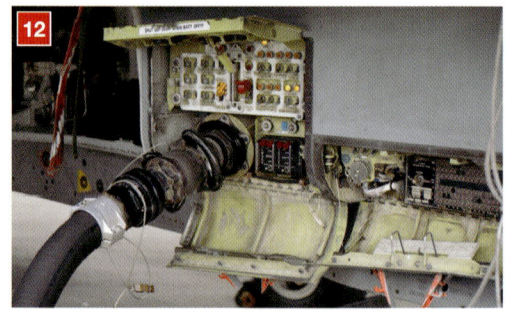

15 ADV fatigue meter inside the main gear bay.

16 27mm Mauser cannon and external power attachment.

17 Hydraulic reservoir level indicators.

18 Skin accumulator gauges.

19 External pressure gauges.

- Check rear of engines.
- Check all weapon pins are fitted.
- Ensure the canopy is open.
- Check that all external skin gauge pressures are within limits.

Once all checks are complete the ground crew person fills in the paperwork (RAF Form 725) stating the aircraft is fit to fly. Should the aircraft be left overnight the LOX is disconnected and aircraft covers fitted, if possible taping the canopy, which is prone to leak when not pressurised.

Tyre pressures

(depending on all-up aircraft weight and tyre type):

- Nose wheel – between 165–195psi
- Main wheel – between 210–335psi

System fluids

- Fuel – NATO F34 or F40
- Engine oils – O-160-OX-26
- Gearbox/SPS – O-160-OX26
- Hydraulics – H-515-OM15
- Windscreen washer – AL-36
- External power sources – Standard RAF GPU, also USAF GPU AM/32A-60A and 86D or MC1A

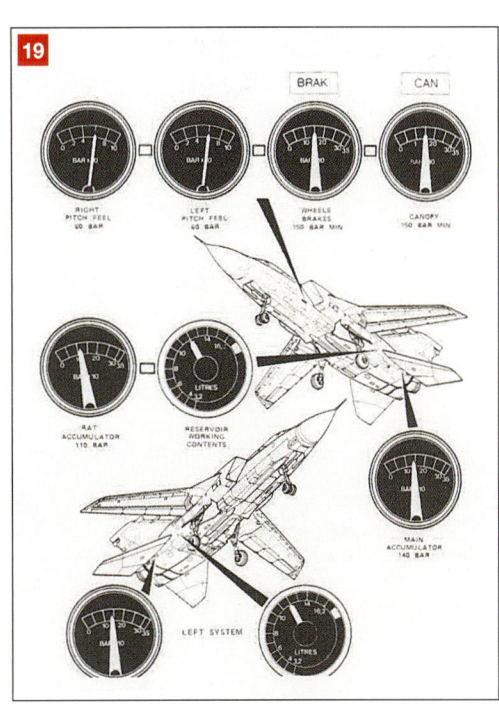

153

MAINTAINING THE TORNADO

Appendices

RAF Tornado GR4/GR4A squadrons (2014)

2 (Army Co-operation) Squadron, RAF Marham
9 (Bomber) Squadron, RAF Marham
12 (Bomber) Squadron, RAF Lossiemouth
15 (Reserve) Squadron, RAF Lossiemouth
31 Squadron, RAF Marham
617 Squadron, RAF Lossiemouth

(Data: http://www.raf.mod.uk/equipment/tornado.cfm)

Specifications

Panavia Tornado ADV (F3)

General characteristics
Crew: 2.
Length: 61ft 3½in (18.68m).
Wingspan: variable geometry wing, 45ft 7½in (13.91m) at 25° wing sweep, 28ft 2½in (8.60m) at 67° wing sweep.
Height: 19ft 6½in (5.95 m).
Wing area: 286.3sq ft (26.60sq m).
Empty weight: 31,970lb (14,500kg).
Max take-off weight: 61,700lb (27,986kg).
Powerplant: 2 × Turbo-Union RB199-34R afterburning turbofans.
Dry thrust: 9,100lbf (40.5kN) each.
Thrust with afterburner: 73.5 kN (16,520lbf) each.

Performance
Maximum speed: 920mph (1,480kmh, 800kts) IAS, Mach 2.2 at altitude.
Combat radius: more than 1,000nm (1,853km) subsonic, more than 300nm (556km) supersonic.
Ferry range: 2,300nm (4,265km) with four external tanks.
Endurance: 2hr combat air patrol at 300–400nm (560–740km) from base.
Service ceiling: 50,000ft (15,240m).

Armament
Guns: 1 × 27mm Mauser BK-27 revolver cannon with 180 rounds (internally mounted under starboard side of fuselage (2 × BK-27 mounted on Tornado IDS).
Hardpoints: 10 total (4 × semi-recessed under-fuselage, 2 × under-fuselage, 4 × swivelling under-wing) holding up to 19,800 lb (9,000kg) of payload, the two inner wing pylons have shoulder-launch rails for 2 × ASRAAM each.
Missiles:
4 × AIM-9L Sidewinder or AIM-132 ASRAAM.
4 × British Aerospace Skyflash or AIM-120 AMRAAM (mounted on 4 semi-recessed under-fuselage hardpoints).
ALARM.
Others: up to 2 × drop tanks for extended range/loitering time. Up to 4 drop tanks for ferry role (at the expense of 4 × Skyflash/AMRAAM).

Sensors
Radar – GEC-Marconi/Ferranti AI 24 Foxhunter radar.
Targeting – JTIDS.

(Data adapted from *Royal Air Force Aircraft and Weapons* (2007, Defence PR (RAF) Publications) and *Jane's All The World's Aircraft 1993–94*)

Panavia Tornado IDS (GR4/GR4A)

General characteristics

Crew: 2.
Length: 54ft 10in (16.72m).
Wingspan: variable geometry wing, 45ft 7½in (13.91m) at 25° wing sweep, 28ft 2½in (8.60m) at 67° wing sweep.
Height: 19ft 6½in (5.95m).
Wing area: 286sq ft (26.6sq m).
Empty weight: 31,620lb (13,890kg).
Max take-off weight: 61,700lb (28,000kg).
Powerplant: 2 × Turbo-Union RB199-34R Mk103 afterburning turbofans.
Dry thrust: 9,850lbf (43.8kN) each.
Thrust with afterburner: 17,270lbf (76.8kN) each.

Performance

Max speed: Mach 2.2 (1,490mph, 2,400kmh) at 30,000ft (9,000 m); 800kts, 921mph, 1,482kmh indicated airspeed near sea level.
Range: 870 miles (1,390km) typical combat.
Ferry: 2,417 miles (3,890km) with four external drop tanks.
Service ceiling: 50,000ft (15,240m).
Rate of climb: 15,100ft/min (76.7m/s).
Thrust to weight: 0.55.

Armament

Guns: 2 × 27mm Mauser BK-27 revolver cannon internally mounted under each side of fuselage, each with 180 rounds.
Hardpoints: 4 × light duty plus 3 × heavy duty under-fuselage and 4 × swivelling under-wing pylon stations holding up to 19,800 lb (9,000kg) of payload, the two inner wing pylons have shoulder-launch rails for 2 × ASRAAM each.
Missiles: Storm Shadow cruise missiles, Brimstone, ALARM, AIM-9L Sidewinder.
Bombs: Paveway II or III, or Enhanced Paveway II or III, Paveway IV, BL755, General Purpose.

Defensive aids

Sky Shadow-2 ECM, BOZ 107 chaff dispenser, BOL-IR decoy chaff dispenser.

Sensors

Radar – ground mapping;
Targeting – TIALD, LRMTS, Litening II;
Reconnaissance – RAPTOR, DJRP, Litening III.

Others:

Up to 4 drop tanks for ferry flight/extended range/loitering time.

(Data adapted from *Royal Air Force Aircraft and Weapons* (2007, Defence PR (RAF) Publications), John Fredricksen, *International Warbirds: An Illustrated Guide to World Military Aircraft, 1914–2000* (2001, ABC-CLIO) and Doug Richardson *Tornado, Modern Fighting Aircraft* (1986, Simon & Schuster).)

ABOVE A pair of Tornado GR4As fitted with TERMA and BOZ pods, and long-range fuel tanks.

Index

ADGE (UK Air Defence Ground Environment) 35
Aeritalia 20, 81
Aero engines (power plants):
  Bristol
    M45G 112
    Olympus 112-113
  General Electric 112; J79 112-113
  Pratt & Whitney 112
  Rolls-Royce 111
    Avon 112
    Pegasus 114
    RB211 112
    Spey 15, 112
  Turbo Union (Fiat, MTU and Rolls-Royce) 112-114; RB199 18-21, 111-119; Mk 101 115; Mk 103 38, 57, 115; Mk 104 31, 39-40, 115, 118
Airbases, overseas
  Al Jarrah 67, 69
  Al Kharj 72-73
  Ali Al Salem, Kuwait 73
  Ar Rumaylah Southwest 68
  Dhahran 7, 27, 64-66, 68, 71-72
  Gioia del Colle 72, 78
  Kandahar 51, 58, 76
  Manching 20
  Muharraq, Bahrain 64, 66, 68-69, 71
  Nellis, USA 92
  Shaibah 66
  Solenzara 73
  Tabuk, Saudi Arabia 6, 66, 68, 70-72
  Tallil 68, 73
Airborne test beds 19, 21
Airbrakes 95, 97-98, 109, 115, 142
Air Intake Control System (AICS) 117
Airbus A330 Voyager tanker 107
Aircraft projects:
  AFVG 14-17, 112
  Buccaneer 2* 15
  Heston JC-9 14
  P45 16
Aircrew:
  Black, Wg Cdr Euan 64
  Black, Ian (Author) 6, 8, 12
  Broadbent, Wg Cdr John 68
  Brown, Paul 6
  Brownlow, Bob 7
  Buckley, Sqn Ldr Gordon 69
  Collier, Flt Lt Max 68
  Eagles, Dave 7
  Elsdon, Wg Cdr Nigel 68
  Garwood, Sqn Ldr Dick 71
  Graham, Sqn Ldr Mark 15
  Hill, John 71
  Ingle, Flg Off Nigel 68-69
  Kenward, Roy 37
  Knowles, Sqn Ldr David 'Noddy' 74
  McKernan, Flt Lt Paul 68
  Myers, Sqn Ldr 74
  Nichol, John 68
  Peacock Edwards, Gp Capt Rick 26, 64
  Peters, Jon 68
  Robertson, Wg Cdr Dave 74
  Teakle, Flt Lt Paddy 69
  Torpy, Wg Cdr Glen 71
  Turk, Flt Lt Andy 74
  Waddington, Dave 70
  Witts, Wg Cdr Jerry 68
Air intakes 17-18, 31, 38, 43, 57, 95, 113, 115-117, 140, 152
Air-to-air refuelling, (AAR) 31, 33, 35, 37, 40, 45, 65, 67, 69, 73-74, 91, 104, 107-109, 138, 145, 151
Allison, AVM Sir John 46
Angle of attack (AOA) 95, 117, 139, 142
APU 91, 100, 103, 112, 115, 119, 139-141, 142
Armament – see Weaponry

Armourers 127, 129-133, 148
Arrester hook 98
Avionics 18-19, 21, 53-54, 66, 81, 83-84
Avro
  Shackleton 33
  Vulcan 13, 15, 19-21, 24, 112-114
AWACS 33, 35, 47, 53, 60, 78

BAE Systems 59-60, 81, 149
Battle of Britain 12
Berners-Lee, Tim 40
Bird strikes 83-84, 114
Blackburn Buccaneer 15, 19, 21, 24-25, 52-53, 71, 123, 144
Blue-on-blue casualties 77
Blue Steel nuclear missile 13
Boeing
  E-3D Sentry 47
  KC-135 tanker 16
British Aerospace (BAe) 34, 38, 42, 45-46, 54-57, 82
  Harrier 26, 44, 52, 57, 60, 72-73, 76, 79
  Hawk 52, 84, 142, 144
  Nimrod 33, 38, 53
  Strikemaster 34
British Aircraft Corporation (BAC) 14, 16-21
  Weybridge 14
British Aircraft Corporation (BAC) aircraft:
  Lightning 6, 19, 21, 31-32, 34-35, 38-40, 42-43, 112
  TSR2 12-14, 16, 18, 20, 22, 112, 114
Cameras 56
Cockpits 19, 33, 40, 43, 54, 59, 84-87, 96, 99, 104, 108, 117, 132, 136-145
  autopilot 69
  canopy 83-84, 100-101, 138, 140-142, 151, 153
  Head-Up Display (HUD) 20, 41, 54, 84, 108, 124, 142-143, 151
  Night Vision Goggles (NVG) 44, 49, 54, 57, 59, 71, 145
Cold War 14, 25-26, 31-32, 39, 53-55, 64, 99
  Soviet Union/Warsaw Pact area 15, 104
Colour schemes and markings 7, 20-23, 26, 43-44, 47, 53, 65-66, 70-73, 75-76, 97, 132
  ARTF (Alkali Removable Temporary Finish) 65-66, 76
  re-coding 56-57
Communications 40, 49
Computers, on-board 40-41, 46, 53, 55, 59, 145
Concorde 112-113
Crashes and losses 21-22, 41, 56, 67-68, 70, 75, 104
Crew training 23, 129, 133, 144-145, 149
  TTTE 23-24, 144

Dassault
  Mirage IV 15
  Mirage 2000 25; 2000C 7
Defence White Paper 1957 14
Design criteria 17
de la Billière, General Sir Peter 8

ECM (electronic counter measures) 32, 43, 68, 125
  ALE-40 43, 66
  BOZ pods 59-60, 70, 73, 78, 121, 124, 126, 155
  chaff and flare dispensers 43-45, 74, 125-126
  Sky Shadow 2 ECM pod 59, 121, 125-126
  TERMA pods 60, 77, 125, 155
  Wild Weasel 52

Ejection system 74
  Command Eject System 70, 142
  Martin Baker seats 84, 90, 133, 138, 140, 151
Electrical systems 37, 55, 82, 103-104, 115, 136
Emergency Power System (EPS) 101-102, 104
Engine bay 98
Engines 152
  bleed air 117
  changes 18, 98, 111-112
  Digital Engine Control Unit (DECU) 40, 118
  exhaust system 116
  flame-outs 22, 37-38, 104
  Main Engine Control Unit (MECU) 118
  oil system 118-119, 137, 152-153
  re-heat (afterburner) 5, 40, 111, 113-116, 118-119, 142
  starting 115-116, 119, 139, 141
  thrust reversers 114-116
  vibration detection 118
English Electric Canberra 48
Entry into service 38, 40, 57, 115
Environmental Control System (ECS) 117
Eurofighter Typhoon 2 20, 30, 33, 61, 76, 78-79, 122, 133, 144

Farnborough Air Show 34; 1980 115; 1988 35
Fiat 17, 112
  G91 20
Fire detection and suppression 95, 140, 152
First (maiden) flights 13, 19-20, 22-22, 36-38, 90, 113-114
Flying clothing 44, 74, 90, 137
Flying control systems 91-104
  Command and Stability Augmentation System (CSAS) 96-97, 136-137, 141
  fly-by-wire 18, 81, 92, 96-97, 104
  primary flight control system (PFCS) 96-97
  secondary flying control system (SFCS) 91-95
  utility system 100
Flying the Tornado 135-145
  briefings 136-137, 142, 145
  chocks away 141-142
  control checks 141-142
  Form 700 (logbook) 137-138
  kitting up 137
  mission planning 136
  pre-flight checks 74, 78, 138-139, 142
  strap-in and final checks 140
  walk-around 139-140, 152
Fokker 17
FRAG (Fragmented Operation Order) 67
French Air Force 7, 16, 25, 73
Fuel system and consumption 40, 82, 104-105, 107-109, 113, 115, 117, 140, 153
Fuel tanks 22, 31, 34, 36, 44-45, 55, 58-59, 66, 68, 70, 74-75, 78, 92, 98, 104-105, 108, 121, 155
Fuselage 82, 113, 140
  access panels 81-82, 136, 147, 149
  centre section 46, 91-93
  front nose section 83, 91, 152
  rear 95, 98, 114

Gaddafi, Col. 79
General Dynamics 14
  F-16 31-32, 46, 66
  F-111 16, 18, 82, 92, 99; F-111K 13-14, 20, 91; EF-111 Raven 68
German Air Force/WGAF 20, 23, 33, 45

German V-weapons 14
Gloster Meteor 82
Ground Control Stations (GCS) 35
Ground Controlled Interception (GCI) 35
Ground crew 44-45, 74, 78, 82, 84, 98, 136-140, 148, 151-153
Ground earthing 152
Grumman F-14 Tomcat 16, 32-33, 92, 98-99
Gulf Air 75
Gulf War 1 6-7, 24, 26-27, 36, 43-45, 48, 52, 54-55, 65, 70, 72-76, 79, 105, 123, 132, 144
Gulf War 2 27, 74-75

Handley Page Victor 13; tankers 20
Handling 20, 143
Hands on Throttle and Stick (HOTAS) 43, 59
Hardened Aircraft Shelters (HAS) 18, 42, 67, 73, 75, 98, 130, 138, 140, 149-150
Hawker Hunter 82, 95
Hot turnarounds 76
Hussein, Saddam 71, 73
Hydraulic systems 17, 37, 92-93, 96, 98-99, 100-104, 115, 136, 138, 152-153

Introduction to service 24-25, 42, 47
Iraqi invasion of Kuwait 26, 64
Iraqi Air Force 64-65, 67, 70
Italian Air Force 15, 23, 33, 72

Joint Strike Fighter (JSF) F35 60-61

Libyan Air Force 79
Lockheed
  F-104 Starfighter 15, 17, 20, 33, 95, 113-114; F-104S 33
  F-117A Nighthawk 72
  TriStar tanker 11
  U-2 48

Maintenance and servicing 137, 147-153
  external inspection 152-153
  ground refuelling 152
  system fluids 153
MBB (Messerschmitt-B lkow-Blohm) 16, 18, 20, 81, 91-92
McDonnell Douglas
  F-4 Phantom 6, 32-35, 38, 95, 112-114; F-4F 33; F-4G Wild Weasel 68; F-4J 43; FG1 42; FGR2 31, 38, 40, 42-43, 112
  F-15 Eagle 31-32, 46, 66, 98-99; F-15C 68; F-15E 70
  F-18 Hornet 99
Mikoyan
  MiG-23 19
  MiG-25 'Foxbat' 32, 36
  MiG-27 'Flogger' 19
  MiG-29 'Fulcrum' 31, 35, 68
MOU (memorandum of understanding) 16
Myasishchev Bison 32

NAMMO (NATO MRCA Management Organisation) 16
National Gas Turbine Establishment, Pyestock 113
NATO 15, 23, 26, 35, 38, 44, 66, 79, 105, 131
Navigation equipment – see Radar, navigation and targeting systems
Navigators 42, 144
Nose art and names 76
  Foxy Killer 27
  Scud Hunter 55
  Snoopy Airways – Debbie 69